Brooke Herford

The Story of Religion in England

A Book for Young Folk. Third Edition

Brooke Herford

The Story of Religion in England
A Book for Young Folk. Third Edition

ISBN/EAN: 9783744772532

Printed in Europe, USA, Canada, Australia, Japan

Cover: Foto ©ninafisch / pixelio.de

More available books at **www.hansebooks.com**

THE STORY

OF

RELIGION IN ENGLAND

A BOOK FOR YOUNG FOLK

BY

BROOKE HERFORD

AUTHOR OF "TRAVERS MADGE, A MEMOIR"; "BAINES' HISTORY OF LANCASHIRE" (THE CONTINUATION); &c.

THIRD EDITION

LONDON
THE SUNDAY SCHOOL ASSOCIATION
37, NORFOLK STREET, STRAND
1883

LONDON:
PRINTED BY WOODFALL AND KINDER,
MILFORD LANE, STRAND, W.C.

CONTENTS.

CHAPTER XXXIV.

CHAPTER XXXV.

CHAPTER XXXVI.

CHAPTER XXXVII.

CHAPTER XXXVIII.

THE STORY

OF

RELIGION IN ENGLAND.

CHAPTER I.

THE FAR-OFF PAST—THE DRUIDS.

For the beginning of the story of religion in England we must go back in thought to a dim and far-off time. Reader, is there an old church or the ruin of some ancient castle in your neighbourhood? We have to go back far beyond the time when that was built—hundreds and hundreds of years further back—to a time when forests and swamps covered the greatest part of our island, and the only inhabitants were tribes of half-naked savages, as rude and fierce as the New Zealanders or the Red Indians.

We must not think of all the ancient world as lying in this kind of barbarism. Away to the East, around the shores of the Mediterranean Sea, were highly civilized nations, with rich, beautifully built cities, and cultivated farms and vineyards; with settled

B

governments and magnificent public institutions, such as temples, colleges, libraries, museums and baths. Italy, Greece, Egypt and Phœnicia, were then the centre of the civilized world, and when people heard of the little island which centuries after came to be called England, they thought of it about as Englishmen or Frenchmen used to think of New Zealand when it was first discovered. The Phœnicians were the great traders of that ancient time, sending out their merchant ships in every direction. The Mediterranean was as well known to them as a great highway. Then they voyaged into the unknown seas, beyond the two great headlands called the Pillars of Hercules which close in the Straits of Gibraltar, and found their way to some islands which we now call the Scilly Isles, and to the neighbouring shore of a new country which they called Britannia, and which in time they found to be also an island. It was in some of the further parts of Cornwall that they landed, and they traded with the natives for tin, and probably established trading posts and mines of their own there. So, from time to time, there came to the geographers and learned men of the civilized world vague tidings of these islands, which people thought of as almost out of the world, or at any rate as on the very edge of it.

A little later, these same islands began to be heard of from another source. The armies of Rome, conquering the peoples of Gaul, and pushing their way ever northward, came to the sea coast, and across the narrow seas which now we call the Straits of Dover could see another land, a land of white cliffs stretching far away to unknown distances. The Gauls told them dreadful stories of the fierceness of the tribes inhabiting this "Albion;" yet, nevertheless, adventurous traders from Marseilles and other rich cities had been making their way there and had brought back rich merchandise not only of tin, but of lead, and skins, and hunting dogs of wonderful breed. Moreover, they told that gold and silver were plentiful among the natives, and it began to be thought of as a land worth conquering. So in the year 55 B.C., Julius Cæsar, at the head of two Roman legions, crossed the Straits, and after a year or two of fighting compelled the tribes along the southern coast to acknowledge the Roman government. Then, however, he had to go back to Rome, and nothing more was done. Nearly a hundred years passed by without the natives being much disturbed, but the traders still went, and the richness of the island came to be more known. At last, in the year 43 of the Christian era, the Romans set to work in earnest to conquer Britain, and from this time we begin to hear something trustworthy.

Our common ideas of the ancient Britons are more like the impressions which the Romans got from the vague stories of the Gauls than like what they actually found. The Britons were by no means such mere savages as they had been described. They had among them something of trade and agriculture. They knew how to fortify their villages with ditches and stockades, and they fought so bravely that in some parts of the country they were able for a long time to defy the Roman legions. They had dresses of skins, and rudely woven shawls of wool much like the plaids of the Highlanders; and golden bracelets and brooches are still sometimes found in their graves, showing how skilful they must have been in finding and working the precious metals. Most of all, however, their chariots, with sharp blades stretching from the axle-trees, drawn by hardy little horses, and used with wonderful agility in their battles, excited the admiration of the Romans, among whom chariots were little used except for shows and sports.

It is their religion, however, with which we have especially to do. The Britons were a very religious people, and it was their fierce religious patriotism which formed the greatest hindrance to the Roman conquest. The Romans had heard of the fame of the British priests before they landed. The Gauls, who were of the same religion, spoke about them with great veneration, and told how those who wished to be thoroughly instructed in their faith used to go over to these British priests, or Druids, as they were called. The Romans found that these Druids formed a strong religious order, and had immense power over the people.

It is easier to say what the Druids were than what Druidism was. Among the different Celtic tribes which inhabited Britain, we can dimly see a race of men of better dress and higher knowledge, who were among all the tribes, but were of no tribe themselves—a separate and higher religious caste, reverenced all over the island, and probably through a large part of Gaul. These were the Druids. They were not chiefs, but the awe with which they were regarded, and the fact that, while the tribes were divided, and often hostile, the Druids dwelling among them all were one united order, gave them a power really greater than that of the chiefs. No tribe dared to touch their persons by its laws, or to touch their property for its taxes. They used no weapon, yet at their intervention every weapon was sheathed and contending chiefs had to stop their quarrels. They were the prophets, priests, and bards of the tribes. The chiefs were proud to place their sons with them to be instructed. They kept the tradition of the ancient laws, which even the chiefs must not violate. They had some knowledge of astronomy; and, reading the stars, were thought by the people to read the future, to have strange powers of blessing and cursing, and to be able to speak with the gods.

The chief abode of the Druids was the island of Anglesea, where the High Priest or Arch-Druid lived in mystic seclusion, and where it is believed that there were great settlements of Druids, dwelling in some sort of monkish communities. But throughout the whole country they had their dark groves, where, beneath ancient oaks, or within sacred circles of huge stones, which some think to have been the work of earlier races still, they offered their sacrifices, performed their magical incantations, and worked themselves up into a religious frenzy which the people, and probably they themselves, took for inspiration. Early traditions tell of great yearly festivals of their religion kept throughout all the tribes, processions of white-robed priests at the new year (which they counted from about the tenth of March) to cut the sacred plant of the mistletoe from the oak with a golden knife, and to sacrifice a white bull. The first of May was a great festival to the Sun, when mighty fires were lighted on their cairns and high places. Midsummer-day also had its sacrifices and prayers, to procure a blessing on their fields and orchards; and on the last night of October there was a great religious celebration, when every household had to put out its fire and to light it again next day with sacred fire from the altar. And, besides these great occasions, each neighbourhood had its smaller local festivals for the gods of its own mountain, lake, or stream.

Some of their rites were of a sterner and more dreadful kind. At times they offered human sacrifices. The Gauls told Julius Cæsar that on the occasion of some great calamity, they would make a huge figure of a giant in basket-work, and filling it with criminals or prisoners taken in fight, they heaped up dry grass and wood about it, and burnt the whole to ashes. If any dreadful crime had been committed, there must be human blood shed to appease the anger of the gods; or if some enterprise of peculiar importance was to be undertaken a human sacrifice must be offered, from the nature of whose dying struggles they thought they could foretell the future. These victims were usually prisoners or persons marked for some crime, but it was told in after times that if there was no one of this kind available, they singled out for their sacrifice the person who had come last to their religious assembly!

Concerning the religious ideas which lay behind all these rites and festivals, very little is known. Some people believe that among the Druids themselves there was a secret wisdom of a very pure and high kind, such as the belief in One Great Spirit, and in the immortality of the soul. What is taken to support this idea is the fact that they had no idols or images in their worship. But then, on the other hand, it is certain that they kept up the belief in many gods among the common people, and the Romans, hearing of these, called them by the names of such of their own gods—Jupiter, Mars, Mercury, and so forth,—as seemed to come nearest to the native idea. These, however, were mere guesses. The nearest approach to certainty is that the Druids held to some kind of worship of the heavenly bodies, and their name of "Bel" for the Sun-god, to whom they lighted their May-day fires, is so like that of Baal, that it has been thought by many to indicate some connection between their worship and that of the Phœnicians and Philistines. Others, however, think it more likely to be connected with the old Teutonic deity Balder.

These Druids the Romans found to be their bitterest and most relentless foes. It was natural it should be so. They alone among the native tribes could understand something of the real character of this Roman power which had been pushing onwards, year by year, so slowly yet so irresistibly, through Gaul and Germany, and was now claiming Britain also for its own. Besides, the Druids knew that the victory of the Roman power would be the destruction of their own subtle and all-pervading authority. So, again and again they roused the tribes to fierce resistance, awed them by their warnings, stirred them to frenzy by their war-songs. It was in vain, however, and their patriotism only made their own fate more bitter. Usually, when the Romans conquered a new province, they left the vanquished people to follow their own religion in peace. But Druidism was too powerful and irreconcilable to be treated in this fashion. After a time severe laws were passed against it by the Roman governors. The Druids were hunted from place to place. At length Anglesea, their last stronghold, was laid waste. Their groves were cut down, their altars were overthrown, and, after fierce and desperate fighting, they themselves, in great numbers, were burned in the huge fires which the historian Tacitus says that they had prepared for the expected Roman prisoners.

From this time the power of the Druids was broken.

Much of Druidism, however, long survived. In the remoter refuges of Ireland and Scotland it remained for a time little disturbed, and in country places throughout the land its superstitions lingered for ages. Nearly a thousand years later, after Saxons had succeeded Romans, and Danes had overwhelmed Saxons, there was so much of the old Druid superstition still surviving that King Canute had to pass laws against worshipping "the sun, moon, fire, rivers, fountains, hills, or trees and wood of any kind;" and centuries later yet, the old stone circles and cromlechs were still regarded with awe and fear by the common people.

Here and there those rude monuments still remain. Most wonderful of all these is Stonehenge, on Salisbury Plain, but smaller circles of stones are found in many places throughout these islands, and indeed similar circles have been found in France and Spain, and even as far as Palestine, Sinai, and India. In some places, also, mounds and circles of earth, too large to have been huts, too small to have been forts, are met with, which are thought to have been at one time covered with the sacred groves of the Druids—perhaps to have served as their places of worship or courts of justice. More curious traces, however, may still be found. Probably our May-day sports originated in the May-day festival of the Druids. The bon-fires of Midsummer-eve, and Hallow-een or All-Saints' Day, which are still kept up in different parts of England and Scotland, are relics of the old Bel-tein, or Bel-fires, which the country people used to light before the Romans came to Britain. And every spray of misletoe that is hung up at Christmas is really an unconscious memorial of that oldest religion of our land.

CHAPTER II.

CHRISTIANITY AMONG THE BRITONS.

How did Christianity first make its way into this country? What an interesting story it would be, if we could know who it was that first stood forth among those ancient British tribes (whose native Druid priests had been almost exterminated by the Romans), and preached to them the simple religion of Christ. In after ages, indeed, many stories about this grew up, nobody knew how, and the monks took them as the best accounts they could get, and wrote them down as history. Thus there was one legend that St. James had come to Britain preaching the gospel; another told of Simon Zelotes as the first British missionary; others ascribed the work to St. Peter or to St. Paul. The monks of Glastonbury Abbey maintained that the glory belonged to Joseph of Arimathea—who, they said, had been sent over with twelve disciples by St. Philip, and, moreover, had founded their own abbey; and they told how he had planted his staff in the ground there, where he made his abode, and it had taken root and grown into a thorn-tree. And there, in the abbey-close, a grand old thorn-tree—that very tree, they said—might be seen still standing, and they handed down a wonderful story of how it always flowered at Christmas, so that their account must be true!

But these are all mere monkish legends. The most

likely thing is that the earliest Christianity came in unobserved among the Romans, and the story of its gradual propagation among the natives is part of the general story of the Roman conquest.

A very interesting story that conquest is. The Britons made a long and noble struggle, but when the Romans once resolutely set themselves to conquer there could only be one end. The tribes disputed their progress step by step, stopped their way with pointed stakes across the rivers and along steep earthworks. It cost Vespasian, the Roman general, afterwards emperor, thirty battles to master the south coast and the Isle of Wight. And when peace was made it was continually broken again. Now Caradoc (whom the Romans called Caractacus) roused up the tribes of South Wales, and made his last stand behind the vast earthworks which still bear his name at Caer-Caradoc, in Shropshire, where they may yet be traced skirting the mountain side for miles; but he was defeated and carried captive to Rome. Now Boadicea, the fierce Queen of the Iceni, the natives of Norfolk and the eastern counties, maddened by Roman outrages, aroused her people, made a desperate effort to throw off the Roman yoke, massacred the settlers in Verulam (afterwards St. Albans) and London, and ravaged all the south country; but only to be crushed at last and to take poison in her despair. Gradually the southern part of the island settled down in peace. Then, in the year 79, came the greatest of all the Roman rulers of Britain, Agricola, who marched northwards and made the great Roman roads which may still be traced in places all through Cheshire, Lancashire, and Yorkshire. Forming camps, and planting settlements as he went through England, and then doing the same through the

Lowlands of Scotland, he reduced the whole country to a Roman province. When they were once fairly mastered, the Britons seem to have settled down peacefully with their conquerors, and to have readily received their higher civilization. Roman towns sprang up in all parts of the country. Wherever we have the name of a town ending in "caster" or "chester," there we may be sure was one of the old Roman *castra*, or camps, around which the towns grew up. Deep below the present surface of London, York, Chester, Lancaster, Manchester, Leicester, Lincoln, Ilkley, and many other places, are still occasionally discovered the foundations of Roman buildings, or fragments of Roman weapons and pottery. Here and there are found the walls and pavement of some villa where lived the Roman governor of the district, and ancient Roman tools have been met with in the disused workings of old mines. So the Roman garrisons and colonists settled down in the midst of the people—a superior race, their leaders and teachers in the arts of peace.

When these peaceful times came, among the things which the natives gradually learned, was the religion held by some of the best of these Roman settlers—Christianity. Christianity had then been in existence in Rome for a hundred years or more, and though despised by the learned and great, had thousands of followers among the common people. Thus wherever the legions of the empire went, there went Christians among them, and these Christians would be, of all the Romans, the only ones who cared much about spreading their religion. Moreover, every time that new persecutions broke out at Rome, Britain, where no such persecutions had been attempted, would be a refuge for many, and all these would help to make Christianity better known.

To such an extent had this gradual missionary work been going on, that by the year 209 we find Tertullian declaring that even "those parts of Britain into which the Roman arms had never penetrated were become subject to Christ."

How this missionary work was done we can only gather from what we know in general of the times and the people. Christianity would be a simpler thing in remote Britain than in the East. It would have little to do with the luxuries, the political intrigues, and the endless controversies which were already corrupting the Churches of Rome and of the learned and wealthy East. We have to picture to ourselves simple-hearted Christian men and women settling down here and there, and trying to convert the natives in their neighbourhood to their faith in the one great God, the heavenly Father, and in the crucified Christ; by-and-by would come wandering missionary priests, in their rude leather jerkins—for ecclesiastical robes were little known as yet—preaching more fully, and contrasting the doctrines of the Gospel with the old Druidism, or with the idol-worship of the Romans. These would urge the people to be baptized, would teach them the commandments and a few simple prayers, perhaps the short creed which was called the Apostles' Creed (though there is no ground whatever for supposing it was really written by the Apostles), and which was the only one then drawn up; and would form them into little churches with some settler or native as elder or deacon over each. Here and there such a missionary would make his home among them, be himself their priest, and gradually convert the country round, till he would come to be looked upon as their bishop, perhaps even as their saint. It must have been a very plain, simple kind of Christianity, with a good deal of the old lingering superstition of the country mingling with it. Such a missionary would find the people still regarding with awe the old stone circles and sacred groves of the Druids, and the days and seasons of the old Druidical year. He would teach them that those places were the haunts of devils, and on the old sacred days he would persuade them to hold, instead, Christian holidays and festivals of their village churches. As time went on, and more of the people fell into the ways of the new religion, it would become more of an organized Church, such as it already was in the more civilized countries about the Mediterranean. There were no regular monasteries as yet, but tidings would be brought of the holy men who lived lonely hermit lives in the Eastern deserts, and the old traditions which would still be told among the people of the sacred communities of Druids and Druidesses, would make it natural for the fervently religious to follow such ways in order to live what was thought a holier life. Some man holier than the rest would take up his abode in a desert place, and people would resort to him for advice and blessing, and some would want to stay with him always, and would build themselves little huts or cells near to his, until there grew up a little community looking to him for guidance and all calling him "abba," or father; this would be the beginning of the system of monasteries, each with its "abbot" which is simply the old word for *father* in a slightly altered form.

About three centuries after Christ, and two centuries after the Romans had finally subdued and occupied Britain, Christianity seems to have made so much way among the people that the British Church had come to take its place among the other branches of the Christian Church, though very little thought of because it was too poor and too far off to be able to take any part in their controversies and rivalries. About this time (A.D. 314), a large council of bishops from different countries was held at Arles, in Gaul, and among those who were present mention is made of bishops of York, London, and Lincoln. These, however, could not have been rich and lordly dignitaries like the bishops of the more important Churches; for, even forty years later, when another council was held and the Emperor of Rome offered to maintain, at the public charge, all who came to it, all the bishops were rich enough to be able to provide for themselves, except three who came from Britain. Then, also, British Christians began to be heard of abroad; Jerome, one of the great Christian writers of those early times, who was living at Bethlehem, speaks of Christians from Britain as having come all the way to visit the sacred places of Jerusalem, and there were some of them who wandered even to Antioch to see the wonderful hermit Simeon Stylites, who for many years had been living on the top of a high pillar there, and who had a great name among men as a saint.

So, very gradually, unnoticed amidst the great movements of history, the Gospel made its way among the British tribes, until the people generally, throughout the Roman part of Britain, were Christians. How we should like to have some trace of them! Here and there, indeed, rude crosses may be seen in parts of Cornwall, where, close by, cromlechs and stone circles tell of the earlier worship, and these crosses may perhaps be traces of that old British Church. And close to some of the places where the Romans had their military stations, ancient headstones have been dug up, with rude carvings of Christian emblems on them, curiously like those found near the earliest Irish monasteries. But Church and Christianity alike perished when the Romans left the land and our old Saxon and Ænglish forefathers came in.

CHAPTER III.

THE SAINTS OF THE BRITISH CHURCH.

How we should like to be able to look back and know something about those little churches of the Christian Britons in the old, old time when the Romans were still in the land! But all is very dim and uncertain. Of the churches themselves not a trace remains; they were only rude buildings of wood, or of reeds and mud, with thatched roofs, such churches as travellers find in Abyssinia in the present day. Of the men and women who worshipped in those churches, of the priests who ministered at the rude altars, of the bishops who ruled over them, all that we have are a few traditions told by the Welsh monk Gildas two hundred years afterwards, or by Bede two hundred years later still. But "the venerable Bede," as he was called, in writing his famous history, was very anxious to learn all he could of the ancient people of the land, and so we get a few interesting glimpses of the holy men whose names had been preserved to his day, though of course we cannot be sure of the truth of all he tells about them. The most interesting of these is the story of

St. Alban the Martyr.

Alban is said to have been the first man who was put to death in Britain for being a Christian. For nearly two hundred years these little churches among the Britons knew nothing of martyrdom, except what some of the soldiers in the Roman legions might tell them of the terrible things that Christians sometimes had to suffer at Rome. At length, however, in the days of the Emperor Diocletian, when a last desperate attempt was made to stamp out the new religion, the Christian Church in Britain had become too large to be overlooked any longer. Bede says "the cruelties of wicked princes were raging against Christians," and though it is not likely that there was any wide-spread and general persecution, there were sure to be some among the Roman magistrates who hated the Christians and would be glad to enforce the edict of the Emperor. Such a man seems to have been the magistrate of the district about Verulamium, one of the Roman garrisons in the southern part of Britain; and so it came to pass that a Christian priest, being threatened with death, took refuge in the house of a citizen there, named Alban. Alban was a heathen, but, being a good and kind man, he sheltered the fugitive, and, moreover, observing him to be "engaged in continual prayer and watching, day and night," the sight of this so touched Alban that he himself "cast off his idolatry and became a Christian in all sincerity of heart." And when, in a while, it came to the ears of the magistrate that the priest was hidden in Alban's house, and soldiers were sent to make strict search, Alban put on the long priest's habit of his guest, and gave himself up in his stead, and was led bound before the judge.

The judge was sacrificing to his gods when Alban was carried before him, and was enraged that he should thus of his own accord have put himself into the hands of the soldiers. So he commanded him to be dragged up to the altar, before the "images of the devils" (as Bede always calls the statues of the Roman gods), and threatened him with the punishment intended for the priest whom he had hidden, unless he would deliver him up. Alban, however, bravely refused. Then the judge asked him who he was. "What does it matter of what family or race I am?" he replied; "if you desire to hear the truth about my religion, be it known to you that I am now a Christian, and bound by Christian duties." And he added, "I am called Alban by my parents, and I adore the true and living God who created all things." Then the judge had him scourged with the terrible knotted whips of the executioners, but he was not shaken. Bede says he bore the cruel torture "patiently, or rather joyfully, for our Lord's sake." So, at last, the judge ordered him to be put to death, and they led him out to a hill a little way beyond the wall of the town, to die. Wonderful stories were told in after times of miracles that took place as he went thither through the crowds of people who gathered about the road, and thronged the little bridge so that he could scarce pass over it; but better than all the miracles is it to hear that the very executioner was so struck with awe that he threw down his sword, and falling at Alban's feet begged to suffer instead of him, or at any rate with him. For some time no one else would take up the sword, but at last one of the soldiers plucked up courage, and there, on the hill-top, in the sight of the multitude, "the head of our most courageous martyr was struck off, and he received the crown of life which God has promised to them that love him." At the same time also was beheaded the soldier who refused to give the stroke. They did not die in vain, for the judge himself was so moved by their death that he ordered the persecution to cease, and ever afterwards that town of Verulamium was counted a holy place and marvellous for the healing of the sick; so that when Bede wrote, four hundred years afterwards, there was "a church of wonderful workmanship" there, in memory of the martyr. In Bede's time the town was called Verlamacester, but in later days it was named St. Albans, and it is called St. Albans still.

St. Ninian the Missionary.

Here and there in Scotland we find churches dedicated to St. Ninian or St. Ninias. There is not much known of him, except that he was one of those wandering missionaries who went to and fro among the villages of the ancient British tribes, winning them to the faith of Christ. The tradition is that he was the son of a British chieftain, and went to Rome to be educated in the Christian faith; but this latter point is very doubtful, for the monks in later times used to take it for granted that every saint and bishop had been to Rome, and set it down so as a matter of course. It is more likely that he was instructed for the priesthood by old Bishop Martin of Tours, in Gaul, another famous saint and missionary of those old times, for it is certain that they were warm friends. Then afterwards Ninian returned to his own land and wandered away preaching into the northern parts, among the valleys and mountains of what is now Cumberland, and even beyond the Roman wall, preaching to the Picts in the Lowlands. These Picts, says Bede, forsook their idolatry and embraced the truth at the preaching of this "most reverend bishop and holy man." Thenceforth he became a sort of apostle among them, and gathered a colony of monks about him, among whom he lived as abba, or abbot, going forth from time to time in his wandering missionary life all through that Lowland country, and sometimes dwelling quietly amid his monks, and writing a commentary on the Psalms, or letters to his old friend Martin of Tours. In Bede's time there was still standing the church which he had built, of stone, "which is not usual among the Britons," at Whitherne, on the coast of Wigtonshire. It is but little that is known of him, but it is interesting to think of him as one of the real workers in those days.

Pelagius the Heretic.

More distinct and more interesting is the name of Pelagius. He was never put on the list of saints by the Roman Catholic Church, for he opposed some of the doctrines of the time, and was counted one of the worst heretics in the world. And yet, perhaps all the more, we may count him among the true saints of God; for he was one who thought for himself, and when he had found what he believed to be the truth, was not afraid to declare it, and would not be put down by emperors, or bishops, or councils; so that, whether he was right or wrong, we are glad to think of him as a Briton.

He, too, like Ninian, was a British monk; Morgan is supposed to have been his native name, and Pelagius, which means the same thing ("of the sea"), his name turned into Greek. From the simple faith and life of the rude British churches he went to Rome, which was then the great central light of all the Christians of the

West. At Rome he found himself among the great controversies about the doctrines of religion, which were already doing so much to divide Christians; and he became a deep scholar, and was regarded as a very holy man, until his learning got him into difficulties. He seems to have been one who read the teachings of Christ in a simple, natural way, and formed his faith by them, and could not receive the doctrines which, it seemed to him, Christ did not teach. The particular point about which he set himself against the common notions, was that of man's nature. The great doctors of the Church in that day were laying it down that the nature of man was totally evil, corrupt in reason and will, and unable to do any good whatever. This, they said, was the consequence of Adam's sin; and as they made out that all mankind had existed in Adam, they asserted that all had sinned in him, and that therefore all deserved to suffer in this way and to be punished in hell for it. This was the doctrine of the great Augustine, at that time the most noted theologian of the Church. Pelagius could not take this in. He maintained that man's nature was not entirely corrupted by Adam's fall, and that men were able to do their duty by their own will, if they would—so much so, that even heathens were able to do it, and he averred that there were many good heathens who had done it.

This is only an outline of a question which was fiercely argued all over the Christian world for many years. Pelagius, having become interested in it, did not return to his own country, but remained at Rome, trying to convince men of what he was persuaded was the truth, and wrote and argued and held his ground.

So it was, until the fierce Gothic barbarians came down upon Italy and laid it waste, and there was no longer any home there for peace-loving, studious men. Then Pelagius went to Egypt, where there were great colleges and libraries and numbers of learned men. With him went, as his disciple and helper, Celestius, also a youth from Britain, whom Pelagius had found studying law at Rome, and persuaded to give himself to a religious life. Celestius shared his master's opinions, and together they became the leaders of a great party, for there were many who thought that they were right. Augustine, however, was too strong for them. No man in all the Church was so powerful as he was. The Pope condemned them, and councils and synods condemned them, and all bishops who held with them were deposed, and gradually the obnoxious doctrines were put down and disappeared—for the time!

Pelagius and Celestius also disappeared. They had returned to Rome, but the Emperor Honorius banished them in the year 418, and probably they sought some retired place where they might be safe from persecution. Some said, in after days, that Pelagius had died in Palestine; others that he went home to his native land. How that may be we know not; only Bede says, that a little later his doctrine had "sadly corrupted the faith of the Britons." But then Bede was a very zealous Catholic!

CHAPTER IV.

SAINT PATRICK AND "THE ISLAND OF SAINTS."

JUST beyond the island of Britain, the old-world explorers found another island, which they called Little Britain. It was also called Ierne, then Hibernia, and in later times Ireland. Its inhabitants were other tribes of the same Celtic people whom the Romans found in Britain. These tribes were never conquered by the Romans, and remained undisturbed in their ancient religion, long after the Britons had become Christians. In course of time, however, Christianity was introduced among them, and it took such strong root, and produced so many good and famous men, that Ireland came to be called "the island of saints." So that, as we know so little of the Christian Church in Britain, it is the more interesting to look at this branch or offshoot of it, which must have been very much like it.

The missionary who carried the gospel to Ireland was St. Patrick, and the Irish have reverenced him as their patron saint ever since. Indeed, so many foolish and marvellous legends grew up about him, that many people have fancied the whole story of him untrue. But quite independent of these legends, we have a very simple and interesting account of Patrick, one of the best and most beautiful stories of those early times; and there are even one or two works which, there is little doubt, were written by him. His story is as follows:—

About the end of the fourth century, while the Romans were still in Britain, there was growing up in a little village called Bonavem (believed to have been on the Clyde) a boy then named Succath,—"Patricius," or "Patrick," being only his monkish name, given years afterwards. He must have grown up a Christian, for his father, Calpurnius, is named as having been the deacon of the little community, which very likely was one of the villages converted by the preaching of Ninian. Succath, as a Christian child, would be taught the Creed, some sort of little catechism, and a few prayers. Very likely he did not pay much attention to these at the time, but afterwards something happened which made them very precious to him. Rovers from the far north, sailing the seas in their great war-galleys, seeking plunder and slaves, found their way up the Clyde and landed, and fell upon the little Christian village where Succath lived. Among their booty they took this lad, and carried him off with them, and sailing away to the opposite side of the sea, sold him for a slave to one of the chieftains in the north of Ireland. Here he was sent out on to the hills, keeping sheep, and in his lonely shepherd life he thought, as he probably had never done before, of his home, and of the religion of his childhood, of which these wild people among whom he was knew nothing. One of the works of his which has been preserved is called his "Confessions," and in it he tells about his life at this time. He says: "I was sixteen years old, and I knew not the true God; but in a strange land the Lord brought me to a sense of my unbelief, so that, although late, I minded me of my sins, and turned with my whole heart to the Lord my God, who looked down on my lowliness, and had pity on my youth and my ignorance." After six years of slavery he escaped, and found some way of getting back to his own land. Then the traditions are confused. Some say that he went to Rome, and obtained consecration from the Pope; but that is very uncertain. Patrick himself does not say anything in his Confessions about having gone to Rome at this time. It seems quite as probable that he remained at home, and that it was there that, after some years, the thought began to grow up in his heart that he ought to go back, and preach the Gospel to the rude people among whom his captivity had been passed. At one time there seemed to come to him in a dream the united voices of the Irish who dwelt near the sea, crying, "We beseech thee, child of God, come and walk again among us." Another time there came a message to him in his sleep: "He who gave his life for thee, He speaks in thee." Ireland was then looked upon, by those Britons who had been civilized by the Romans, as the wildest and most barbarous country in the world, and his friends tried to keep him back, thinking that one captivity there was enough. The voice within, however, was too strong to be resisted. "It was not in my own power," he says, "but it was God who conquered in me and withstood them all;" and so he sailed away over the sea, and landed in Ireland, and the rest of his life was spent in preaching the Gospel amongst its wild clans.

There had been another missionary before Patrick, a monk named Palladius, said to have been sent from Rome; but he was a foreigner, and did not know the language, and had not made any way. Patrick, however, was at home in Ireland. He had lived among the common people as a shepherd lad; he knew their speech and their ways, and soon his preaching began to tell. He used to gather the people together, in the places where he came, by beating a rude drum, and then he told them the story of Christ and preached his religion to them. Sometimes the Druids excited the people against him. At one time, he says, "Daily I expected to be seized, to be carried into slavery or killed." Once he was seized by one of the heathen chiefs, and for a fortnight was kept a prisoner, but in the end he was freed and came safely through all dangers, and gradually a great fame of him went through all the country. Usually he went first to the chiefs and tried to convert them, for if the chief received the Gospel, the whole clan soon followed. In one chieftain's hut, the young son of the household was so attracted both by his looks and words, that he gave himself up to the religious life, and thenceforth went everywhere with Patrick, who baptized him Benignus, made him his companion and helper, and afterwards named him as his successor. As years passed on, a great veneration for Patrick as a holy man of God spread among all the tribes. The poor looked on him as their champion; the kings—every tribe in those times called their chief a "king"—sought his blessing and his advice. Few dared incur his anger. Once a roving chief from the coast of Christian Britain—from the part afterwards called Wales—carried off a number of Patrick's newly baptized converts; but straightway the saint wrote him a terrible letter, excommunicating him from the Church till he should set them free. In their veneration, the chiefs often gave him lands, but he kept none of these for himself, and devoted them to forming little religious communities, which became the beginning of the Irish monasteries. One of the best things told of him is, that he gave the Irish their alphabet and taught them the art of writing. A true man of God, he laboured in this way many years—so many years are set down to him that it is thought there must have been others of the same name after him. Once he went over into Gaul, to visit some of the holy monks there, and perhaps at that time he may have gone on to Rome. But for most of his life he was wandering to and fro in Ireland, labouring through perils and hardships, never flagging—a patient, fearless, devoted man, well worthy of the name of "Saint."

The *work* he did is even more visible to us than the *man*. For, from the example and influence of Patrick, the wild wastes and forests of Ireland, and even the lonely islands along its shores, became dotted over with monasteries. There they built those lofty round towers which still remain, and round about these clustered the rude cells which were all the dwellings the monks had for some centuries, and there they lived together under the rule of some holy man. Wonderful traditions have been preserved of those old monasteries. In some cases whole clans were gathered into a sort of monastic community. The monastery of Bangor (near Belfast) was one of the most celebrated, numbering, some accounts say, three thousand, others, four thousand monks—who, divided into courses, kept up perpetual sacred song and service night and day.

Thus, one by one, were most of the Celtic peoples who inhabited the British Isles converted to Christianity. As the new religion spread from one of these tribes to another, it kept very much the same character, so that they, altogether, made up a little family of simple primitive churches, closely connected together, but having very little to do with the rest of the Christian world which looked to Rome as its head. They had customs and usages of their own, different from those of others. They all looked to Rome, indeed, with something of the old awe which that mighty name had created through the world; and it seemed a specially holy place, because it was said that there St. Paul and St. Peter had lived and had been put to death. And very proud their priests and monks were to go on pilgrimage and get the blessing of the Bishop of Rome, but they did not acknowledge his authority, or regard him as chief over all bishops, as most of the Churches were beginning to do.

Of all this group of Churches, thus growing up in these islands apart from the rest of Christendom, the Irish Church became the most important. For, after a while, the Christian provinces of Roman Europe began to be overrun by bodies of barbarians, and Britain was being desolated by the Saxons, and the quiet useful life of learning which the monks in these countries had generally followed became no longer possible. But Ireland lay too far out of the way to be much troubled by these heathens, so thither came for refuge many a learned monk from Gaul and Britain. Thus the Irish monasteries were strengthened, and the monks, who had not yet fallen into the corruptions of later times, passed their days in studying such learning as they knew, and copying the works of holy men like St. Patrick, or writing down with beautiful illumination the laws and poems and traditions of the bards. From among them, too, went forth during several centuries many a fearless and devoted missionary, like Columba,—the founder of the monastery at Iona, and Columbanus and Gallus, who, with little colonies of monks, preached to the barbarous heathen tribes who had settled amidst the ruins of the old Roman civilization in Burgundy and Switzerland and Northern Italy. Thus, while the British Church was being swept away, and Roman Europe was gradually sinking back into barbarism, Ireland was the home of a simple peaceful faith. The fame of its strong churches and great communities of holy men, —of its poets, and musicians, and philosophers, spread through the lands. Doubtless these reports would lose nothing in the telling, but enough remains of the buildings, the poetry, the traditions of those old times to enable us to understand how the admiring reverence of the world gave it the name of "the Isle of Saints."

CHAPTER V.

THE SAXON INVASIONS—BRITISH CHRISTIANITY SWEPT AWAY.

A SAD story has now to be told, the story of the over-running of Britain by the barbarians; the story of how the ancient British people, with their Christian Church, were almost destroyed, or driven to the mountains, by our heathen forefathers the Saxons and Ængles, who then settled down and became the people of the land.

It is a long story, though it does not take long to read, because so little is known of it.

For three hundred years, as long as from the days of Queen Elizabeth to the present time, Britain remained a Roman province. It was a peaceful, happy province. Once fully conquered, the people were bright and quick, and seem to have been willing learners of the Roman ways. Orderly and well-built cities arose, where garrisons were stationed, and these were connected by fine, well-made roads, some of which still remain in use as high-roads to the present day. Forests were swept away, mines were opened, manufactures were introduced. All this lasted so long that the people came to have very little idea of any other order of things, except that there were traditions handed down by the old men, of a far-off time when their fathers had kings of their own race, before the Romans were in the land. But at length a change began to come. Tidings of disturbance and disaster came from

Rome. Stories began to be whispered among the people of how that great, strong, wonderful Roman land from which their rulers came, was beginning to be beset by vast hordes of warlike barbarians from unknown countries in the North and East. Then signs of weakness began to appear in the government of Britain. The troops in the great garrison towns were no longer exchanged as regularly as formerly. The district governors did more as they pleased, and seemed no longer afraid of being called to account by the home government. Legions were sent for back to Rome, and none took their places; and the garrisons became smaller and smaller. Great endeavours were made to induce the British youths to enter the legions, and numbers of them enlisted and were drafted off to defend the provinces nearer Rome, and few ever came back. From time to time new efforts were made to establish the Roman power as before, and once or twice fresh bodies of troops arrived. But each time some pressing emergency soon occurred. Every soldier was needed at Rome, and so, little by little, the military stations were deserted, the richer settlers went home, and at length, by the year 440, even the show of Roman government was given up, and the Britons were left entirely to themselves.

At first there was great rejoicing among the people. They recalled the traditions of their older time, set up a king from the old royal race, and were very proud of their independence. But troubles soon began. Beyond the Roman and Christian part of Britain were fierce barbarous tribes, very much like those who were overrunning Italy. To the North were the savage Picts, whom the Romans had never been able to subdue, but whom they had kept away by a great wall and chain of forts, which can still be traced, stretching right across the island from sea to sea. The Britons had now to protect themselves, however, and this they had not been accustomed to do, so that, though they made a long and brave defence, they failed. Year after year the marauding bands came swarming down from the North, ravaging the country to its very centre.

Here and there a brave stand was made. Bede tells how, one time, when a great body of Picts came where a number of Christians were holding their Easter festival, their bishop, Germanus, put himself at their head and led them on. With loud shouts of "Hallelujah" the Britons rushed forward and put the Picts to flight. A field near Mold, in Flintshire, is still pointed out as the place which tradition says was the scene of this "Hallelujah Victory." But such single instances of courage could not stay the invasions. Then the Britons looked abroad for help. They sent pitiful appeals to Rome, but not a legion could be spared. Then, in desperation, they turned from one race of the barbarians to another. They asked the aid of the Saxons, and a new chapter in the history of this island began.

The Saxons were tribes of brave, hardy adventurers, who, from the shores of the Baltic and the Northern seas, were roving far and wide in their war-galleys, slaying, plundering, conquering, and, when they came to any pleasant land, settling down upon it. Even in Roman times their forays were not unknown on the British coast. Some of these roving sea-warriors were cruising about in the Channel just at the time when the Picts, in greater numbers than ever, were laying waste the country, and to two of their chiefs, whom the ancient chronicles call Hengist and Horsa, the British king, Vortigern, applied for aid. The aid was willingly given, a body of Saxons landed, the Picts were driven back, and the Saxons obtained the Isle of Thanet for their services. From the moment the Saxons thus got a foothold in the country, the misfortunes of the Britons were doubled. Their warlike allies soon quarrelled with them, and from Thanet won all Kent. Then tidings of the new settlement spread among the other Northern tribes, and soon other bands of warriors came swooping down on the defenceless coast. It was from the country just south of Denmark (part of which is to this day called "Anglen") that most of them came, and they called themselves Angles, or Ængles; but the Britons called them all "Saxons," from the first bodies who settled down; and to this day the Welsh, who are the descendants of those Britons, call all English people *Sassenach*—"Saxons." Saxons, or Ængles, however, their invasions never ceased, till nearly the whole country was in their hands.

These Saxon and Ænglish forefathers of ours were fierce heathens. Their gods were the magnified likeness of their own rough heroes, and their heaven was a mighty "Wal-halla," or "Hall of the Fallen," where those who fell in battle, which they thought the only death fit for brave men, were to spend their days eternally in furious battles, and their nights in feasting and drinking mead out of the skulls of their enemies. They despised the Britons for their Romanized dresses and ways, and they despised them most of all for their religion. A religion which taught that people should be patient under injuries, and forgive their enemies, seemed to those fierce children of the North only fit for cowards. So they destroyed with savage exultation everything connected with Christianity.

As they spread over the land in their great war parties, nothing seemed able to resist them. They broke through the defences of the towns which the Romans had left, and swarmed over the ditches and earthworks of their fortified stations. They massacred all who resisted them, only saving captives to torture by their camp-fires, or make them into slaves. The people fled in terror before them. Beautiful Roman villas, where petty British kings had set up their palaces and aped the Roman fashions, lay empty and deserted. Husbandmen left their farms, serfs their rude huts, seeking refuge in the old hill forts where, ages before, their fathers had resisted the Romans, or flying, with wives and children, towards the shelter of the Western hills. There the native British tribes dwelt on unmolested, and the fugitives were absorbed among them. But over the rest of the country, from the German Ocean to the Severn, the invaders spread themselves, and settled down where they would in the almost deserted land. The native race had well nigh disappeared. Those who were left were probably for the most part only the serfs of the soil, the poorest, the least raised above the old British barbarism and the old Druid superstitions. The churches, the priests, every trace of the despised Christianity, had been ruthlessly swept away. It is little wonder, therefore, that we know so little of the Christianity of the Britons. The Saxons partly, but in far larger proportion the Ængles, became the people of the land. Those of the native Britons whom they had amongst them they called *Weallisc*, or "strangers," from which the hill-country whither most of these had fled came to be called "Wales." There, and there only, the remnant of the ancient British churches survived. Cut off more than ever from communication with the rest of Christendom, they drew still more closely to the churches in Ireland, and nourished their religion and their patriotism with memories of the old time before the heathen came into the land. But from that land which had been theirs, their religion, their very name almost, perished. It came to be called, from those who now inhabited it, "Ængla-lande." Its people knew no religion but their own rude heathenism.

But, it may be asked, did not the ancient Christian Church, thus still surviving beyond the Severn, exercise some influence over these heathen Ængles and gradually convert them? That was what Christianity did over a great part of Europe. As the barbarians spread through the Roman provinces, the one thing which stood its ground—not everywhere, but in many places—was Christianity; and over a great part of Spain, Gaul, and Italy, it gradually absorbed the new populations into the Church. But it was different in this country. The Britons were a sturdier race than the more Romanized natives of the provinces nearer to the capital. Britain resisted the invaders as no other part of Europe did, and instead of its people mingling with them, they drew back before them, remained still a separate people, and regarded the invaders with undying hate.

The consequence was that the British Christians, from their mountain refuge, made no attempt to convert the Ængles. They did not want them converted. They did not wish that they should be saved. Driven out from the best part of their own land on earth, the Britons comforted themselves by thinking that at least they should have heaven to themselves. They even bound themselves by oaths, says Bede, never to reveal the saving truths of religion to the "Saxons," as they called them. And they kept their oath, for not a single attempt, by any British monk or priest to convert the heathen settlers of the land, is recorded.

CHAPTER VI.

THE MISSION FROM ROME—AUGUSTINE.

Now we come to one of the most interesting parts of the story of those old times, the winning of this newly settled Ængla-lande to Christianity.

Like all the Saxon tribes, the Ængles were fierce heathens. Their chief name for God was Odin or Woden, but they thought there were many other gods, whom also they worshipped. The names by which we still call the days of the week are most of them derived from those old Saxon deities. Wednesday is Woden's day; Thursday, the day of Thor, the god of thunder and storm; Friday, is Freia's day, the goddess who blessed the fields and harvests; while Tuesday and Saturday are also called from the names of two other gods. Moreover, every mountain, river, and wood was thought to have some lesser deity of its own, and the belief in these as "fairies," "brownies," and "bogarts" lingered long among the common people, and may even yet be found in out-of-the-way places. They had no regular system of temples and priests, though there were priests and seers among them. The most part of their religion was done in the home by the head of each family, who was a sort of house-priest. Such a kind of people were these Ængles—or Anglo-Saxons, as they have commonly been called in history—who had spread over most of this country, settling on the land,

and occupying the villages and towns. Strong and brave were they, and loving the simple institutions of self-governing freemen in which they had grown up, and which they brought with them across the sea, but still fierce heathens, utterly despising Christianity.

At this time—we have come to the end of the sixth century—Gregory the Great was the head of the Church at Rome. He was one of the best of the Popes, and longed very much to make the Gospel known throughout these heathen tribes that had settled all over the Roman empire, and that dwelt in the lands beyond it to the north. He especially desired to have this island become Christian again, as it had been in the former times of the Britons. There is a story told, that, even before he was made Pope, he was one day walking through the slave-market at Rome, when he was struck by the sight of some little slave children standing there for sale, whose rosy cheeks, blue eyes, and flaxen hair were very different from those of the dark little Italian children. "What people are these?" he asked. "Angles," was the answer, for that was the way the name was pronounced in Italy. "*Non Angli sed Angeli*"—not Angles, but Angels—"would they be if they were Christians," he cried; and he had them bought that they might be trained up to be Christian monks, with the idea that some day they might be sent home to convert their countrymen. Whether those children ever did so return we do not know, but from that time forth Gregory was always planning for the conversion of that Ængla-lande. It was no easy task, however. The Anglo-Saxons were regarded in France and Italy as merciless savages, very much as the Malays and the New Zealanders have been regarded in modern times. After Gregory had been Pope for six years, however, news came that Ethelbert, the chief or king of one of the little Saxon kingdoms on the English coast opposite to France, had married a Frankish king's daughter, and that she was a Christian, and had taken a monk with her to her new court, so that she might keep up her own religion. Immediately Gregory determined to wait no longer, and choosing Augustine, the prior of a Roman monastery, he sent him off with his forty monks to go and live in the Ænglalande and try to win the people to the gospel. Away they went, journeying on foot through France, but everywhere as they went the people told them such dreadful tales of these savage Anglo-Saxons, and drew such pictures of their ferocity, that at last the monks became afraid, and stopped, and persuaded their leader Augustine to go back to Rome and ask that they might be released from so dangerous and useless an enterprise. But Gregory, who was a firm, brave man, and would gladly have gone himself, would not hear of any turning back, and encouraging Augustine with many words, he sent him on his way again. This time they all went forward, and, crossing the narrow sea, landed on the coast of Kent in the spring of the year 597.

Kent was then a separate kingdom, and to Ethelbert, its king, Augustine sent, on landing, to tell him that he and his companions had come from Rome as an embassage on the subject of the king's eternal welfare. It was a strange message, and the name of Rome had still something awful in it to the people of those far lands, and so the king wondered greatly.

The pagan priests about him whispered doubts to him, and though he consented to give the monks a hearing, he would only meet them in the open air, being half afraid of witchcraft. Out in the open air, therefore, under a great oak-tree, high seats, or thrones, were set for Ethelbert and his Christian queen, Bertha; and there, with his chiefs and priests around him, the king waited for the monks to approach. Augustine and his forty companions wished to make as much of a show as they could, so they came in solemn procession, two by two, with a great silver cross and a picture of the Crucifixion carried before them, and chanting their Latin psalms as they advanced. So there they uttered the message of Christianity to Ængla-lande. They could not speak a word of the Ænglish or Saxon tongue, and Ethelbert and his people were just as ignorant of Latin, so that everything they said would have to be interpreted, sentence by sentence, by some Frankish attendant of the queen. It was preaching under great disadvantages, and yet they made a strong impression. Ethelbert was not prepared all at once to adopt their faith, but he spoke fairly to them, and promised them hospitality, and gave them leave to preach freely to his people, and to convert all whom they could.

It was an encouraging beginning; the missionaries were allowed to go inland to Canterbury, and there they found an old ruined building which had been a Christian church in the Roman times; they repaired it, held worship in it, and built huts to live in close by. Great was the wonder of the common people all about; they saw the simple hardy life of these monks; they witnessed their worship, so strange to pagan eyes and ears; they were awed by the very eagerness and certainty with which these men entreated and warned them. Within a few months Ethelbert, their king, became an open convert and was baptized, and then the people began to come in crowds to follow his example. At the first Christmas festival it was said that as many as ten thousand converts were baptized. Augustine sent word back to Rome of the encouragement he was meeting with. The Pope was overjoyed; immediately he sent back a large band of monks to help on tho work, and began to map out Ængla-lande into bishoprics. His intention was to make London the seat of the archbishop, who was to be at their head. It was easier, however, to make plans in Rome, than to carry them out in a new country. Augustine and his followers were already preaching here and there, sometimes far away from Canterbury; but London was in one of the little Saxon kingdoms where the king and people were still heathens. They had, therefore, to content themselves with Canterbury as the seat of the archbishop, and it has continued so to this day, the Archbishop of Canterbury being still called the "Primate of all England."

It will be easily imagined that Augustine and his monks would find here and there traces of the Christianity which had been the religion of the country a hundred years before, while the Britons still held the land, and they would be curious to know what had become of those native Christians. Augustine himself had been received in such a friendly way by the Anglo-Saxons that he would not be able to understand the fierce hatred with which the Britons regarded them. These Britons he would hear of as dwelling beyond the Severn, in the wild mountainous region of Wales; they were a strong settled people there, with many churches and large monasteries, and he could not understand how it was that they had never made any effort to convert their Anglo-Saxon neighbours. The Pope had given him authority over all Christians in Britain, so he determined to try and unite his movement with that ancient native Church. The British Christians, however, showed little desire to have anything to do with him; they had some customs different from those of Rome, as to the time for keeping Easter, and the way of shaving the heads of priests. They were indignant, moreover, at a foreigner claiming to have any authority over them, and they could not help looking upon him as an ally of those hated Saxons, among whom he and his monks were dwelling so peaceably. Thus it was a long time before Augustine could get any access to them, but at length he procured a conference with the leading bishops and doctors of these British churches in Wales. It was held in Gloucestershire, near the Severn. Augustine urged them to join with him in preaching the gospel to the heathens, and to submit to the authority of the Pope as delegated to him. Long was their discussion, but it ended in a refusal. Then Augustine proposed an appeal to miracle to see on which side God would manifest himself. Bede tells how a blind man was brought in, and the Britons prayed over him, but he said he was still blind; then Augustine's turn came, and after his prayer the blind man found he could see. As Bede, however, tells us that the blind man was of the race of Augustine's Ænglish friends, and as it was thought in those days that deception was not wrong when done for the advancing of the Church, we may well doubt whether there was any miracle in the matter. The British bishops, however, professed to be struck by it, but still would not yield without consulting their people, so the conference separated to meet another day. In the meantime, they consulted a venerable hermit as to whether they should abandon their traditions and submit to Augustine. "Yes," was the old man's answer, "if he is a man of God." But how were they to settle this? "True Christianity," said the hermit, "is meek and lowly: if Augustine is so, he is of God; if he is proud and haughty, then do not heed him." To test this, he bade them let Augustine arrive at the place of meeting first, and then let them notice whether, when they approached, he would rise up to meet them with respect. But when they drew near, Augustine kept his seat; so Bede says they began to upbraid him with pride, and would have nothing more to do with him.

How far all this can be depended on as true, is quite uncertain, but one thing is certain, that the two Christian movements kept quite separate from each other, and that for centuries the Britons of Wales hated the Ænglish just as much after they became Christians as before.

Though, however, the British Christians would not help in the missionary work, it went on none the less eagerly. Soon after this conference Augustine died. The monks persevered with their mission, however. Supported by Ethelbert, who was *Bretwalda*, or Overlord among the chiefs of the various kingdoms, they went far beyond the limits of Kent. Into the kingdom of Essex, or the East-Saxons, they went, and converted the king, and close to London they founded the great "West-Monastery," now "Westminster." Away into Wessex, too, they wandered, through the parts settled by the West-Saxons—Hampshire and Wiltshire—and sometimes were roughly treated, for we are told how, in the Dorsetshire fishing villages, an "impious mob" tied fish-tails to their cowls and chased them from the neighbourhood. On the whole, however, it seemed as if they were making great progress, and for nineteen years after Augustine's landing all went well.

Then came a great change; Bertha had already been dead some years; now Ethelbert died. His son was a pagan, a man of violent temper and evil life. With such an influence at the head of the people, they fell back from Christianity as easily as they had come into it, and the monks, afraid of the feeling which was rising against them, fled into Gaul.

A few remained, indeed, and among them Augustine's successor, Laurence. He seems to have been a brave man, and at last he got some hold upon the king, and persuaded him to give up his heathenism and be baptized as a Christian. Then the monks came back again, and Canterbury remained a Christian settlement as before. But Ethelbert's strong influence over the other kingdoms was no longer at their back, and all the work of conversion in distant parts of the country had fallen through; it seemed as if darkness was again settling down over the land, and all that remained of the once bright prospect of Christianizing Ængla-lande was the one little Christian district of Canterbury and the immediate neighbourhood.

CHAPTER VII.

LIGHT FROM THE NORTH—PAULINUS—ST. AIDAN.

JUST at the time when the missions from Rome, in the South of England, appeared to be turning out a failure, light appeared in another quarter. Away in the North was another of these Anglo-Saxon kingdoms called Northumbria, which then included not only the present Northumberland, but Durham and Yorkshire, and parts of Lancashire also, and stretching northwards over the Lowlands of Scotland as far as the Frith of Forth. Over this great tract of country ruled one of the most powerful of the Anglo-Saxon kings, Eadwine, or, as it is usually written now, Edwin, from whom the great fortress at the north of his kingdom was called Eadwinesburh, now Edinburgh. Edwin became the most powerful king in the Ængla-lande, and sought for a daughter of Ethelbert and Bertha to be his wife. She was given to him, but only on the same condition on which her mother had been married to Ethelbert—that she might be accompanied by a Christian priest, and have freedom for her own religion. So among these rude people of the North-Humber-land came a Christian queen, and in her train one of Augustine's old fellow-missionaries—

PAULINUS.

Little is known of Paulinus, but he was probably an Italian, by the description which is preserved of him.

For, a century afterwards, the old people used still to tell of him as their fathers had seen him—a tall, thin man, with stooping shoulders and dark, piercing eyes, and long black hair falling round a thin, eager face. He had full liberty to preach, and he was a man of untiring energy; but for a long time he went to and fro over the country without making any converts. At last his patience and his holy life were rewarded. The king was saved from the dagger of an assassin, and the queen brought through the perils of childbirth, and Paulinus urged upon them both that these were mercies of the God whom he preached to them; and these things made a deep impression upon the king. Even yet, however, Edwin hesitated, until he should have taken counsel with his people; so the "Witena-gemote," or wise men's "mote" or meeting, was summoned; and here, surrounded by his priests and nobles, Edwin called on each in turn for his opinion. It must have been a curious scene. The most remarkable thing, perhaps, was that the chief of the heathen priests, Coifi, at once answered that, for his part, he was quite ready to try the new religion, for he verily believed there was no good in the old. No one, he said, had given himself more busily to their old religion than he had, yet it had not made him prosperous, nor brought him into favour with the king. If the gods were good for anything, it must have been different; so he was quite willing to give them up. An interesting indication, this, of the way in which idolatry was losing its hold by the mere presence of Christianity. There were others there, however, who looked at the subject in a worthier way. One of the thanes, or nobles, rose and said, "The life of man, O king, compared with all that lies beyond unknown to us, is like a sparrow flying into your great hall, when you are feasting with your thanes in winter. A moment it is safe from the storm, in the midst of the light and warmth, and then it passes out of sight again, into the darkness from which it came. So is our life; we see it for a short space; but what went before, or what is to follow, we know not. If this new religion can tell us something more certain, it deserves to be followed." Paulinus was then called in to explain his faith more fully, and the story, which is told at some length by Bede, ends with Coifi—for whom, as a priest, it was unlawful to mount a horse or carry arms—calling for the king's own charger; then, mounting it, and with a spear in his hand, to show how completely he broke with the old superstition, he rushes to the neighbouring temple and casts the spear into it, exciting the people to burn it to the ground. From this time the work of Paulinus went on apace. King Edwin was baptized. A little wooden church was hastily built up at York for his baptism, and here, immediately afterwards, he began to erect a large church of stone, which was the original of the present Minster. The thanes mostly followed his example. Then the people began to flock in crowds to be baptized. Their Christianity could not have been very deep, but it had some effect. It made both rulers and people more humane and civilized than before; and Bede tells how it used to be a saying that in Edwin's time there was such perfect peace that a woman with her new-born babe might walk from sea to sea without meeting with insult or injury; and another chronicler records that Edwin had cups of brass or iron hung up by the wells for the refreshment of way-goers, and no man ever took them away.

It seemed, at last, as if Christianity, baffled in the South, was to find its success from the North. But here, also, it was to meet with a reverse like that which had almost overthrown Augustine's work in Kent. The king over all the midland parts of England, then called Mercia, was still a fierce heathen, and he attacked Edwin. With this heathen chief, Penda, came the mountain tribes of Wales, who, though they were Christains, did not hate their old Saxon enemies the less; and whose fierce chieftain, Cadwalla, hoped, by helping one Saxon king against another, to end by destroying them all. Together, they were too powerful for Edwin; he was overthrown and killed, and for a year the Northumbrian kingdom was wasted with fire and sword. The Christians were the object of special hatred to the conquerors, and it seemed as if the work that Paulinus had spent his life in doing were all scattered to the winds.

But again light appeared from an unexpected quarter. The chief who, after a space, succeeded King Edwin, though only obtaining part of his kingdom, was Oswald, a man who for seventeen years had lived among the missionary monks of Iona. The great monastery there had been founded by Columba, a monk from Ireland, who, from his island home, had gone forth among the Picts and converted them. Dwelling at Iona among the monks, Oswald had learned to love their faith; and when he came to the wasted kingdom of Northumbria, and found how Christianity had been beaten down and almost trampled out by the heathen, his first thought was to send to his old friends in Iona for help in winning the people once again to the true religion.

St. Aidan.

Among these monks dwelling in their little island monastery at Iona was one Aidan, to whom, far more than to Augustine or any other, really belongs the glory of converting the Anglo-Saxons. He was not indeed the first who was sent from Iona. A priest named Corman was sent first, but he soon returned and reported that the people were so stubborn and barbarous that he could do nothing with them. "Brother," said one of the monks sitting by when he made his report, "perhaps you were too severe, and did not remember the apostle's rule to feed men first with milk." This monk was Aidan, and his words so struck the brethren, that with one accord they appointed him to go on the mission which he seemed so well to understand, and accordingly he was ordained a bishop and went forth into Northumbria.

A true man of God was this; one who well deserved the name of *Saint* Aidan. Gentle and brave, self-sacrificing and pious, he was just the man to deal with the strong rough forefathers of the miners, and fishermen, and dalesmen—still a strong rough race—of those northern parts. It might have been expected that he would fix the seat of his bishopric at York, as Paulinus had done; and indeed all through the troubled time a brave deacon had held his ground there and kept up a little centre of Christian life. But those Scotch monks loved wilder solitudes than the priests from Italy did, and so St. Aidan chose out a wild lonely island on the coast of Northumberland, Lindisfarne, ever after called Holy Island; and here he gathered a colony of monks about him and laid the foundations of the monastery, the ruins of which still remain. And then for sixteen years he went up and down that northern land from the Forth to the Humber, and from the shores of the German Ocean to the hills of Westmoreland and Lancashire, everywhere preaching to the people. Bede, who was born only twenty years after Aidan's death, gives a beautiful account of his character, though he cannot help putting in a word against some of his heresies; for those Scottish monks, sprung originally from the ancient British Church, had still kept to some of their peculiar customs different from those of the Roman Church to which Bede belonged. Aidan was a marvel of austerity and self-denial. The king and nobles heaped gifts upon him, but he gave all away in alms, or spent it in ransoming slaves, for the Anglo-Saxons were great slave-dealers. Sometimes great gifts of land were made to him, but he wanted nothing for himself beyond Lindisfarne with its few barren acres, and all that he retained of each estate was a site for a church, with a small chamber by it for his use when he came there preaching, and in every church or monastery thus formed he set up a sort of parish school, where the children of the people round were brought up by teachers whom he sent for from Iona. In looking after these churches and monasteries and schools, together with preaching in districts where the people were still heathens, he took long and weary journeys on foot. Now he was among the rich, whose sins he rebuked with a sharpness and plainness which were still remembered in Bede's time; now he was with the poor, whom he specially loved—Bede calls him "The father and worshipper of the poor;" and always, on his journeys, whenever he fell in with any strangers, he held them till he had found out whether they were still heathens or had already been baptized. All who went with him, whether monks or laymen, had to spend part of each day in reading the scriptures or learning the Psalms. Foremost of all who thus went with him was King Oswald himself, who was a beautiful example of what Christianity could make of the strong hard Teutonic nature. He was as pious and charitable as he was brave—a man of whom it is told that he was so used to praying or giving thanks that whenever he was seated his hands would be resting on his knees without his thinking of it, upturned as if for prayer. When Aidan first came from Iona, knowing nothing but the Celtic speech, King Oswald, who had learned Celtic during his long residence among the monks, would go with Aidan, and, sitting at his feet as he preached, acted as interpreter to the audience of thanes and people. It was a sad day for Aidan when this true friend was taken from him; but Oswald, too, had to fight against the fierce heathens who had overthrown Edwin, and after a good reign of seven years he was slain in a great battle with them at Macerfeld, (supposed to be the Makerfield near Warrington,) and ever after was reverenced as a Saint.

Though thus once again the Christian King was conquered, Christianity was not this time overthrown. It had made way too widely and too deeply, owing to the character of Aidan and Oswald. Aidan did not fly, and the two princes between whom the kingdom of Northumbria was now divided were both Christians. With one of them, Oswin, Aidan formed a strong friendship. Oswin was not such a man as Oswald had been, yet he loved this holy man whom all the people reverenced as a Saint. Hearing of his long journeys on foot the king pressed his own favourite horse upon him, and Aidan took it and used it for awhile, till one day some sudden call for charity arose, and he gave it away, with the rich royal harness and all. Upon this, Bede tells us, the king was vexed—as he well might be, indeed—and rather sharply told Aidan that he thought a horse of less value would have been good enough to give away. But the Saint answered, "What is it you say, O King? Is that foal of a mare more dear to you than the Son of God?" and the king could not withstand such goodness, and fell at his feet, praying to be forgiven for his hasty words. Soon after, King Oswin was murdered, and it was but twelve days later that Aidan himself went to his rest. He died as became so true a soldier of Christ. He fell sick on one of his missionary journeys, and they hastily stretched a tent for him, against the wall of a little timber church which he had just built. There, resting against one of the logs which formed its buttresses, he breathed his last, August 31, 651.

His body was taken to Lindisfarne and buried in the low ocean-washed graveyard there. It did not remain there long, however. A few years after, when the struggle which arose between the Celtic and the Roman parties in the Church was settled by the Anglo-Saxon Church joining with the Church of Rome, the Scottish abbot of Lindisfarne was one of those who would not give way to the Roman customs. He withdrew to Scotland, and among the treasures which he refused to leave behind him were the bones of his sainted predecessor. So Saint Aidan lies buried among the unknown graves of Iona.

CHAPTER VIII.

THE GREAT NAMES OF THE ANGLO-SAXON CHURCH.

WITHIN a few years of the death of St. Aidan, Christianity began to spread rapidly through the rest of the little kingdoms into which the Ængla-lande was divided. Even the rude people of Mercia, as the whole midland country was called, whose king, Penda, had been the fiercest foe of Northumbria and its Christianity, had to yield to it at last. Penda's son went into Northumbria to seek the daughter of its king, Oswi, as his wife. Oswi would not give his daughter to a heathen, so the young prince began to study Christianity, and soon declared himself so earnest a convert, that even if the maiden had been refused to him he must still have continued a Christian. However, he was not tried so sorely as that, and he went home with a Christian wife, and four monks from Lindisfarne. Contrary to what might have been looked for, King Penda raised no persecution against them. He himself never changed his religion, but he let the monks have freedom to preach, and to convert all whom they could; only, if any would receive the new religion, he sternly required that they should practise it. A few years after, the aged Penda was killed in battle, and then Christianity had full sway, a monk of Lindisfarne, named Ceadda, or Chad, preaching here and there around Lichfield, where he fixed his bishopric. With such earnestness and power did he preach, that all the country called him "Saint;" and when afterwards the cathedral at Lichfield was built it was dedicated to him, and is called St. Chad's to this day.

Gradually Christianity became the general religion of the whole people. The change was made easier by its not destroying all their old associations, but rather turning them to account. Augustine had found that at various times in the year there were great religious festivals kept up all over the land, and he knew that it would be very difficult to put these down, for they had been so kept up for centuries, yet he did not like them because they were associated with the old heathenism and helped to keep it alive. So he sent to Rome to ask what he must do. The Pope wisely replied that he had better let the people keep them as before, and indeed keep their old customs generally, but that he must teach them new meanings for them, and turn them into festivals and customs of Christianity. Thus there was a great religious festival kept by the Saxons in honour of the goddess Eostre, in the spring, about the time when the Christians kept the festival of the Resurrection, so it was changed into the Christian festival, but the old name, Eostre—our Easter—remained for it among the people, and still remains. Then in the winter, the Saxons, like all the northern people, kept the great Yule-feast, so this was turned into a festival for the birth of Christ, and by-and-by people forgot that Christ-mas had ever been anything else. Gradually churches were built throughout the country. These were not fine stone buildings. These Saxons, from the fens and forests of northern Europe knew nothing yet of stone architecture. Even their castles were only timbered houses, with stockades round them, usually on small mounds, such as we still find in many parts of the country, often close by the churches. As these churches were built, the districts round them were put in their charge as their parishes, and over each larger district of the country there was a bishop. Generally those bishoprics in the old Saxon times arose from the labour of some holy man who had come into the district while it was yet heathen, and gradually converted the people and built churches here and there, the place where he first settled keeping its place as the seat of the bishopric. Thus Canterbury was the first Saxon bishopric, and when bishoprics were set up in London, and Rochester (604), and Winchester (648), Canterbury was made an archbishopric. So, when the second great missionary movement in the north was made, York became its centre; and the fact that the bishoprics of England are to this day divided into two "provinces" as they are called, of Canterbury and York, each with its archbishop, arises from the Christianity of the country having in that ancient time had this twofold origin.

Then these churches had to be supported. At first this was done by free offerings and gifts. The Saxon thanes or nobles, when they were converted, often made rich offerings, sometimes out of piety, sometimes in remorse for wicked and lawless things that they had done. Many made grants of land. Later, some of the kings gave to the churches rights over the people of their parishes; sometimes a right to call upon them for labour, just as their lord himself could; sometimes a right to tax a part of their earnings for what was called the "kirk-scot." Thus Offa, King of Mercia, the midland district, commanded (about 760) that all his people should give a tenth, or tithe, to the Church; and a hundred years later, when all the kingdoms were united, Ethelwulf ordered this payment of tithe to be made all over England. From these different sources the Church grew rich. There were some churches, in the later Ænglish times, in which the sacred vessels were of gold, and the priests' robes were of gorgeous colours, and all embroidered with silk and gold.

In close connection with all these churches, monasteries also spread. Sometimes they were great settlements of monks, sometimes of nuns; often, in those times, they were double communities, monks and nuns dwelling close together and under one head. As time went on, so many of these monasteries were set up, and such numbers of people joined them, that at the beginning of the eighth century Bede says he began to be afraid there would soon not be enough laymen left in the land to do its work, and to furnish soldiers to keep away their enemies. Indeed, in time many people adopted the monastic life in order to escape working and paying taxes, for the monks were free from all claims of their lord or king. This was a great mischief, and caused a great deal of corruption, and some of the monasteries became haunts of idle and pleasure-loving men, with a great deal of wickedness going on in them. Still it must not be thought that they were all of this character. Many of them were always the home of humble godly men, or of gentle Christian women, who wanted to live a quieter life of worship and of learning than they could do in the midst of the world. Let us recall the names of some of the greatest men of that Church which grew up among these Anglo-Saxons.

Wilfrid

is one of the earliest of these great men. He is most notable for the part he had in bringing the Church, which was being extended through the Anglo-Saxon kingdoms, into full subjection to the great Church of Rome. Wilfrid was the son of one of the northern thanes or nobles, and, as a boy, was a sort of page or attendant to an aged man who had withdrawn from the world to the lonely monastery of Lindisfarne. Thus he himself became a monk there, and as he grew up he heard the monks eager about questions which were rising up between those who held by the old ways which their holy founders had brought from Iona, and originally from Ireland, and those who thought that these ways ought to give place to the customs which were followed in Rome. The whole question was only a small one, the two chief matters in dispute being as to how a monk's head should be shaved, and when exactly Easter ought to be kept. The Roman monks used to shave the top of the head, leaving a rim of hair all round as an emblem of the Crown of Thorns; while the Irish Church had never learnt this practice, and its priests and monks simply cut the hair very short in front and let it grow behind. Then a change in the way of reckoning the calendar had been introduced at Rome in the year 525, and the Irish and Scottish Churches had heard nothing of it, and went on keeping Easter after the older reckoning. As long as they were separate this did not matter much, but now the southern part of the country was being converted by monks from Rome, and the north by monks from Iona; and their work was beginning to touch. Already, in the very midst of the district which the Scottish monks were working, a colony of Roman monks were settling down at Wearmouth, and establishing a monastery there. So the customs which they taught clashed, and people did not know which to follow. The difficulty came to a head when King Oswi of Northumbria married a princess from Canterbury, for she brought her priests with her, and they kept her to their old Roman ways; so that the king was holding Easter with his Church at one time, and the queen was holding it a week or so later.

Wilfrid heard all these things and determined to go to Rome and try to find out for himself which way ought to be followed. He was but a youth of nineteen, but was quick and clever, and when he came back he declared that the Roman customs were the right ones, and that the monks and priests everywhere ought to yield to the authority of the Pope. Thenceforth he became famous as the warmest partisan of Rome, and never rested till the question was settled.

The place where it was settled is one of the most famous spots in that Anglo-Saxon Church. On one of the boldest hills of the Yorkshire coast, where, even so early, a lighthouse had been built near a harbour which was called Streaneshalh, or "the Bay of the Lighthouse," a large settlement of monks and nuns had gathered about the Abbess Hilda, a strong-hearted Northumbrian lady of royal race. Long afterwards the Danes called the place Whitby, the name it still bears, and a noble abbey was built there. There was no such magnificent building in Abbess Hilda's time. The monasteries of that day were merely groups of wooden buildings around a church, built of cleft oak trunks, and roofed with a thatch of reeds. Hilda was accounted one of the wise women of her time, and her abbey was a sacred place. Hither, therefore, King Oswi summoned the leaders of the two Churches, Colman, Bishop of Lindisfarne, Aidan's successor, and Wilfrid, who was the life and soul of the Roman party; and hither the King came himself with his thanes and courtiers, in the year 664. Long was the discussion, which is given at length by Bede, and it ended in a curious way. Colman set forth what had been the practice of Aidan, and especially of the holy Columba, the great founder of Iona. Wilfrid, however, urged the claims of Rome as having been founded by St. Peter. "Will you," he cried, "set the practice of Columba against the authority of St. Peter, to whom are given the Keys of the Kingdom of Heaven?" At these words the king interposed, "Is it true, Colman, that Christ gave the Keys of Heaven to St. Peter?" He answered, "It is true, O King." "Then, for my part," said the king, "I must obey him who has the keys, lest when I come to the Gates of Heaven, I find him my adversary, and there be none to open to me!" Such an argument could not be got over; Colman retired, and with his more obstinate followers left Lindisfarne, and carrying the body of his predecessor, Aidan, with them, they went back to Iona. On so small an argument hung the fate of the Christian Church in England! Thenceforth it became fixed as one of the branches of the great Church of Rome; and one of the busiest in enforcing the decision of the king and bringing the churches everywhere into the Roman ways, was Wilfrid. Underneath Ripon Cathedral there is a long narrow crypt, called "St. Wilfrid's Needle," which is thought to have been built by him, especially as it is very like the little oratories in the Catacombs, which he would see when he was in Rome. For some time he was Archbishop of York, and later in his life he laboured much among the South Saxons, in the part now called Sussex. A strong man he was, but made many enemies by his partisanship for Rome.

A nobler character than Wilfrid was

St. Cuthbert.

About the same time that Wilfrid was growing up in a noble household, a simple peasant boy was living in a poor widow's home at the foot of the Lammermoor hills, and was dreaming dreams and thinking of holy things in the loneliness of his shepherd lot. He felt his heart drawn towards that religious life which he heard people speak of as followed by the Christian monks. So, while still only about sixteen years old, he found his way to Melrose, where a few missionary monks from Lindisfarne had settled down, in what was then a desolate wilderness, and were living in the poor log huts which were the beginning of all monasteries in those times. All the other monks loved him for his piety and goodness, and when their prior died, a few years after, they chose Cuthbert to be their head. He was no longer subject to others, then, and could spend his time as he liked, so he began to wander far and near, through all that Lowland country, teaching the peasantry, and especially loving to go to the most remote hamlets among the hills, where no other preacher ever went, and where the people were Christians in little more than in name. His desire was to bring them to some real understanding and love of the Gospel. And he was very successful in this ; for, while he was a thorough man of the people, one who could talk to them in their own broad country speech, and with a ready humour too, he was at the same time so humble, and charitable, and devout, that the villagers were delighted when he came among them. After a time he was called to Lindisfarne, and thence went preaching all about Northumberland. A hardy, untiring man he was, one who shrank from no hardship and feared no danger. When the hearts of others fainted he always cheered them. Once, when he was without food, an eagle flying to its nest with a fish in its mouth dropped it near to him, and it seemed to him a miracle of God's care. Another time he and his companions were snow-bound on the shore, with the sea impassable because of the storm. His attendants said there was no way either by land or sea. "The way of Heaven is still open," cried the brave monk. As his life passed on, however, he longed for rest and meditation, and left the busy monastery of Lindisfarne for Farne, a still smaller and wilder island miles away out at sea, where he built a little hut with his own hands. A man so good, however, could hardly be spared from that troubled northern land, and, after eight years of hermit life, the King of Northumbria himself went to Farne and brought him back by his entreaties. So, once more, first at Hexham and then again at Lindisfarne, he laboured for two years as bishop. Then, once again, he retired to his beloved retreat; not for long, however. In a few months he had entered into the holier rest which he had earned by his saintly life.

But all through that northern country his memory remained dear to the people. The place where his body was laid in Lindisfarne became a sacred spot, to which sick people were carried in the belief that they would be healed there. And when the monks had to fly from there, two hundred years later, in order to escape from the attacks of the Danes, they took St. Cuthbert's coffin with them as a precious treasure, and carried it about with them as they took refuge first in one place and then in another. At last they settled down with it at Chester-le-Street, and there it remained for a hundred years. Then more perils and more migrations. For a little time it was at Ripon, and then it was taken to Durham. At Durham it still rests, in a great tomb behind the high altar of the cathedral. A few years ago it was opened, and among the mouldering bones were found remains of beautiful embroidered work—faces and names of saints, wrought in silk and gold thread. These may still be seen in the library of the cathedral, and they were undoubtedly the borders of the robes which the good old Bishop of Northumbria used to wear eleven hundred years ago.

Cædmon.

In telling of the great names of the Anglo-Saxon Church we must not leave out Cædmon, the first writer of any note who wrote in this mother tongue of ours. He was only a poor peasant to begin with, a cow-herd employed by the monks of Whitby, at the time the Abbess Hilda was head over the great monastery there. A poor ignorant man he was, who could not even make such songs as his fellows used to sing, when they gathered at the lower end of the great hall at night, so that Bede tells how when the harp was passed to him, he would get up and go out ashamed. Perhaps it was, however, that there was something in him which made him wish to make some nobler song, and yet he could not make it amidst the noise and jesting of the hall. One night after he had thus gone away in shame, as he lay sleeping he saw a vision in his dream of one who came to him and said, "Cædmon, sing me something." "I know nothing to sing," replied Cædmon, but the vision would take no refusal and bade him sing of "the Creation." Thereupon the dreaming man began to pour forth verses glorifying "the Guardian of Heaven" for his wonderful works; and when he woke the verses were still fixed in his mind, and he went on and on with them, with a feeling of awe, for it seemed to him that the poetry was not made by him but, as it were, given to him. This came to the hearing of Abbess Hilda and the monks, and they all believed he had received the gift of song from Heaven. So they took him from his farm work, received him among them as a monk, and taught him all the old Bible stories, which he passed his days in thinking over and turning "into most harmonious verse," says Bede. It does not seem very harmonious to us, for it is in the short, rugged, broken style of the Saxon war-songs, which was the only kind of poetry Cædmon knew, but to the people of that time it seemed divine. And indeed it was so strong and racy that, centuries after, Milton did not disdain to learn of it, and many passages in "Paradise Lost" were plainly suggested to him by the verses of the old Anglo-Saxon singer. A simple-hearted pious man he was, too, as well as a poet, and when the last sickness was upon him, and he felt that his end was near, he asked them to make ready a place for him in the house where people sick to death were usually carried. They could not understand why he wanted it, for, said they, "You are not like to die, since you talk so merrily with us, as if you were in perfect health." But they did as he wished, and when he asked for it, they brought him the sacrament, and then he lay down and asked how near it was to the hour when the monks gathered to sing the midnight service. "It is not far off," they answered. Then he said, "Well, let us wait for that hour;" and as he lay waiting for it he fell into a slumber, and so passed peacefully away.

The Venerable Bede.

About the time when Cædmon was making the last of his Bible verses in his monk's cell at Whitby, a child was born in a village a few miles further north, who was to do a still more important work in the literature of those old Anglo-Saxon times. This was Beda, or Bede, afterwards called the Venerable Bede, from the great reverence which men felt for him. He was born on the lands of that great monastery at Wearmouth, which has already been mentioned as having been founded, not by the Scottish monks from Iona or Lindisfarne, but by monks from the south, of the Roman party. At seven years old the brethren took him into the monastery among them. It was a time when they were famous for their skill in arts and learning, for their "Abbat Biscop, surnamed Benedict," had been often in Rome and foreign lands; and he had brought home with him masons and glaziers, and taught his monks to build great stone buildings, instead of the timber houses and churches that were all that the Ænglish had before. He taught them, also, better chanting for their service, and finer lettering for copying the books in their monastery library. So here

Bede grew up, and loved to learn everything he could, not only writing and singing, but Latin and Greek, and even Hebrew, and came to be so highly thought of by all in the monastery, that at nineteen years of age he was ordained a deacon. A quiet life it was that he lived there; sometimes taking his share in winnowing corn or threshing it, or in the various employments of the garden, the bakehouse, or the farm, as all had to do from the abbot downwards; "but in the intervals of discipline," he says, "I always took pleasure in learning, or teaching, or writing something." In this Wearmouth monastery he passed his whole life. He became its teacher, and such a famous teacher that six hundred scholars are said to have gathered about him there. Books of hymns he wrote, and books upon the art of poetry, and a life of St. Cuthbert, and many a book of commentaries on different parts of the Bible. The most valuable book that he left, however, is a long Ecclesiastical History of those early times in this country. It is a curious rambling book, for the way to write history was not much understood in those days, and the monk seems to have put down all the old traditions that came to his ears without much sifting. But still it is very valuable, as it is almost the only source we have of information about those very early times, and along with much mere monkish legend, it contains a great deal that there is no reason to doubt is true; and it gives us many interesting particulars about the old Ænglish times and people, and all is told in very pleasant graphic style. He was so brave, and cheerful, and devout, that all loved him; and though a very feeble man, troubled with ever increasing sickness, he busied himself with his books till the last. His last work was a translation of the Gospel of St. John, from the

Latin, in which the priests used to read it, into the tongue of the common people. One of his scholars, Cuthbert, afterwards abbot of the monastery, has left a beautiful account of his anxiety to finish this work, and of how he kept labouring at it all through his last illness. He was too feeble to write himself, so he sat or lay in his cell, translating, while some of his scholars read to him—often through their tears—or wrote down what he dictated to them. Very careful he was,—for, said he, "I will not have my scholars read a lie after my death." With failing strength, and his breathing getting shorter, he still kept at his task: "Go on quickly," he said, "I know not how long I shall hold out." And thus came Ascension-day (A.D. 735), and he had been awake all night, spending the hours in thanksgiving. The monks were walking in procession that day, but one remained with the old man, and said to him, "Most dear master, there is still one chapter wanting. Do you think it troublesome to be asked any more questions?" He answered, "It is no trouble; take your pen and write fast." After a time the monks came back, and he sent for them, and gave among them the few little articles he had in his chest, and spoke to every one of them; and they mourned and wept, but he said that he desired to die and be with Christ. "And having said much more," says Cuthbert, "he passed the day joyfully till the evening." And then the youth ventured to remind him—"Dear master, there is yet one sentence not written." "Write quickly, then," he answered: and soon the writer looked up—"Master, it is finished." "Yea," said the dying monk, "thou hast well said. *It is finished.*" Then with much help he was raised up, for he wanted to sit looking on the spot in his cell where he used to pray. And thus, on the pavement of his little cell, with his head resting in the young man's hands, he chanted the "Gloria," and with the last words of it on his lips, he died. This was how the New Testament first began to be translated into our old Ænglish tongue.

King Alfred.

We have not to go to monasteries for all the great names of the Anglo-Saxon Church. There is no greater name shining out in all those centuries than that of Alfred, who was king about a hundred and fifty years after the time of Bede.

By this time, when Alfred was growing up, you must understand that the various Angle and Saxon tribes which had settled in the land, had almost blended into one Ænglish people, and their little separate kingdoms had all fallen under one rule. Egbert, Alfred's grandfather, had been the first king over the whole country. But now that their wars among themselves had ceased, a new trouble was coming upon the land, in the invasions of the Danes. The Danish war-galleys were swarming about the shores of Ængland, just as those of the Saxons had done three hundred years before; and their fierce warriors were landing at every unprotected spot, plundering the country, destroying the churches, murdering the men, carrying off the women and children for slaves. All through the reigns of Alfred's father and brothers, these hardy Northmen, from Norway and all the Baltic coast as well as from Denmark, were ravaging Ængland. They were often beaten back, and in Alfred's day were for a time effectually checked.

Still, they kept coming again, until, as we shall see, a hundred years after, they finally overcame the Ænglish, and a Danish king, Cnut or Canute, became king over all the land.

It was in the earlier part of this long struggle that Alfred lived and reigned. He was the youngest of King Ethelwulf's four sons, and when he was a child of four years old his father went on a pilgrimage to Rome and took Alfred with him. Afterwards he lived with his father at Paris, which was already a considerable city. He was of course too young to understand much of what he saw, but the magnificent buildings which still remained in Rome, and the grand doings of these cities, and all that he must have heard of arts and learning, left impressions upon him which set him trying, through all his after life, both to improve his own mind and to elevate his own country and people. There is a story, too, of his early life, that one day when his mother, Osburgha, who was one of the sweet Christian women of that age, was sitting with her boys about her, she showed them a book of Saxon poetry, all written out fairly with pen and ink, and with beautiful gilded and painted headings, and offered to give it to the one who should first learn to read it. Alfred sought for a teacher and won the book. Certain it is that he became one of the best scholars of his time. As he grew up to manhood, however, other things than scholarship had to occupy him. His father had died years before, and then his two eldest brothers had each reigned for a little time and died. And now the third son was king, and Alfred stood next to him, and the Danes were ravaging the kingdom, and it was a life-and-death struggle for all the king's house. In the midst of the struggle (871) the third son, Ethelred, died, and then

Alfred was king. Many stories were told in after days of the courage with which he carried on the warfare, and of his wanderings when defeated. That was the time when he is said to have been hiding in one of the peasant's cottages, and to have sat by the fire so busy with his own thoughts, that he forgot the cakes which the peasant woman had bidden him look to, and let them burn. In a while, however, he gathered more followers about him, made another brave effort, and at last defeated the Danes so thoroughly that they were glad to make peace. They were routed and beaten back, but he could never drive them out of the country. If you draw a line on the map from Liverpool to London, that will show about how ÆEngland was divided, for the Danes were lords of all the northern and eastern part, while the kingdom over which Alfred ruled was all the country to the south and west of that line. It was not even half of what we call England now, but he ruled it so well that people forgot how small it was, and he became more famous than any other of the kings of that old time.

For, instead of spending his life as a foolish or ambitious ruler would have done, in trying to win back the rest of the land, he set himself to make his people wise and happy. He taught them how to build better houses. With his council of wise men—"Witenagemote"—he made good laws, putting the ten Commandments at the beginning of them to be part of the law of the land. Moreover, he set himself to have the laws carried out, and was always ready, in his court, to hear the appeals of his people. A mild, kind, cheerful man, he was only pitiless to corrupt magistrates and judges, whom he hanged without stint; and he was very watchful in putting down wrong, and exacting justice through the courts of the counties, and hundreds, and tithings. There was a law in those times called the law of frankpledge, by which, if any one in a village committed a crime, all the people of that village had to answer for it, and to join in giving redress; and Alfred was so strict about this that robbers had no chance, and it was said that men might leave golden bracelets hanging by the wayside for weeks without their being taken. He established schools, too. Then he sent out travellers over distant seas and lands, some of whom went even as far as India, and he himself wrote down for his people the information that they brought back.

At the heart of all this good life was religion. Alfred gave eight hours of every day to sleep and meals and exercise; and eight hours more to the cares of his government; the other eight were passed in study, and in the exercises of piety and religion. He earnestly longed for his people to be good Christian people, and to this end tried to have wise, good monks and ministers among them. The services of the churches were all said in Latin in those times, as they were indeed for hundreds of years afterwards, and when Alfred came to the throne he found that very few of the priests knew the meaning of the Latin words they mumbled over, or could tell their people anything about them. The King set himself to remedy this. He gathered about him learned monks, who might teach the others; he translated, into the Ænglish of his time, a good book of Pope Gregory's on the duties of pastors. Indeed, he urged that all useful books "should be translated into the language that all understood," and himself set the example by devoting the study of many a year to this work of translating.

Yet all through these manifold labours King Alfred

was only a weak, ailing man. All through his manhood he suffered from a tormenting malady which no one could understand or heal, which racked him with constantly recurring pains. Sometimes it utterly prostrated him, and it never left him till he died, at the age of fifty-two. He had said once, that he wished "to leave to those who came after him a remembrance in good works." And he did so; he was a wise, good, Christian king.

CHAPTER IX.

THE CHURCH IN THE DANISH INVASIONS—DUNSTAN.

What a strange story of successive conquests the History of England is! We have seen the Britons invaded by the Romans, and the ancient Druidism passing away before the Christianity silently introduced among the Roman settlers. Then we have seen these Romanized and Christianized Britons invaded by the Angles and Saxons and Christianity almost swept away, only to be brought in again among the new people of the land by long missionary labours. Now we are to see the Anglo-Saxon Christianity attacked in its turn and nearly swept away by the invasion of the Danes. Round the coast they came in their great war-galleys, from their homes on the shores of Denmark and the Baltic, landing at the fishing towns and harbours, everywhere slaying and plundering. Year by year they became bolder. Soon, they sailed up the rivers, right into the heart of the country; then, landed, made fast their ships, set up camps, round which they raised vast earthworks, which may still be traced; and seizing the horses of the country people, went on their plundering raids far and wide, spreading terror and desolation through the land. For many years they used to go back to their own country every autumn; but at last, in 851—just when Alfred was two years old —the Saxon Chronicle sadly says, "This year the

Heathen men, for the first time, remained over winter, and from this time there was no peace for Ænglend."

Especially there was no peace for the churches and the monks. These Danes were fierce Pagans; indeed, they were just what the old Teutonic ancestors of the Ænglish had been originally, and because they were of the same stock, they hated and despised the Ænglish all the more for having forsaken the religion of their forefathers and become Christians. It may easily be understood what a welcome prey to such cruel and covetous invaders were the monasteries, which were dotted all over Ængland, with their fertile fields and well-filled granaries, their rich altar-stuffs and their sacred vessels. Nowhere else was the booty so plentiful, and nowhere was it so easy to take. The Danes had no pity for age or sex. They would torture their prisoners horribly to make them give up their Christianity. Thus, after they had defeated Edmund, the King of the East Angles, they dragged him from his hiding-place, and beat him with clubs and whips while they taunted him with his faith. Edmund held firm, however, and then they tied him to a tree and made a mark of him for their arrows, and ended by beheading him. In after times he was counted a saint for his fortitude, and the place of his death still bears his name—Bury St. Edmunds, St. Edmund's "burg" or town.

Long the Ænglish people struggled bravely against the Danes, but gradually they seem to have become cowed, by the ferocity of their vengeance when opposed. It is a pitiful story how the Danes spread over the land, and how churches and monasteries fell before them. First those near the coast were plundered, and then those inland. Holy Island, Lindisfarne, was wasted, and the bishop and his monks fled, carrying with them the precious relics of St. Cuthbert. Then the great monasteries at Wearmouth, Jarrow, and Whitby were left mere heaps of ruins. York was stormed and taken, and Beverley, and all the other rich churches and monasteries founded by the northern kings and thanes, till it is said there was not a single monastery left standing, north of the Humber. South of the Humber, the struggle was continued longer.

One little glimpse of that struggle, taken from the old Chronicles, will give an idea of the sorrow and danger of the time. It was just two years before Alfred became king that there was a great landing of the Danes in Lincolnshire, and word soon spread that they had pillaged Bardney Abbey and killed its monks. The country was roused. From all directions men came together with their arms, and among others came a body of men sent by the monks of Crowland, or Croyland, with one of the lay-brothers at their head. All one day they fought the Danes and held them back, but in the night more Danes came up, and many of the Ænglish peasants fled. Still, a brave band were left, however, and at daybreak these all took the sacrament, and then linked their shields together, and all day long, through the second day, they held their own and stood their ground. In the evening, however, the Danes pretended to retreat, and so got the wall of Ænglish shields broken, and then turned again and defeated them. The slaughter was terrible, but a few young men managed to escape into the woods, and fled all night towards Croyland, to warn the monks there of the danger coming upon them. They came to the monastery at daybreak, just as the monks were at their morning prayer, and rushing in told them, with cries and tears, the Danes would soon be upon them, and warned them to fly. There was no time to be lost. The white-haired old Abbot, Father Theodore, bade the younger monks get a boat ready, and load it with their most precious relics and treasures, and said that those who could should escape with it; but he and others who were too old for flight would remain, and the little children might be left with them, for surely no one would harm them. So they set the boat, with its load, off through the winding channels among the fens, and then the old men and the children went back into the church, and began singing mass with what heart they could. Just as the service was closing, there came wild war-whoops and the rush of many feet, and the Danes were upon them. No mercy had they for old or young. The Abbot in his robe was struck dead upon the altar steps, and some of those about him were beheaded, and some were tortured to make them tell where the treasures were; and when the Danes found that there were no treasures left, they were so mad that they killed all whom they could lay their hands upon, and set the monastery on fire, and left it blazing and strewed with corpses, to burn on, until after seven days the whole group of buildings was burnt through, and nothing was left but a waste of charred and fallen timbers.

Meanwhile the Danes hastened southwards to another rich monastery at Medehampsted, now called Peterborough. There the retainers and followers of the Abbey had been gathered together and something done to fortify it; but the fierce warriors soon broke through the defences, and, maddened by the death of one of their leaders, ordered every one they found to be slain. Not a monk was left alive; the altars were overthrown, the relic-cases ransacked; the library, which was rich in beautifully illuminated parchments, was strewed about, and then all was set on fire, and it went on burning for a fortnight before all was destroyed. Then the fierce Heathens went on their course, marked by blazing churches, pillaged farms, and mutilated corpses,—on to Ely, where they found a nunnery, and, after shocking atrocities, slaughtered all the women.

This was but the story of what went on in different parts of the country, year after year. Sometimes, as was afterwards the case in this particular foray, the invaders were at length met by a strong force and routed; but more often they got back safely to their camps or to their ships, laden with plunder. The fear they inspired was terrible; the farmers had no heart to till the ground; the monks, even when they escaped with their lives, had no means to rebuild the monasteries. By the time Alfred made the stand which at last rescued a part of the country to be his kingdom, it was said there was not a monastery left in all the Ænglish land, except at Abingdon and at Glastonbury.

Alfred's reign was the turning point, as far as the danger to Christianity was concerned. For, when he had defeated Guthrum the Dane, and had him and all who were left of his routed band at his mercy, one condition Alfred exacted of him was that he should be baptized. Guthrum went to the King's camp, with thirty of his chief men, for his baptism, and there they stayed twelve days, and Alfred so won the heart of his former enemy, that Guthrum kept his vows and continued a faithful ally of the Christian Ænglish thenceforward. And from this time great numbers of the Danes, being peaceably settled in their own part of Ængland, which was called the Danelagh, gradually mingled with the Ænglish people, who were after all originally of much the same race, and became Christians. After this it became possible for churches and monasteries to be rebuilt. Where the body of the martyred Edmund had been laid, a few generations later the Danish King, Canute, built a magnificent monastery, round which gathered the town of St. Edmund's burg or bury; and in many another place the Danish nobles, having once become Christians, shared the same admiration and reverence for the monkish life which had dotted over the land with monasteries in the earlier time.

The revival of the Church, however, from the depression caused by the Danish invasions, is very largely connected with the name of one great man,—

Dunstan.

Such a haze of marvellous legend has gathered about Dunstan, and he made such bitter enemies by the hard, high-handed way in which he carried out his measures, that it is difficult to get at the simple facts of his life. Yet he seems to have been one of the strongest and ablest men of his time, both in reforming and strengthening the Church, and in helping to govern and defend the kingdom.

As a boy, the son of a powerful thane, he grew up near Glastonbury, and when, as a man, he was persuaded to become a monk, it was the monastery at Glastonbury he entered. There he became one of the most noted of the monks, learned for the times, skilled in music, and skilled, too, in smith's work, and almost every other art and craft of the age; noted, too, he was, for the severity of his life, his only dwelling-place being a little sunken cell, about five feet long, more like a tomb than a living-place, where he studied and wrought at his anvil. Here he won such saintly fame by the hardness of his life, and his struggles with his temptations, that all sorts of stories came to be told of how the devil himself tried to tempt him there, but was always put to flight. One of the best known is, that on one occasion when the tempter came, the saint seized him by the nose with the red-hot pincers he was using at his forge. Perhaps such traditions shadow forth some deeper fact, of how, in that hard hand-labour, he found refuge and safety from the tempting thoughts which are sure to attack any one who tries to live a lonely meditative life. However, men came to think of Dunstan as a strong, learned, capable man, and when he grew a little older, he was made Abbot of Glastonbury, and also the King's Treasurer. It seems strange to us in these days to hear of monks being chosen for such an office of state, but they were the only class, in those rude times, who had scholarship enough for such a post, and so all such offices fell to monks and priests. As the King's Treasurer, Dunstan was at the height of power; for Edgar was only a weak king, and though Edgar reigned, Dunstan ruled. In such power his good qualities and his bad ones both came out. For, while he was a very able man, really loving his country, desiring to see it strong and prosperous, and still more vehemently loving his Church, which he wished to reform and make more united and powerful, he was at the same time wilful, intolerant, and often unscrupulous in carrying out his measures. He made the kingdom stronger than it had ever been before, did much to knit its different parts into one compact whole, and raised a great fleet of warships, which he kept so active that for many years the northern pirates dared not show themselves. And he was just as busy with the Church; he persuaded the King to found and endow no fewer than fifty great monasteries, and into all these he introduced the strict and settled order of the Benedictines, while the double monasteries of the older times, which had been swept away, were heard of no more. Let it not be forgotten, too, that he required the King to send copies of the Scriptures into the different provinces of the kingdom, to be placed in those churches which were without them. He was a zealous upholder of the doctrine, which was beginning to be enforced through the Western Church, that priests should not marry. Anciently, priests were allowed to marry like other people, and in the Eastern Church, which would not submit to Rome, this has never changed. Even in the West, the custom of celibacy, which the Popes began to enforce, was long resisted, in spite of all that here and there some zealous advocate of the stricter way could do. With Dunstan went, hand in hand in his work, the Archbishop of Canterbury, a fierce, rough Dane, named Odo, and together they ruled the Church. Great numbers of the married priests were forced to put away their wives, and Dunstan did all in his power to get the churches and cathedrals into the hands of monks, and, in fact, to make all the clergy into monastics. To a great extent he succeeded; the Church flourished; Church dues and offerings were demanded so urgently that they became more and more like a regular tax, and monasteries sprang up everywhere, until nearly a third of the whole land of the country was in the hands of the clergy. In the reign of one King, Edwy, Dunstan used his power at court so roughly, that the King turned against him, took away his offices, and chased him from the country. But Edwy soon died, and his successor finding he could not get on without the strong, shrewd counsellor, recalled him. So, through nearly five reigns Dunstan was the one strong, able man in Ængland. But at last there came a time when "Ethelred the unready" was on the throne—a man too weak and shiftless to value such counsel, or to like having such a counsellor about him; and then, after a long and vain attempt to keep things right, the old monk retired, sad and hopeless, to his monastery, and there soon died.

And so, once more, the Church in Ængland settled down very much into its old ways. For the moment Dunstan had brought it into line, as part of the great Church that was spread through all the countries of Europe, and whose head was the Pope of Rome. For a while the monasteries were carried on regularly by the strict Benedictine rule, and the awe of the great ecclesiastical councils of the time, with their injunctions of celibacy, and "canons" about the government of the Church, was felt far and wide over the country. But it was only for the time; the kings had something else to do besides looking after the monks of distant monasteries, or the priests of far-away country parishes; and Rome was a great way off, and the Popes of those times were not very powerful, so that gradually Dunstan's reforms and new ways were forgotten, and monks and priests, whether Ænglish or Danish, fell into very much their old kind of life. Thus we come towards the end of those old times before the Norman Conquest. The monasteries had become once again settlements of people living on the lands which the piety of a former age had given to them, living very much like other folk, but with something of monastic order, and with masses sung more or less regularly in their abbey churches. Besides these, were scattered here and there over the land, parish churches, still mostly rude timbered buildings, rebuilt after the wasting by the Danes just as they had been hundreds of years before, and, always hard by, the house of the priest. Not very learned these priests, many of them knowing very little about the Latin service, which they said in no very regular order; but they baptized the children, and married the up-grown, and shrived the dying, and buried the dead in what the people called "God's acre," and kept up such religion as they knew. Perhaps not many of them were very learned or very saintly, like some of those holy men in foreign parts, of whom pilgrims now and then brought back such wonderful stories; and no doubt they knew little of Theology, and were often over eager about their tithes; yet, at any rate, they were Ænglishmen, caring little about Rome or the Pope; living mostly with wife and child about them, as men should do, and thinking it no wrong. And so things went on till the Norman came.

CHAPTER X.

THE CHURCH UNDER THE NORMANS.

THE Norman Conquest was almost as great a revolution in the English Church as it was in political and social life. Not only did it bring numbers of foreigners into the abbeys and churches, but it altered the whole religious life of the country. It introduced a new element of art and dignified order into the worship; and brought in that passion for noble architecture which covered England with fine churches and magnificent cathedrals. What was, perhaps, still more important, it made the Church and the priestly order more independent and separate from the rest of English life than ever before, and drew them into much closer connection with the rest of the Catholic world.

The very character of the invasion, indeed, was full of warning to the English Church. Everything was done that could be done, to make it appear a holy war. The fact is that the Pope of that day was glad of any excuse for bringing England under Norman rule. Nowhere was the Church more rich, powerful, and submissive to Rome than in Normandy. Nowhere was it so independent and so difficult to bring under any kind of subjection, as in England. So, at the mast-head of William's ship floated a holy banner, which the Pope had sent along with a license to invade England; and in return the Pope had received—at least so he ever claimed, afterwards—a solemn promise that the land to be conquered should be held as a fief of the Papacy, and render a yearly tribute to Rome. Thus blessed, priests crowded with other adventurers to take part in the expedition. Such an one was Remi, who offered a ship and twenty soldiers on condition that an English bishopric should be given to him. Such, too, was Odo, Bishop of Bayeux and William's half-brother, who, after saying mass before the army, threw off the priestly robe which he had put on over his armour, and, mounted on his great white horse, led the Norman cavalry. Only, since it was forbidden to a priest to shed blood, he bore no sword, but a heavy iron mace with spikes at the end of it! The day before the battle Harold's spies brought word that there were more priests in the Norman camp than there were men-at-arms in the English one.

On the other hand, the priests and monks of the threatened land were thoroughly English in character and sympathy. None resisted the Norman invasion more sturdily than they. Many of them put on coats of mail and came forth to fight for their native land. Thus Alfwig, Abbot of Winchester, with twelve of his monks, stood by King Harold at the battle of Hastings, and they died there, every man of them. So, also, did Leofric, Abbot of Peterborough, "dear to all people," as the "Anglo-Saxon Chronicle" says of him. And when the Normans had got the victory and were on their way northwards, tradition tells that they were stopped at St. Albans by the multitude of trees which Frithic, abbot of the great monastery there, had felled across the road. William sent for this abbot and asked him how he dared to do this. "I have done my duty," was the answer, as it was long told among the people; "if others had done the like, it had not been in thy power to come thus far." And in the insurrections which, from time to time, burst forth in desperate attempts to throw off the Norman rule, the English monks and priests were always found helping, if not heading, the struggle.

It will be easily understood that all this brought down the iron hand of the Conqueror upon the native Church and clergy. William was a strong man, of great ability, and he meant to be king of this land which he had won. Yet he was far from being a mere tyrant. He wished to rule well. In his fourth year he summoned the Witan, to declare what were the ancient laws of England, and in middle life he set to work to try to learn English, that he might be better able to do his kingly part for his new realm. The "Anglo-Saxon Chronicle," which was written in those very times, by one who says he had looked on William and had once lived in his court, may be trusted in its account of him; for the writer speaks plainly of the harder side of his character. He was "very stark towards those who withstood his will," says the Chronicle, and one who "loved the tall deer as if he were their father;" and it adds that he "was given to avarice, and greedily loved gain." Yet it also says that he was "a very wise and good man," and "mild towards those good men who loved God." So there was no general persecution or depriving of the native clergy, and some of them kept their places all through his reign; but every abbot, or bishop, or priest who showed the slightest sign of resistance or disloyalty was swiftly removed; and many more were displaced for not coming up to the Norman ideas of the learning a priest should have; and into every vacant abbey or see was put some Norman follower of the king.

Let us take a scene from that old time. The Bishop of Worcester, when William conquered England, was a sturdy old Englishman named Wulfstan, one of the truest-hearted and most religious of the native bishops. Like many others, however, he was a man of very scanty learning, and so he was summoned to a Synod at Westminster Abbey, by the Norman archbishop, and there, on the ground that he was not able to speak the Norman tongue, he was called upon to resign his bishop's staff. The old man replied that he could only give up his office to him from whom he had received it, and straightway he rose up and strode to the tomb of Edward the Confessor, which was close by. Solemnly invoking the dead king, whom Normans and English alike counted a saint, he addressed him as his master who had made him a bishop, and said that to him alone could he surrender his staff and his flock; and with that he laid down his crosier on the tomb, and went and took one of the lower seats among the common monks. Such an invocation of a dead saint was, in those days, regarded as a very awful thing. No one dared to take up a staff so laid down. A legend grew up afterwards that no one *could* take it up, that it was miraculously embedded in the stone and could not be moved. It was not taken up, however, till Wulfstan himself was bidden to resume it, and he remained Bishop of Worcester till his death. An active, godly man he was, revered by both races alike, and making his influence felt far and wide. To Bristol he went often, and preached so much against the slave trade, which was carried on by the burghers there, that they forsook it. And when no Norman bishop could be found who dared to risk himself in the wild districts about Lichfield, where the people were almost as untamed as in old Penda's time, Wulfstan went and did a bishop's work there.

Such another as Wulfstan was Egelwine, the English Abbot of Evesham—a prudent, kindly man, who continued in favour with William, as he had been with Edward and Harold; so much so that he was put in charge of the government of several counties, and of another abbey as well as his own. Such men were able to do a great deal to soften the rigours of the Conquest, and to help on the better day when the two races should be blended into one.

These, however, were the exceptions. Throughout the churches in general there were gradual but very great changes. It was not merely that men were wanted who could be trusted to be loyal to Norman rule, but also that the Normans wanted the churches and their services altered to the ways they were accustomed to.

William's great helper, in dealing with the conquered Church, was Lanfranc, whom he had put in the place of the English Archbishop Stigand, as Archbishop of Canterbury and Primate of all England.

Lanfranc was the most famous scholar, and one of the most remarkable men, of his age. He had come originally from Italy, where all that was left of art and refined civilization had its home; and becoming a monk in Normandy, he had been one of the foremost in advancing learning and piety in the Norman abbeys and churches. William had known his high character and ability as Abbot of Bec, and chose him to aid in the changes that had to be made in the new kingdom. Lanfranc became the second man in the realm, and when William was out of England was the one who stood in his place as Viceroy. He entered into the king's work for the Church with his whole heart. The native English Church, with its slack order, its little respect for Rome, its rude timbered structures, and its irregular and poorly performed ritual, filled him with pious horror, and he set himself zealously to put it in order. Sometimes the clergy gave way quietly, sometimes they resisted, but give way they must! The churches and monasteries were looked into. Everything must be in the Norman fashion. Even the favourite saints of the old Saxon times were struck out of the calendar. Then the Church services were brought into order. Previously there had been little uniformity. The mass was recited quite differently in some churches and monasteries from what it was in others. Henceforth the service must be the same all through the country, and the chanting must be done in the foreign fashion. The people often resisted, but it was of no use. The new ways had at the back of them not only Lanfranc, but every Norman lord or knight throughout the country. Robert of Chester entered his new diocese at the head of a troop of men-at-arms. In the monasteries the men were more stubborn, and it was not so easy to fill their places with Norman monks as to put a Norman priest into the parish church—but they had to yield. Sore work there was sometimes between the Norman abbots and the English monks whom they had been set to bring into order. Here is the story of what took place at Glastonbury when Abbot Thurstan would introduce the new Norman fashion of chanting the mass. It is told us in the "Anglo-Saxon Chronicle:" how, when the monks gathered in the chapter-house refused to learn the new way, Abbot Thurstan "sent for laymen (neighbouring Norman knights), and they came in, all armed, upon the monks in the chapter-house. Then the monks were greatly terrified, and knew not what to do, and some ran for refuge into the church, and locked the doors, but the others followed them and would have dragged them forth when they durst not come out. Rueful things happened there on that day, for the French (so the Chronicle always calls the Normans) broke into the choir and threw darts towards the altar, where the monks were collected, and some of their men-at-arms went upon the upper floor (the open gallery round the chancel), and shot down arrows, many of which stuck in the crucifix which stood above the altar; and the wretched monks lay around the altar, and some crept under it, and they earnestly called upon God and besought his mercy, since they could obtain no mercy at the hands of men." And the end was that "three were smitten to death and eighteen wounded." This was an extreme case, however. Thurstan was even deposed for this ferocity by William; but it was only for a little time, for the next king, William Rufus, allowed him to return to his office as abbot, for a bribe of five hundred marks.

Let it be told, too, that not all of William's Norman priests would consent to be the tools of what they looked upon as spoliation and wrong to God's Church. There was a brave monk named Wimund, whom the Conqueror summoned from Normandy to place in some rich English living. Wimund came, but refused to accept the benefice, and spoke up before William and his nobles, bidding them remember that God hated robbery for burnt-offering, and warning them that by such spoiling of the native Church they were in danger of the judgments of God. To William's honour, Wimund was suffered to go home in peace.

Not many, however, were so scrupulous. The changes went on. Gradually a new service book, drawn up by

Osmund, Bishop of Salisbury, came into use throughout the country. The services became more regular and dignified. Schools were established here and there, and the churches were almost everywhere rebuilt in a nobler style.

Some of the changes brought about by the Norman rule were of a deeper character. Now, for the first time, with the exception of Dunstan's ineffectual efforts a century before, began that steady movement to do away with the marriage of the clergy in England, which at last succeeded. It did not succeed at once. So universal was marriage among the English clergy in England, that the change could only be gradually introduced. Lanfranc, indeed, at once obliged the married clergy of the cathedrals and chapters to resign, and put celibate monks in their places, but in the ordinary parish churches the priests were allowed to keep their wives; only he was very strict that no more of the clergy should marry, and that no more married men should be ordained. Yet it was long before this could be universally enforced, and, even a century or two later we find exceptions in remoter places, such as Whalley, in Lancashire—where the living descended from father to son for generations,—and Blackburn, where, says an ancient record, "the rectors were generally married men" until the time of King John.

From Lanfranc's day, however, this work went steadily on, and it told upon the character of the Church in many ways. It made the priesthood more of a separate order, quite apart from the rest of the people; and it drew them closer together in a Church-life separate from, and henceforth often antagonistic to, the general life of the State. "Under the native English kings," says Mr. Freeman, whose "History of the Conquest" gives a wonderfully living picture of these times, "the Church and the State had been absolutely the same thing. Kings, earls, and bishops were elected and deposed by the same all-ruling assembly. Under William, all things were tending towards a separation between the ecclesiastical and temporal power." Separate courts began to be held by the bishops, and all causes in which priests were concerned were left to these. In the end all this was very mischievous, and these special ecclesiastical courts became in later days instruments of great corruption and oppression, besides shielding priests and monks from punishment even when they had committed great crimes. But it is right to remember that in the earlier time there was another side to this; for, as the same author says of these Church courts: "Their claim, which was to judge not only all ecclesiastical persons, but also the widow, the orphan, and the poor, placed the most helpless part of the people under a milder rule than that of the Norman kings and their officers."

CHAPTER XI.

THE NORMAN CHURCH-BUILDERS.

There was nothing in which the Normans introduced greater changes into England than the art of building, and especially the architecture of churches and cathedrals. The Angles and Saxons had brought from their native plains and forests, ideas which reached no higher than a hut for a dwelling, and a mound or ditch for defence. Here, in their new land, remote from the noble architectural remains of Roman Europe, they learned little, and for centuries kept up their old ways of building. Here and there some monk from foreign parts tried to teach them the art of building in stone, as Paulinus, who built a stone church at Lincoln, and "Biscop Benedict," the founder of the monastery at Wearmouth. Thus, gradually, a few of the larger monasteries and cathedrals had come to be built of stone, and Canute rebuilt in stone many of the little wooden churches which had been burnt in the Danish invasions. But still, throughout the country, even up to the eleventh century, the churches and monasteries generally were very poor rude buildings, and many of them still of squared trunks of oak trees, roofed with reeds. The Normans, on the other hand, had caught something of the spirit of the old Roman architecture. There were many noble ruins of the Roman times in the parts of France where they settled. Some of these ruins—Temples, Theatres, Halls of justice, Baths, and Aqueducts—still remain, and there were many more remaining then, and in a much more perfect condition. The earliest Norman architecture is simply the copying of the old Roman work. What we call the Norman arch is really the round arch of the still older Roman buildings. They were not mere copyists, however, and gradually a passion for fine buildings grew up among them. To this day there is no part of Europe so rich in beautiful old architecture as Normandy.

Already, before the Norman Conquest, the influence of this Norman taste for fine buildings was beginning to be felt in England. Edward the Confessor had been brought up at the court of Normandy, and when he came over to England he brought with him many Norman ways, and tried to teach them to these rough Saxon folk, as he considered them, among whom he had to reign. The people did not like this, and though they made a saint of him when he was dead, they were always resenting his new-fangled foreign fashions while he was living. Yet it was thought a wonderful thing when he began to rebuild the church of the great abbey at Westminster, in what was called "the new manner"—that is, of stone; and they could not complain, for he gave for its building a tenth part of his whole possessions. This became the type of the new architecture. And yet even this was a small thing compared to what the people were to see before many years were gone by.

As soon as the Normans were settled throughout their new English land, they began to want to have about them the same kind of strong stone buildings to which they had been accustomed in Normandy. Then it was that there began to rise, wherever William settled his great nobles, those strong castles by which they afterwards held down the people of their counties. Then it was that Roger of Poictou began to build the great castle at Lancaster, and Duke Robert the New Castle on the Tyne, and William Peverel "of the Peak" the old keeps at Bolsover and Castleton; while Ralph Guador almost rebuilt Canute's old fort at Norwich, and similar works were going on at Skipton, Stafford, Leicester, Lincoln, Warwick, York, and many another place.

But more remarkable than the castles are the magnificent churches and cathedrals which are the pride and wonder of England. We owe those cathedrals mainly to the Normans.

It has been told, already, how William, as soon as England was fairly conquered, began gradually to displace the native English bishops and put his own followers in their Sees. One of the first things the new Norman bishop set to work to do, was, in almost every case, to build up his cathedral on a nobler scale and plan.

Canterbury Cathedral was the first of these great works of the Norman church-builders. When Lanfranc was made archbishop he found his cathedral a desolate ruin. Twice already within the memory of the old men of the place it had been destroyed. In 1011 the Danes had attacked the city, murdered Archbishop Elphege, and burnt his great church. It had been restored, and then in 1067 a great fire had laid the city in ruins, and the cathedral perished with the rest. It was three years afterwards that Lanfranc came there to be archbishop, and though he was so busy with all the changes that the king had set him to carry out through the country, he began that very year to rebuild his cathedral; and, to the wonder of all men, he had completed it in seven years, after which he rebuilt the great monastery there, with lodging for a hundred and fifty monks.

Almost at the same time, far away in the north, Thomas of Bayeux, appointed to be Archbishop of York, began to build the great Minster, which he also had found a bare and roofless ruin. The Norman barons and knights all through the country round helped him, and the citizens were laid under contribution too, and the poorer folk had to help with labour; and when means ran short, recourse was had to the Jews, who were already the great money-lenders, and made a rich harvest out of the difficulties in which this passion for fine buildings involved many an abbot and bishop of those times. Very busy must the old city—for it was an old city even so long ago—have been with carpenters and masons and smiths. There were no regular "architects," as we call them, in those days. The architect was simply the master-workman among the band of builders, mostly some monk who had learned his skill in masonry or carpentry by labouring in the building of his monastery abroad. He would map out the general dimensions and design, and then each part would be committed to some other of these monkish master-builders, with others under him in turn, each of whom chiselled out the ornaments of pillar or window as he thought would be most beautiful; and under all these were the great body of mere labourers and bearers. It is not till later that we begin to hear of some who became so famous for their skill that they were called to other places, to plan out great buildings; as, for instance, Gundulf, a monk of Bec, who was made Bishop of Rochester, and after rebuilding his own cathedral there, was sent for to build the great Tower of London; and "William of Sens"; and another, called "William the Englishman," so that he must have been one of the native monks, of whom it is pleasant to read that he was "small in body, but in workmanship of many kinds acute and honest."

Thus, by the labour of many minds and many hands, that great church at York rose up—walls and arches, and windows and pillars; and then the great oak beams were carried across, and the wooden roof laid on. It was not till a hundred years later, that the Norman builders dared to arch over the great central space with the ribbed and groined stone roofs which most of our cathedrals have to-day. That is the reason why the history of those old churches is, at first, such a story of constant fires and rebuildings. Thus Archbishop Thomas's minster had not been finished above thirty years when it was again burnt down. Then men got discouraged, and for a long time it lay in ruins, till, after forty years, Archbishop Roger began to rebuild it on something of its present plan. If you go to York Minster to-day, they will show you Archbishop Roger's work in the strong arches and pillars of the crypt, but all above has been built or altered since. For, generation by generation, the taste for architecture grew, and new fashions of it came in; and soon the strong massive work of the Normans seemed clumsy, and must be removed to make way for the lighter and more ornamented work called "Early English," and this, a little later, for each new development of beautiful decoration. Thus one archbishop rebuilt the south transept and the chapter-house; and another the north transept, putting in that beautiful window which is called "the five sisters." Then, fifty years later, in

1291, Archbishop Romaigne began to rebuild the great nave, and it was building for sixty years before it was finished; and it was still another hundred years before the two noble towers of the western front were finished, and the great Minster stood as it has been standing ever since. Over the west porch you may still see a sculpture that tells part of the story of that rebuilding: two mail-clad figures, one bearing a block of wood, and the other an unwrought stone, memorials of the two great families, the Percys and the Vavasours, one of whom gave all the wood needed in the rebuilding, and the other all the stone.

The story of almost all our great cathedrals was very much of the same kind as this of that mighty Minster at York.

To Rochester came Gundulf, one of Lanfranc's Norman monks, and found no cathedral at all, only a great waste of ruins which had been lying there for two hundred years, just as they had been left after one of the Danish raids. First he built up the keep of the old castle, and then set to work at the cathedral, which was only finished and consecrated after fifty years' building, when he had long been dead. Perhaps it seems a strange thing for a bishop to have to begin by building a castle. But the country people were still fierce and bitter against these Norman usurpers in church and hall, and William's bishops would not have been safe unless they had dwelt in strongly fortified places. For the same reason it was, that several of the bishoprics were moved from country places to the larger towns and cities. Thus, in the Saxon times there had been a bishopric at Dorchester, a little village in Oxfordshire, and William gave it to that Remi who had bargained to furnish, for such a reward, a ship of war and twenty men-at-arms towards the invasion. The English were little likely to take peaceably the rule of one who had bought his bishopric in such a manner, and so Remi transferred his Episcopal seat to Lincoln, where there was a strong castle, and built his cathedral on the hill there, towering above the city.

In like manner, from Selsea, a little village on the South coast—where an old Saxon cathedral once stood on land now lying underneath the sea—the new bishop removed his dwelling to Chichester, and used the abbey church there for his cathedral. His successor, Bishop Ralph, was not content with this, and built up a separate cathedral by fifteen years' labour; and when, after standing six years, this was burnt down, he set sturdily to work at it again, and before he died he saw it once more far advanced towards completion.

About this time, too, it was that the first of the great Prince-bishops, whom the Conqueror settled at Durham to keep order in the turbulent North, began to build the massive pile of Durham Cathedral. The first seat of that bishopric had been in the little island of Lindisfarne, where holy St. Cuthbert had lived, and had been buried. But when the Danes came, ravaging the monasteries along the coast, the monks took up the body of the saint, which was counted a most precious relic, and wandered off with it inland. For years they bore it with them from place to place, and wherever the saint was there the bishop dwelt. For above a hundred years it was at the little village of Chester-le-Street. For a while it was even so far away as Ripon. Then it was removed to its present site, seventy years before the Conquest; and here, first a little hut of branches, and then a wooden church, sheltered the relic; and then, in 995, the bishop, helped by Uctred, the Earl of Northumbria, and by all the people round, built a better church of stone, and the town of Durham grew up about the sacred spot. When the Conquest was complete, William placed one of his followers, as both Bishop and Earl, there, and side by side, on the steep hill above the city, rose the great Castle and the majestic Cathedral, very much as they are standing now.

Down in the fen country, too, at Ely, which had been a sacred place before the time of Alfred, Simeon, the Norman abbot, though he was an aged man of eighty-eight years when appointed to the See, was not too old to begin a similar work, and he went on with it till he died, at a hundred. It was his brother Walkelin who was Bishop of Winchester, and there is a curious story of how he got the timber for his cathedral—for he was building, like all the rest. He went and begged it of the king, and William granted him out of one of his great woods as much timber as his carpenter could take in four days. But Bishop Walkelin immediately collected "an innumerable array of carpenters," and in the time given, felled and carried off the whole wood! At first the king was very angry, but the bishop went to him so humbly, begging for forgiveness, that he was let off with a sharp rebuke for his grasping ways.

So it was everywhere! Away in Wiltshire, in the old hill-fort of Sarum—so wild a place, that, as the old tradition says, "when the wind did blow they could not hear the priest say mass,"—Bishop Osmund built a cathedral. After a hundred and fifty years, owing to the scarcity of water, the present Salisbury was built, in the plain two miles away, with its beautiful cathedral, which has the loftiest spire in England; and the old town was deserted, and fell to ruin, and gradually became a mere space of grassy mounds, amongst which may still be traced the site of Bishop Osmund's church. At Hereford, too, Bishop Losing was rebuilding his cathedral, on the model of a famous church which had been erected by Charlemagne at Aix-la-Chapelle. In London, Bishop Maurice was beginning the vastest and grandest of all the Norman cathedrals, old St. Paul's—on such a scale, indeed, that it was beyond his power to finish it. And at Exeter, Gloucester, Norwich, the same work was going on. Even Wulfstan, the Bishop of Worcester, of the old English race, caught the spirit of the time, and began to build a new cathedral by the side of the old church which his predecessor, Oswald, had erected a hundred years before. There is a touching story, however, which shows that Wulfstan had more feeling for the monuments of the past, than William's Norman bishops could be expected to have. For, when, on the completion of the new church, the workmen began to pull down the rude structure of the earlier time, Wulfstan was seen weeping, and he said, "Alas! we deface the monuments of our holy predecessors, not so much to glorify God, as to glorify ourselves."

And yet even this was not all. The abbey churches, or "minsters," many of them as large as cathedrals, were also mostly rebuilt. At Chester, Hugh Lupus was building St. Werbergh's Abbey, which four centuries and a half later, was to become Chester Cathedral. On the Sussex Downs, near Hastings, rose the great monastery which, after the famous battle which had won him the kingdom, the Conqueror vowed should stand as his memorial offering to God. The monks, indeed, did not like the bleak hill-top where the victory had been actually won, and would have chosen a site in the valley near. The king, however, would have it there, and nowhere else, and when they objected that it would be difficult to get water at such an elevation, he swore that wine should be as plentiful in that abbey as water was in others; so there stand the ruins of that old Battle Abbey to this day. At St. Albans, the great minster was rebuilt out of the bricks of the ancient Roman Verulam; and one of the old monkish chroniclers tells how two of the bells in the minster tower were the gift of Ligulf, a rich thane, and his wife. Rich in sheep and goats he was, and he had to sell many of these to buy the bells; and it was told that when he used to hear those bells ringing, he would say merrily that his sheep and goats bleated sweetly. So that here and there we gather that the native English had a hand in all this church-building, besides the labour to which they must often have been compelled as serfs and slaves.

It is wonderful to think of all the building that was done in those first fifty years after the Conquest. It was not only the great cathedrals and abbeys; there was hardly a little parish church that was not rebuilt during the same period. Here and there, those little Norman churches are still standing, with their massive walls, and narrow loophole windows, and zig-zag mouldings, and grotesque corbels and finials. Even where the oldest church has been destroyed, and built up again—and many of those old parish churches have been so rebuilt several times over—you may still generally find traces of the Norman builders. Whenever you visit some little village church, look carefully, and you will find some Romanesque window or doorway in the midst of later work, telling how the builders of the later age liked to build in again the most beautiful parts of the older structure. Sometimes, where there is not so much as a whole arch or pillar left, if you look carefully at the walling, you may find here and there a single stone that still shows upon it a Norman fret or moulding; and so you may spell out some fragment of the silent story of those old mighty builders.

CHAPTER XII.

THE MONASTERIES—THE CISTERCIAN REVIVAL.

THE monasteries of England deserve a chapter to themselves, and it should come in here, because it was at this time, some sixty years after the Norman Conquest, that there arose a great revival of religion, through which the monasteries became more numerous and more living than they had been for centuries before, or ever were afterwards.

We have seen that there were monastic institutions in England from very early times. The great changes which had from time to time swept over the country, had prevented them from sinking into quite so corrupt a state in England, as on the continent. No sooner had the Saxons planted them all over the land than the invasions of the Danes came, and the monasteries lay waste and deserted for generations. Then the Danes gradually became Christians; the monasteries began to be restored; many of them became more powerful and prosperous than ever. From the time of Dunstan they had all been under the "Benedictine Order," but that order had never been very strictly followed in this country, and, by the time of the Norman Conquest, they had very generally lapsed into a sleepy kind of inactivity. There is no doubt that the Norman archbishop, Lanfranc, was sincerely desirous to improve them, and especially to put them under a stricter religious discipline; but the new men whom he put in to carry out this work were regarded with such jealous dislike, as Normans, that they had small influence in the direction of religious revival or reform. Outwardly the great abbeys were prosperous, but they had little religious life in them. For the most part, they had settled down into great ecclesiastical corporations, some of whose members supplied the priestly offices at the churches the livings of which belonged to them; but they were chiefly busy with the management of their great estates, holding their manor courts, and looking after their rents and tolls, their granges, markets, and fisheries.

On the continent, throughout a great part of France and Italy, the monasteries were far worse than this. They were rich, luxurious, and corrupt. A cell in one of the great monasteries was a comfortable sinecure for life. The abbots lived like princes. They were no longer chosen by the monks for the devotedness of their lives, but were put in by emperors and kings for the sake of the rich revenues. If, here and there, some monk, touched with the old religious spirit, attempted reform, he was soon got rid of, often by being sent away on some distant and dangerous mission.

It was when this state of things was about at its worst that there arose a new order of monks, which was destined to bring about a wonderful revival of monastic life throughout Europe. Just at the end of the eleventh century, a little community of really fervent and pure-hearted men had banded themselves together to live a true monkish life, at Citeaux—or *Cistercium*, as it was written in Latin—a bare, lonely valley in Burgundy. They had little influence upon others, however, until, after some twenty years, they were joined by a young man whose name gradually became one of the brightest and greatest names of that age—Bernard of Clairvaux, better known as St. Bernard. Bernard's eager asceticism and fiery enthusiasm soon attracted attention to the new movement. From one place and another, sometimes from other monasteries, sometimes from the throng of the world, men began to come to them, sick of pretence and luxury, and longing for a sincere and noble religious life. All that Bernard and his companions had thought of, was, of living by the old Benedictine rule, only restoring it to its earlier strictness; but soon their movement drew to it such numbers that it outgrew any such subordinate character, and became in reality and in name a new monastic order. Bands of these "Cistercians," as they were called, went far and wide setting up new monasteries; and many of the old communities, catching the fervour of the movement, sent to ask Bernard for counsel and direction, and were glad to place themselves under some monk appointed by him, who had caught his spirit and would teach them to live together after his rule. This rise of the Cistercian Order was really a mighty religious reformation which spread over Europe. It made way with wonderful rapidity. Many hundreds of its offshoot monasteries sprang up in Italy, Germany, and France; and this was not all, for their zeal rekindled much of the ancient fervour in those of the older orders which had previously been sunk in luxury and indolence, and everywhere the monastic life became purer and better than it had been for centuries before.

Soon this new Cistercian Order spread to England. England was ripe just then for such a movement. The existing Religious Orders had, as already explained, ceased to have much life or influence, and any religious revival from within would have had too much the character either of the Norman or of the English, to draw all classes together. But these strangers, who lived only for God and heaven, and, in their fervent zeal, knew neither rich nor poor, Norman nor Saxon, were just the men to gather both around them, and to kindle a religious life in which difference of race might be forgotten. Such was the work they actually did. Everywhere the people flocked to these stranger monks; the eagerness for the life of meditation and prayer to which they called men, penetrated both races and all classes. Nobles gave them lands, the traders money, farmers and yeomen helped them in their buildings. Monastery after monastery sprang up. Among the most noted of their abbeys are Furness and Whalley, in Lancashire; in Yorkshire, Fountains Abbey, founded by thirteen monks who had come away from St. Mary's of York; Kirkstall, now nearly surrounded by the factories and smoke of Leeds, but then in a lonely tract of forest and moor; Rivaulx, Byland, and others; T tern, by the river Wye; Melrose, in Scotland. But these are only a few out of hundreds, great and small, that rose up far and wide over the kingdom, and especially among the moors and valleys of the north.

Let us take the story of one of the first of these abbeys and one of the best known, and it will tell us very much the story of them all. Just sixty years after the Norman Conquest a little band of monks, under the impulse of this new religious spirit, craving a harder and lonelier life, withdrew from a rich abbey in Normandy, and coming over to Lancashire, obtained from Earl Stephen, afterwards king, a grant of lands amid the wild wastes of Furness Fells, and settled down there to found a monastery under this reformed Cistercian rule. It is a fertile and beautiful place now, and people are rather in the habit of speaking with a half sneer of the comfort-loving sagacity of the old monks in choosing out such comfortable quarters, with rich meadows, woody sheltered valleys, and pleasant, well-stocked streams. This, however, is very unjust. It would be about as just if, centuries hence, when the interior of Africa shall have been opened up and settled, people should sneer at Dr. Livingstone for having chosen such a pleasant country for his labours. The fact is that those beautiful sites in which we find the ruins of the old abbeys, of the Cistercian Order at any rate, were, when the monks first settled there, the wildest, most deserted spots, in all the country. It was the monks who made them what they are now—made them so by the hard labour of generations, by labours that no noble or yeoman of the time would have thought of expending on them. So it was at Furness. The monks desired such lonely situations, because the rules of their order required that they should dwell quite away from the cities which had had so much to do with corrupting the monks of the past; they settled in that spot, because it was a tract of land so waste and worthless, that one of the great nobles, having no use for it himself, was not unwilling to consecrate it to God!

So hither came thirteen of these devoted men, brave and strong-hearted—into the dense forest that had hardly a path in it but the tracks of wolves and deer, into the deadly swamp, and among the wild hills that looked out upon the wild northern seas;—thirteen poor monks, with Ewan their abbot, to pray and to work, to cut down the trees, and drain the swamp, and plough the clearing, and channel the streams, and, when they had made good their foothold, to build Furness Abbey.

It was not built in a day, or a year. At first they would have a rough log hut to house in, and a better building, still only of wood, in which to chant their matins and vespers. But they would not long be left to labour alone. Gradually the tidings spread, through the scattered farms and huts of all that wild hill-country, and into the castles of the nobles, of these stranger-monks so different from those whose luxury and indolence had been a by-word through the land. There is always something touching in true piety, and the simple hardy life of these monks would take hold upon the half-savage Thanes and Ceorls of the district, win their almost superstitious reverence, and gradually draw offerings of many kinds. One man gave them a few acres of cleared land; others offered service with man and beast upon their farm or in their quarries; here and there one joined their number. More important still, the reverence they inspired brought back to them rights of lordship attached to the great grant of land, which had before probably been little exercised. And so in a few years they were ready to build the great church which they had planned out in their enthusiastic piety.

From this time the story is one that can be best studied on the spot, amongst the ruins themselves. Those ruins do not tell it to the visitor of a day; but any one who goes again and again, and looks carefully and thoughtfully at wall, and arch, and traceried window, and old masonry patched up with later work, may spell it all out. And the story to be read there is this—of the stern, bare simplicity in which their church and monastery were builded at first, and how, little by little, they fell away from that primitive simplicity, into ornament and into luxury. The old Cistercian rule carried a sort of Puritanism into everything. It mapped out the arrangement of their buildings, in order that they might be kept to one simple hardy plan of life; and if you look into a hundred of their ruined monasteries, you always find that that arrangement was at first adhered to. The monastery was ranged about the four sides of a square court, or quadrangle, round which on the inside ran the cloisters, a wooden penthouse shelter built against the wall. On the north side of this square court, sheltering its grassy walk from the wildest storms, was the great church. On the east side, joining to the transept of the church, came the chapter-house (where the business of the abbey was transacted), with the Scriptorium, or writing room, over it. Continuing in the same line, extended the monks' common room, with their dormitory over it, a passage and flight of steps leading from the dormitory into the church, that the monks might be able to go to and from their midnight services without leaving the building. On the third side, facing the long side of the church, stood the refectory or dining-hall, and the few rooms which at first were all that the abbot required for his separate use. And the west side of the quadrangle, joining up to the other end of the church, was one long range of buildings for the abbey servants and retainers, and for the entertainment of strangers; the lower story being their day-room, and the upper for their sleeping quarters. All this you find has originally existed at Furness, and Fountains, and Kirkstall, and wherever ruins enough of the buildings are still standing for the old plan to be made out. The curious thing is to trace how gradually that old plan was departed from. At first the great church was built strictly according to Cistercian rule—stern, simple, and unadorned. They might have no tracery in their windows, no images of saints, no sculpturing of the human figure at all, no pretty ornamented stonework, such as the great architects of the time delighted in, and were putting into the magnificent cathedrals. And, looking carefully about the church at Furness, you find that, originally, it was even so; there is, indeed, plenty of the forbidden ornamentation to be seen, but it is all of a later style and date. You can see the patched masonry, where the plain Norman windows have been replaced by traceried ones of later style, or where the small chancel has been enlarged into the magnificent choir and lady-chapel, to admit of the wide and lofty east window with its forbidden painted glass. They might not have any lofty tower, only a low belfry or lantern tower in the centre; and if you examine the massive tower which now seems to form one of the finest parts of the Furness ruins, you find it is of a style which dates only just before the Reformation, so that probably it was still unfinished when the final blow came and the monasteries were abolished and swept away. All through the buildings you come upon traces of the same gradual change. Only one more instance, however, but it is most significant of what the hardness of their life must originally have been. If you look at the long building still left standing at Furness, which was the monks' day-room—their common room for assembling and sitting when they needed more shelter than the wooden cloisters—you find that this long day-room originally had no fireplace, and was entirely open to the weather—open at the southern end by six great archways, in which there is no trace of door or closing of any kind. At some time, however, these arched openings were walled up, leaving a single doorway, and the stonework built into one of them was formed into a fireplace and chimney. But it is evidently of later work. You can see where the newer masonry has been joined on to the old. It is a startling testimony to the original hardihood and zeal of these Cistercians, that a door and a fireplace were among the effeminacies of their decline!

Thus, then, grew up this community of monks, the successors of the first brave men who had taken Earl Stephen's grant of Furness. Down the stairway that still stands, worn and broken, in the corner of the church adjoining the dormitory, they came when the bell wakened them soon after midnight, for the day's first prayers. In that Scriptorium, or writing-room, through the centuries before printing was invented, they wrote down the Abbey record or "Register," and copied, in firm clear black letter, with much pride in their illuminated headings, the few manuscripts which came into their hands, the only kind of book they knew. In that chapter-house they sat in conclave round their abbot and settled the business of their Order. In the long day-room, with its narrow windows, they sat or walked, and felt the cold a little more as their first hardness kept wearing off; and out in the cloister they paced in meditation, and, in later and less pious days, played bowls upon the green. In the long guest-house they welcomed prince or peasant, gave free hospitality alike to the noble with his band of retainers, or to the simple yeoman journeying from a distant fair. Away on the coast, a few miles off, through the wild times of the border raids, they kept up their castle of Piel Fouldrey as a refuge for themselves and their tenants. Here, at the Abbey gateway, they kept grammar-school and song-school for the children of the Abbey labourers and tenants; and, at a time when poor-laws were unknown, they gave liberal dole of bread and beer to any who were in want, and, it is to be feared, to many "valiant beggars" who were *not.* And here, in the great church, they chanted their Litanies and Masses, carried their Relics round on Saints' days, and kept up the old forms with ever-increasing splendour, but ever with a little less of the piety which had given them their position in the land.

In their best times their position was very high. They helped to civilize these rude remote districts where they were planted. They did something to check the rough tyranny of the barons, and were the protectors, instructors, almoners of the poor. In their long list of abbots, names of poor men from the neighbouring villages stand side by side with names of noble families that had endowed them with lands and lordships. In course of time, the very wealth that their first zeal brought them proved their corruption and their ruin. But they remained living active institutions for above four hundred years, and their decline, and at last their downfall, belong to an altogether later period in the story of the religious life of England.

CHAPTER XIII.

THE STRUGGLE WITH THE PAPACY.

The Pope hoped for great things from the Norman invasion of England. The Normans had been amongst the most loyal children of the Church. Already Norman knights had been fighting in the wars of the Church in the south of Europe, and Italian priests and monks were at the head of the greatest Norman churches. Among the Pope's counsellors was a young priest, Hildebrand, who was already dreaming of the Church becoming the greatest power among all nations, and nothing would seem more likely to help this on than for that turbulent England, with its rough, independent Church, to become a part of Normandy. So the Pope gave his blessing to the expedition, and sent Duke William a banner, and a sacred ring with a hair of St. Peter in it; and, on the other hand, William promised—at least so the Popes ever after maintained—that he would hold England as a subject province of the Church, and pay to Rome a large tribute every year.

When, however, the Conquest was complete, the Normans seemed, in religious matters, to catch something of the independent spirit of the conquered race. They became just as impatient of any real subjection to Rome as the English had been. Rome, however, was becoming more and more powerful, and was not willing to let slip the advantage which she had counted on from the Norman Conquest. Thus there began a contest which was renewed again and again for four hundred years, and which was only ended in the time of Henry VIII. by England joining in the Reformation, and breaking off all connection with the Church of Rome.

It is impossible, in these brief chapters, to give any full account of this long struggle with the Papacy, a struggle the incidents and fortunes of which were changing with every reign; but some sketch of the leading interests and incidents in its course will help to make the rest of the story easier to realize and understand.

William the Conqueror was no sooner seated on the throne of England than he began to find it inconvenient to admit that he had ever made any promises of vassalage to the Pope. He meant to be lord of his new land himself; he had no more idea of letting a foreign power decide who should be bishop over the churches in the north, than of letting such a power appoint the great feudal lord who should keep the unruly people in order. He would have the bishops obey him, as well as the barons. When some years had passed, and the Conquest had as yet brought to Rome little money and no homage, a legate came from Hildebrand, who had now become Pope, as Gregory VII., to demand, first, a more punctual payment of "Peter's Pence," as the tribute was called, and, secondly, that the King of England should do homage as the Pope's "man." William consented to send the "Peter's Pence," but denied that any promise had ever been made, and utterly refused to let the money be regarded as a doing homage for his kingdom. He asked the Pope to pray for him, and declared that he would give him the same love and reverence as he had given to previous Popes, but no homage. The Pope endeavoured to move the king through Lanfranc, but the Archbishop said he had already done his best, but without effect. In reality, however, Lanfranc himself seems to have paid the Pope only a decent reverence, and to have sided with the king in his independent course. Hildebrand was too busy with similar disputes nearer home to be able to enter on a contest with England just then; but he could wait. So he merely re-affirmed his claim, and left its enforcement to a more favourable opportunity.

Such opportunities were not long to wait for. If the kings of those days had resisted the authority of Rome merely in order to keep the Church more independent, the case would have been simple, and the people and the Church would have been on their side. But very often the kings only wanted to keep the Church independent of Rome in order to make it less able to resist themselves. They were constantly trying to use the Church for their own evil purposes, to enrich themselves out of its wealth, and at such times people and clergy were often glad to fall back for protection on the power of Rome. William the Conqueror, indeed, with Archbishop Lanfranc as his counsellor, ruled the Church on the whole fairly and well, and put many good and able men into the benefices. But no sooner had William Rufus come to the throne than his rapacity appeared. Lanfranc was still alive, though a very old man, and for two years he managed to keep some restraint upon the king; but then he died, and at once the king began to plunder the Church. In those times, so long as an abbey or bishopric was vacant, the king received the revenue; and since he claimed, as his father had done, that no abbot or bishop could be appointed except with the king's consent, he was able to enrich himself by keeping the benefices vacant as long as he liked; then, when he did appoint men to them, he required them to pay him enormous sums of money, which were called "offerings." Thus, when Lanfranc died, the king vowed there should be no Archbishop of Canterbury but himself, and for years none was appointed, and meanwhile all the rents and tithes—a great sum—came to the king. After four years, however, the "Red King" fell dangerously ill, and the illness wrought on his superstitious Norman nature, and in an agony of remorse he vowed to make amends for his evil deeds to the Church. The most pressing wrong to be atoned for was that of his having so long kept the see of Canterbury vacant, and the king sent for Anselm, abbot of the great monastery of Bec, in Normandy, to occupy it. Anselm was a man noted far and wide for his gentleness and goodness; and the king thought, if he must have an archbishop, he would have one not likely to give him much trouble.

Anselm is one of the great names of that time. A high-born Italian, with a fervent religious mind, one of the great scholars and theologians of his age, spending his nights in study and deep philosophic thought, while in the daytime the busy tender-hearted head of his monastery, he was revered and beloved of his monks as a saint. Such a man—an old man now—might well shrink from the difficult task of ruling the English Church under such a king; and, moreover, he doubted if the fit of royal repentance would continue. So, when they sought him out to lead him to the bedside of the sick king, Anselm earnestly protested. "Why will you yoke a feeble old sheep with a mad young bull?" he cried; and it was said that they had to use force to make him accept the post. Events justified his distrust of the king's repentance. As soon as William got well, his first act was to demand the usual "offering" for the Archbishop's promotion. Anselm pleaded poverty, but offered five hundred pounds. The king contemptuously refused it, on which Anselm gave the first indication that he was not quite such a "feeble old sheep" as he had represented himself, by ordering the money to be bestowed on the poor, and sturdily refusing to pay anything at all. In other ways, too, he began to withstand the king's power; he fearlessly urged upon him that he was committing grievous sin in keeping the places of abbots and bishops long vacant, and then, when he did fill them, farming them to the highest bidders. He urged that such a way of appointing men was filling the churches with hirelings, and he fearlessly warned the king to repent. The only answers that the Archbishop received were violent threats, and thus he was thrown back upon allegiance to the Pope as the last refuge against the king's greedy despotism, and he set off on foot as a simple pilgrim to appeal to Rome.

All through the reign of William Rufus this dispute went on. It turned especially upon the question whether the right of "Investiture"—that is, the presentation of the ring and crosier of office to a bishop—belonged to the king or to the Pope. Upon this depended, really, the power of the king to keep the benefices vacant. Under the next king, Henry I., the question seemed for the moment to be settled, for Henry was really a usurper, his elder brother Robert being still alive; and so, in order to strengthen his position, he agreed to the papal claims, and recalled Anselm to his side. But as soon as he was firmly established, Henry also repudiated all his concessions; and so the struggle began again, and was only ended years after, by the compromise that the Pope should have the actual right of investing the bishops with the ring and crosier as the sign of their spiritual appointment, but that the bishops should do homage to the king for the lands and property of their sees like any other feudal vassals.

The next great scene in the struggle was that in which Henry II. and Thomas Beket were the chief actors. Henry II. was an able, busy, resolute man, who was bent upon building up his dominions into a strong, united kingdom, and would brook no rival authority either among the nobility or the Church. When he appointed his favourite companion and counseller, Beket, to be the primate of his Church, he thought he was securing a pliable and submissive servant, through whom he could rule the Church along with the rest of his kingdom. Beket, however, as Archbishop of Canterbury, proved himself a stronger man than he had ever appeared before, and showed that he meant to rule the Church himself. The point on which they at last came into conflict was, as to the trial and punishment of the clergy. The old practice was for priests charged with crime to be dealt with, not by the general courts of the country, but by special church courts held by the bishops. As might be expected, these courts favoured their own order, and it was one of the great scandals of those times that priests who had notoriously committed even the greatest crimes were always lightly punished, and often not punished at all. Henry II. resolved that this state of things should cease. Even he, strong as he was, dared not propose that the church-courts should be altogether deprived of their jurisdiction, and so he left it to them to try whether any accused priest was guilty; but, if declared guilty, he required that he should be turned over to the regular courts of the land to be dealt with like any other criminal. Beket, however, violently resisted any such change, but at last was obliged to give way and to sign the new "Constitutions of Clarendon," which, not only in this matter but in many others also, did away with the special privileges of the Church and the priesthood. The assassination of Beket, by some of Henry's over-zealous courtiers, for a time forced Henry to humble himself and do penance, and in part to give up the new "Constitutions;" but it was only in part, and the result of the whole struggle was a solid gain to general law and order, and to the power of Englishmen over their own Church affairs.

Reign after reign such struggles as these went on. The worse a king was, the more the Papacy gained power in the kingdom, because then priests and people for a time made common cause, and in order to justify and strengthen their resistance, were glad to acknowledge the claims of the Papacy. King John tried to defy the Pope, as he disregarded his own people and nobles. But the long interdict which the Pope laid upon the kingdom at length overcame him. For more than two years, all religious services were forbidden; no mass was said, no absolution given; the dead could have no Christian burial; a blight and curse seemed to rest on the kingdom, and at length John, reduced to terrified submission, allowed the Pope to appoint an Archbishop to Canterbury, and himself gave up his crown and kingdom to the papal Legate, to receive them back as a subject and vassal of Rome.

Stephen Langton, indeed, the new archbishop, was a strong and able Englishman, and it was largely owing to his putting himself at the head of the movement of the people and nobles, for the restoration of the ancient English liberties, that Magna Charta was obtained. But this caused the affairs of the Church to be administered more and more as those of a province of Rome. Henceforth the bishops were appointed from Rome. Even the parish priests were often recommended by the papal court; and as, to bishops so appointed, such recommendations were little less than commands, the custom kept growing, until at length, in 1266, the Pope asserted his right to appoint priests to all church-livings. Of course, most of those thus appointed were foreigners. In three years, more than three hundred Italian and French priests had been put into the churches in the cities and villages of England. Many of them, indeed, never came over to their livings, but drew the revenue and paid some poor English priest a few marks a year to do duty for them. This did not make the system any the better liked, however. The people could not see so much good English money carried out of the country to foreign priests, year by year, without asking the reason why. Besides, it must be remembered that the rule of the Church had in those days to do with many more matters than it has now. When a man died, his children or heirs could not touch his property, till his will had been proved before the bishop or his deputy, and if he had left no will the church-courts had to settle how his possessions should go. Marriage, too, was entirely in the hands of the Church, and if the parties were at all akin, heavy fines had to be paid for a dispensation from the Pope. Moreover, all causes and disputes relating to the payment of tithes and church-dues were under the jurisdiction of the church-courts. It was bad enough to have such matters, which touched the people at every point, in the hands of priests; it was intolerable when those priests were not even Englishmen. It was hard enough for peasants and farmers to have more and more money extorted from them for the support of the Church, but when it came to seeing their tithes and dues sent abroad to Rome, it was more than men could stand. In the time of Edward I. this had become so unbearable, that he forbade monks and priests to send any money to religious superiors abroad. It would seem, however, that he could not really prevent it, for, seventy years later, we find the Commons, in a remonstrance to one of his successors, representing that the taxes paid to the Pope amounted to five times as much as the taxes paid to the Crown.

This "remonstrance" of "the Commons," however, is itself a sign of a new power which was springing up in the country, and which eventually was not only to be fatal to the claims of Rome, but to revolutionize the Church itself. This new power was the power of the people. A middle class of burghers and traders was growing up. In the constant struggling between king, barons, and ecclesiastics, the towns found their opportunity for gradually winning new liberties. At first these towns, consisting of the houses which had grouped around the castle, or the abbey, were entirely dependent upon the baron or the abbot, could not buy or sell, grind their corn, or try their criminals, without paying some fine or toll to the manorial lord. But when the baron was needing money for the wars, or the abbot or bishop had a large sum to raise as an "offering" on his appointment to his benefice, the townsmen found it easy to bargain for freedom from this toll or that fine, or for a charter to build a corn mill or hold a market, in return for a round sum of money. Thus, one by one, the little settlements of vassals grew into free, chartered towns, with their own officers and their own self-government. All this nurtured a spirit of enterprise and freedom; there grew up a race of well-to-do citizens who were not afraid of baron or priest; who could both think and speak for themselves; who, in course of time, dared to make remonstrances even to the king himself. People thus trained began to think for themselves, about religion as about other things. They saw the abuses of the Church with growing indignation. Worst of all abuses, were those which came from Roman interference; worst of all taxes were those which were squeezed out of them to be spent by priests in Italy or France. Men began everywhere to ask, who was this Pope of Rome who claimed to lord it over their property and their souls? what were these monks and priests that they should not be treated as other men if they broke the laws, and that they should hold their great estates without paying taxes as other men had to do? Many dangerous questions began to be asked, among the burghers in the towns and the yeomen in the farms, and generation by generation the power of the Papacy in England kept growing weaker.

This weakening of the hold of Rome on England was helped by the character of the Popes. When they began to meddle with the peoples, the peoples began to talk about them, and judge them just as they would other rulers. Men began to see that this Pope of Rome, who claimed to rule for Jesus Christ, and to be the mouth-piece of God, was really only a very ambitious priest, who made his advantage by keeping the nations quarrelling with each other. Journeys to Rome became more common, and the gossip which the baron's or bishop's followers brought home, spread among the people. It was found that the Popes were no better than other men—some of them were much worse. John XXII. was an extortionate miser. Benedict XII. was a great wine-bibber. Of some, darker things were told. Probably the dark things were not all true, but they set people questioning and doubting. In 1376 two Popes were elected by rival parties, and for fifty years after that no one knew who was the true Pope. There were always two and sometimes three Popes, holding courts at different places, each of whom had been elected by a body of cardinals, and each of whom was supported by one or more of the great kingdoms. Of course, with such divisions, all attempts at enforcing any claim of real papal power were out of the question ; and even when the division was at length healed, and the long scandal was done away, the old authority was hopelessly gone. It was impossible for the ancient claims of Rome ever again to be maintained as they had been at first. There was still controversy, and scolding, and excommunicating enough, and even down to modern times the Papacy has professed to have, of right, its ancient power, and sometimes it has attempted to exert it in mischievous ways. But the real "struggle with the Papacy" was over.

CHAPTER XIV.

THE REVIVAL BY THE PREACHING FRIARS.

In the middle of the long period during which the kings and people of England were struggling with the Papacy, occurred one of the most remarkable religious revivals that history has ever had to tell. Some revival was sorely needed, for religion was losing its hold upon the people. It was nearly a hundred years since the Cistercian monks had roused up a new fervour of piety throughout Europe, and called so many out of the corrupt and struggling world to the life of holiness in their quiet far-away monasteries. Even at the time, the very fact that these monasteries were placed so far away from the busy cities hindered them from exerting any very lasting good effect upon the great world which did not go to them; and now, after eighty or ninety years, though they had not as yet become specially corrupt, yet their first simplicity and piety was gone, and they had become little better than communities of rich landholders, living an easy, comfortable life, doing very little good or harm to anybody, and having no religious help for the neglected life of the time. The poor people in the neighbourhood of the monasteries went to the wicket-gate on dole-days for alms of bread and beer, and now and then on the great saints' days they crowded the abbey church to see the procession of the monks and hear the chanting; but there was little that took hold of their hearts, helped them to live Christian lives, or even taught them to understand what Christianity was.

In the towns and cities things were worse. There stood the parish churches scattered over the country, and here and there the grand cathedrals. And the bishop dwelt in his palace like one of the barons, and near the churches lived the mass-priests. But the bishop was nothing to the common people, and the priests, as we have seen, were often foreigners put in by the Pope. Even where the priest was an Englishman, his service was not said in the tongue of the people. Everything was in Latin; no one understood it; many of the priests did not understand it themselves. There was no preaching, nothing to tell the people plainly anything about religion. Almost the only thing connected with religion which was put into common English was the demand for tithes and dues, and fees for masses to deliver dead men's souls from purgatory. Every one could understand this part of the matter, but it did not make the Church more beloved. And, meanwhile, here and there bold men were beginning to ask why these things should be, and denouncing the monks and priests as drones and thieves; and they did not say these things in Latin!

It was when all this state of things was about at its worst, some five years after the death of King John, that some monks or priests of a very different fashion came over into England. These were the friars—the "Preaching Friars" as they were called by some—while others called them the "Begging Friars." There were several varieties of them, but the two principal orders were those who named themselves Dominicans, after their founder Dominic, and who were called by the people, from the colour of their rough serge dress, the "black friars;" and the Franciscans, so called after Francis of Assisi, and better known as the "grey friars," from the coarse grey frock they wore.

Dominic was a Spaniard, a fiery, fanatical man, who saw with horror how the Catholic religion was losing its hold upon the world, through the luxury and corruption of its priesthood. He dreamed of winning men back by an order of men who should be as poor as Christ himself, go down among the very lowest of the people, devote their lives to calling men to repentance, and urge religion upon them in the plain speech of the street and market. Himself setting the example of what he meant, clothing himself in rags, refusing to have any property, living upon what people would give him in alms from day to day, he drew many to follow him by his vehement earnestness, and soon his Dominican friars were preaching all over Europe.

A very different man was Francis of Assisi—a dreamy, poetical, loving enthusiast. He began by being a wild reveller, though even in his prodigal days he was noted for his kindness to all who were in want. By-and-by a change came; illness struck him. A longing for a nobler life took possession of him; it seemed to him that the Saviour had appeared to him, and thenceforth he gave himself up to poverty, and the service of the poor, and to entreating men to a religious life. He did not care what rags he wore; he rejoiced to wait upon lepers, and in his love for them would kiss their loathsome sores. "Most blameless and gentle of saints," Dean Milman calls him. Gradually, the thought of subduing the whole world to the religion of Christ beamed upon his soul; he fired others with his loving enthusiasm. He would begin with the hardest and noblest task. Those were the days of the Crusades, but the crusading armies seemed to make little head against the fierce Mahomedans, and Francis set off to try the effect of persuasion. He preached before the Sultan himself, offered to enter a fire with the Moslem priests, that God might show which religion was true, by keeping its advocates unharmed; nay, he even offered to enter the fire alone. "If I should be burned, you will impute it to my sins; should I come forth alive, you will embrace the Gospel." The Sultan listened respectfully, though unconvinced, and Francis returned safe, with a promise that Christian captives should be better treated. Some of his followers were more hardly dealt with; five of them were martyred in Morocco. But nothing could daunt the passionate devotion of the new brotherhood.

It was in the dark days which followed the struggles and oppressions of King John's reign, that the followers of these two men made their way to England, and began preaching and working among the common people of our English cities.

Right in the midst of the poorest quarters they took up their abode—not in any fine monastery; rude huts like those of the people round, grouped in a poor enclosure, were the first "friaries," and the memory of them is still preserved in the names "Blackfriars," "Greyfriars," &c., which mark many of the spots where they settled. Thence they went abroad, tending the sick, especially the lepers, of whom there were great numbers in those days; going into the hovels of the poor, hearing their confessions, giving them consolation, entreating them to forsake their sins. In the streets, by the market crosses, they would gather people together and preach to them, not in an unknown tongue, but in plain homespun speech, and in rough-and-ready style, with jest and story, and eager homely appeals, such as all could feel and understand.

At once they attracted attention. These preaching friars, in dress as mean as the poorest of their hearers, with no lands, no property, living from day to day on what people gave them, and meanwhile preaching religion so earnestly and plainly, were very different from the monks and mass-priests, who were all that had been seen before. Men gathered about them in crowds, hung upon their words, begged for their blessing. The churches began to be deserted; the priests complained that no one cared to confess, except to these wandering friars. The monks of the older orders, shamed by the contrast between their own sleek indolence and the active devoted lives of the "poor preachers," denounced them bitterly; but their work went on. Numbers joined them, gave away their possessions, took the friars' vows of "poverty, chastity, and obedience," and went forth, barefooted and ragged, to help in their work. Greater numbers still were admitted to a lower membership, which, without taking them from their ordinary life, bound them to very bare simple living, plain dress, frequent fasts, and loyal help to their order. A new interest in religion penetrated through all ranks of society. A great wave of religious revival passed over the land.

It is sad to read that a movement so pure and noble in its origin, very soon became corrupt; but so it was. For a few years all was fervour, poverty, zeal. Then the vow of poverty began to be evaded; they no longer refused the gifts that grateful followers urged upon them. If individuals could not hold property, the community might. The bare mud and timber huts began to be replaced by fine stone monasteries. The simple, fervent, wandering friars degenerated into meddlesome and sturdy beggars, enforcing their claims in the name of religion, and selling absolutions and indulgences to all sorts of wrong-doers. All were not of this kind, indeed. Some of the noblest minds in England were among the Dominicans and Franciscans. Their peculiar work of preaching set them studying theology, and a few, like the great Roger Bacon, who was a Franciscan friar, laboured in the direction of physical science. But as a religious movement, their strength soon passed away; and within a couple of generations the mendicant friars were even a greater scandal and hindrance to religion than the very orders of the older monasteries which they had begun by opposing and shaming.

CHAPTER XV.

JOHN WYCLIF.

THE spirit of resistance to Rome took many forms. The first outcome was in the spirit of national freedom, which would not submit to pay tribute to the Pope, or to have the kingdom considered a province of Rome. It was only later that the minds of men began to revolt against the subtler claim to headship over men's religious life, and the authority to lay down what must be believed. The demand for Peter's pence touched men, at first, more closely than the claim on their faith. But men could not long carry on a stout resistance to the Pope's lordship over lands and money, without at last beginning to doubt his lordship over souls, and his power of forgiving sins. We are coming now to those times of spiritual resistance, and the first great movement towards this higher independence arose with a priest and scholar of Oxford named John Wyclif.

Wyclif was a man of forty years old when he first began to be known. Always absorbed in his thinking and working, a thin, ascetic, self-forgetting man, he never talked or wrote much about himself, and thus very little is known of his earlier life. There is a little village still called Wycliffe, on the river Tees, near Barnard Castle, where old shields and tombs and effigies of the Wyclifs tell of the knightly family from which he sprang; and only a few miles away are the ruins of an old monastery, Eggleston Abbey, where he would probably go when a boy to the grammar-school of the monks. A little later he was a student at Oxford, and by-and-by a Fellow and teacher there. It was for his proficiency in philosophy and law that he was most known, yet the name that he got there, of the Gospel Doctor, shows that already he was turning to those studies in which his life-work was to be done.

It was when John Wyclif was just grown to manhood that the most terrible pestilence that has ever desolated the world—the Black Death—made its appearance. It had crept stealthily through Asia and over Europe, and now for some years it filled England with dread and awe. It is believed that during those years of its ravages, more than half of the population perished. It may well have been that the impressions of such a time had something to do with that intense earnestness with which, so soon after, we find Wyclif taking his part in the great religious questions of the time. We first hear of him from the stand he took against the Mendicant orders of Friars. These orders had gradually crept up from their lowly beginnings, had become rich, scheming, and ambitious, until now, a hundred and forty years after their foundation, they had grown into mighty ecclesiastical corporations, and were trying to get all the teaching power of Oxford into their own hands This aroused strong resistance, and in this movement against the friars Wyclif took part, and showed such masterly skill that he soon became the foremost man at Oxford. In a while his powers were wanted for yet higher service. Pope Urban V. sent to England a bold claim, that the Tribute promised by John, and which had not now been paid for over thirty years, must at once be paid with all arrears. The whole country was roused to indignation by such a claim, but it was Wyclif from whose pen came the crushing refutation of it, which united the leading men of the Church with the people and the barons in such a sturdy refusal, as left little hope at Rome that it would ever be paid again. Again, a few years later, when the Pope sent over a legate to treat with England on some disputed matters, and it was necessary that he should be met by some of the ablest men in the country, Wyclif was put second on the list of Commissioners. These things made his name widely known, and the rectory of Lutterworth in Leicestershire, which was thenceforth his chief home, was then given him. His plain outspoken opinions against the papal authority, and his ability in expounding the cause of England against the claims of Rome, made him be regarded with favour by some of the great barons, especially by the Duke of Lancaster, the famous John of Gaunt. That rough, wilful noble, must not, however, be credited with any very enlightened desire for pure religion, in taking up the cause of the Reformer. It was, probably, that, like the barons generally, he hated the restraining power of the Church, and was glad to take any side that seemed likely to curb it. However, his favour, even if the motives for it were mixed, strengthened Wyclif to go forward more boldly in his reforming work than he otherwise could have done. The fact was, that the more he looked into the pretensions of the Pope, the more groundless and mischievous he found them; and the more he followed out the subject, the more he saw that the whole pretensions of the Church and the priesthood were very much of the same kind. In his pulpit at Lutterworth and his lecture hall at Oxford, he denounced alike the Pope, and the bishops, and the friars, with a boldness and vigour which made his words eagerly caught up and repeated, until they began to ring through England. He was taken ill, and his enemies bade him prepare for the death which they declared his impiety had brought on him. "I shall not die," cried the sick man; "I shall live and declare the evil deeds of the friars." And he did live, and his words became bolder than ever. It was a new thing in those days to hear the Pope openly denounced as "Antichrist," and as "the proud, worldly priest of Rome." The whole Church took the alarm, and Wyclif was summoned to appear before the bishops in Convocation at St. Paul's. He went up, without a moment's hesitation, but side by side with him went the great John of Gaunt; and when the Bishop of London attempted to treat Wyclif as a criminal on trial, the Duke protested, and the protest grew to a wrangle, until the council was broken up with scolding and brawling before ever coming to any charges. The bishops, however, were not to be thwarted. They appealed to the Pope, and next year, five separate Bulls were sent to king, bishops, and university, enjoining that Wyclif should be straightway put in prison and brought to trial. It had like to have fared badly with Wyclif, but just then the old king, Edward III., died, and with the next accession Wyclif was needed again. Once more there arose the question, of the lawfulness of money being carried out of the kingdom to the Pope; and in this controversy, Wyclif was too useful an auxiliary for the Parliament to leave him to his enemies. So he went back to Lutterworth, and continued his work of probing into the religious errors and abuses of the time, of exposing them and denouncing them. The root of all mischief seemed to him to lie in the great endowments of the Church. These had corrupted the monkish orders; these had turned the bishops into haughty barons; these made the priests greedy for the best benefices. Again and again, with his keen, eager logic, he showed the evils of these great endowments, and pleaded with King and Parliament to take such things away from the Church, and to leave it to be supported by the free-will gifts of the people.

Soon he took a further and bolder step. He began to look into the doctrines of the Church. There was one doctrine which, more than any other, had to do with the hold of the priesthood over the people, and that was the doctrine, that in the Lord's Supper the bread and wine are actually changed by the priest's consecration into the very body and blood of Christ. This was an idea which could be understood by the rudest nature, and which gave to the most ignorant priests a position of awful and miraculous authority that made people afraid to treat them like other men. But as soon as Wyclif began to look fearlessly into this matter, he saw that the whole claim was a baseless imposition, and began to preach and write against it. It is this step which not only marks him out as the great reformer of his age, but as a man of most dauntless courage. For, now, he stood alone. The great men who had supported him in his exposures of the practical abuses of the Church, were not prepared to go thus far, and at once forsook him. John of Gaunt sent to him, to urge him to be silent; but he only answered by a still more forcible setting forth of his views, ending with "I believe that in the end the truth will conquer." The University of Oxford formally condemned him, but he challenged the

University to disprove his teaching, and went right on with his work, staying not for noble or doctor. It was the harder for him, because just now (1381) the great insurrection of the southern peasantry, under Wat Tyler, had broken out, and the cry was raised that it was Wyclif's Lollards who had caused it. The charge was false, but for the moment it served its purpose, and made Wyclif's course more dangerous. He did not falter, however. A number of men like-minded with himself had gradually gathered round him, and to these he taught his views, and kept sending them out to teach them far and wide. Wyclif's "poor priests," or "simple priests" as they were called, were to the new doctrines something like what the Begging Friars had been long before for the Catholic Church. They went about preaching and ministering, not only in churches and churchyards, but in fairs and markets, and wherever men would listen to them, and telling in plain homely style, such as took the ear of the common people, what was the simple Gospel truth on some of the matters which the Church upheld. For, when Wyclif and his followers had once begun looking into these things, it was not possible to stop merely at the doctrine of the Sacrament. The power of priests to grant indulgences or pardons, and the worship of the saints, were just as absurd, and soon the Reformer and his "poor priests" were preaching against everything of the kind. Wyclif's own work was chiefly done at Lutterworth. Here, among his congregation of plain country people, he lived a simple, kindly life. It has been thought by many that it might have been from Wyclif that Chaucer drew his character of the good parson in his "Canterbury Tales"—

"—A clerk
That Christ's pure gospel would sincerely preach
And his parishioners devoutly teach.
Benign he was and wondrous diligent,
And in adversity full patient.—
Wide was his cure, the houses far asunder,
Yet never failed he, nor for rain or thunder,
In sickness or mishap to visit all,
The furthest in his parish, great and small,
Upon his feet, and in his hand a staff.
This noble example to his flock he gave,
That first he wrought and afterwards he taught
The Word of life he from the Gospel caught.
He never set his benefice ahire,
Leaving his flock a'cumbered in the mire,
And ran to London cogging at St. Paul's,
To seek himself a chantery for souls.
He waited not on pomp or reverence,
Nor made himself a spiced conscience.
The lore of Christ and his apostles twelve
He taught, but first he followed it himselve."

It was in his pulpit, however, that Wyclif's light shone out most brightly. Taking the lesson of the day, or some pointed verse of scripture, he would give short pithy explanations, attacking the old errors when they came in his way with keen homespun sentences, with many a sarcasm about Pope and priest as he went along, but trying most of all to bring out the practical lesson for the lives of his hearers. These little sermons, or lectures, were copied out and circulated among his followers far and wide, so that even at the present day there are no less than three hundred of Wyclif's "Postils," as they are called, still extant. But these things were, after all, only preludes to his greatest work. As he went more deeply into those studies which had early won him the name of the "Gospel Doctor," and further in his rejection of one popish error after another, he was led to take his stand more simply on the Bible, and he saw that the one great thing to be done, was to let the people have the Bible to read in their own tongue. Before now, there had been translations of several parts of the Bible made, but practically it still was, to the common people, an unknown book. Wyclif resolved that it should be so no longer. Aided by Nicholas Herford, one of his most attached followers, he set to work to translate the Bible out of the Latin version, or "Vulgate" as it was called, which was used in the churches, into the common English tongue. Printing was not yet invented, and there was very little help for him from the copyists in the monastic writing-rooms. But, as part after part of the great work was done, eager followers in many a home took it, and with loving hands made copy after copy, and these were then circulated far and wide by his "poor priests." Thus in three or four years the whole work was finished, and the first complete English Bible given to the people. And gladly the people received it. Alike among rich and poor it found eager readers. At the court, the queen, Anne of Bohemia, was one of its most diligent students, and through her, this and Wyclif's other works found their way into her native land, and became the seed from which sprang, thirty years later, the reforming movement of John Huss and Jerome of Prague. But it was in the homes of the middle classes, the citizens of London and Bristol, and the other leading cities, that the greatest work was done. So widely were the new opinions spreading, that a panic took possession of the priesthood. They raged for his life. Effort after effort was made to have Wyclif condemned, but the reformer defied them, and petitioned the king for leave to prove his doctrines. At length he was expelled from the University of Oxford, and his opinions were suppressed there, but still he went on with his work at Lutterworth. His great labours, however, and the strain and excitement of his life of constant conflict, were gradually telling upon him. Once and again already, attacks of paralysis had come upon him, and though still strong and vigorous in mind, his body was almost worn out. It was while he was thus that the last blow of his enemies fell upon him in the shape of a solemn Brief, summoning him to answer before the Pope himself. Wyclif was too ill to go, but with his last strength dictated a reply, which shows at once his keen sarcasm, and his indomitable spirit: "I am always glad to explain my faith to any one, and above all to the Bishop of Rome, for I take it that if it be orthodox he will confirm it, if it be erroneous he will correct it." Eagerly his enemies waited for the reply which should finally crush him. But before it could arrive, the reformer had appeared before a higher tribunal. Another stroke of paralysis came on as he was saying mass in his church, and the next day John Wyclif passed away, the greatest and noblest of "the Reformers before the Reformation."

CHAPTER XVI.

THE LOLLARDS.

THE Lollards were the earliest "Protestants" of England. They were the followers of John Wyclif, but before his time the nickname of Lollard had been known on the continent. A little brotherhood of pious people had sprung up in Holland, about the year 1300, who lived in a half-monastic fashion and devoted themselves to helping the poor in the burial of their dead; and, from the low chants they sang at the funerals—*lollen* being the old word for such singing—they were called "Lollards." The priests and friars hated them and accused them of heresy, and a Walter Lollard, probably one of them, was burnt in 1322 at Cologne as a heretic, and gradually the name became a nickname for such people. So when Wyclif's "simple priests" were preaching the new doctrines, the name, already familiar in Holland and Germany, was given to them, and gradually became the name for that whole movement of religious reformation which grew up from the seed Wyclif sowed.

That seed sprang up everywhere. Wyclif's "postils" or commentaries, and especially the copies of his English Bible, were scattered through the land. From their influence, there was continually growing among the more thoughtful people in all classes, the idea of a purer religion, free from the mummeries of the monks and priests—a religion which should take its stand upon the Bible only, and in which each man should be his own priest and serve God for himself.

The death of Wyclif was a great blow to this movement, in more ways than one. It not only deprived the Lollards of the great scholar and thinker who had given the movement a standing before the world, but it took away the strong guiding and inspiring spirit which had kept the movement true to its religious object. For, such a spirit of reform, once awakened, is apt to stir men with other questions besides those of religion. That was a time of widespread discontent among the peasantry of England, and already, before Wyclif's death, it was charged that the insurrection of the Men of Kent was the work of his followers. It is likely enough that, among the multitudes engaged in it, were some of his followers. One of the leaders of it, John Ball, had been going up and down the country, exciting the people against the rich feudal lords, by attacks the burden of which was,—

> "When Adam delved and Eve span,
> Who was then the gentleman?"

It was said that he was a Wyclifite, though this is uncertain. But it is easy to understand how, as time went on, such levelling elements in political life naturally gathered to the Lollards, and frightened away many who would have been willing to stand with John Wyclif in his religious protests. Yet the Lollards never became wild revolutionists. They were religious reformers, touched with a dreamy political puritanism. It is curious to read their own statement of their religious views, as it is given in a petition to Parliament ten years after Wyclif's death. They assert that the possession of endowments by the clergy is contrary to the law of Christ; that the Romish priesthood was not established by Christ; that Celibacy, Masses for the dead, Confession, Absolution, and the professed change of the Sacramental bread and wine into the body and blood of Christ, are superstitions or abuses, and that all outward rites of religion are of little value. To these elements of advanced religious Protestantism they add protests against war and capital punishment, and petitions that certain trades, such as those of goldsmiths and sword-smiths, might be put down, as unlawful among Christians.

The time was not ripe, however, for such principles as these, and the story of the Lollards is the story of a long persecution by which the new opinions, though never entirely trampled out, were so ruthlessly crushed, that it was not till after another hundred years were passed, that they again rose up in a strength which could no longer be resisted.

As soon as Wyclif was dead the clergy endeavoured to bring the powers of persecution to bear against the Lollards, and they got a law passed to punish all persons convicted of heresy in the bishops' courts. They had been too hasty, however, and this was repealed the following year, with a protest from the Commons, which is one of the signs of the time, that they considered it "nowise their interest to be more under the jurisdiction of the prelates than their ancestors were." The fact was, the Ecclesiastical courts were everywhere disliked and distrusted; the king, Richard II., and his queen both rather favoured the new opinions, and the country was in no humour for increasing the power of the priesthood.

In a few years, however, there came a reaction.

Richard II. was deposed, and Henry IV., who ascended the throne, had secured the allegiance of the clergy by promising to advance and protect the Church. Almost at once the Lollards began to feel the change. First, an act was passed empowering the bishops to imprison persons suspected of heresy, and then, almost immediately, this was followed by the horrible statute "for the burning of Heretics." This statute set forth that, "in order that this wicked sect, preachings, doctrines, and opinions should from henceforth cease and be utterly destroyed," all such heretics, if they refuse to recant, or if, after recanting, they relapse, shall be burnt "before the people in an high place." Burning was chosen as a kind of death which did not involve the "shedding of blood," which was unlawful for priests!

The clergy seized on this new and terrible weapon with eagerness, and within a few months of its passing, in March, 1401, the first English martyr was burnt at Smithfield. This was William Sawtre, who had been the priest of Lynn in Norfolk. Two years before, he had been accused of heresy and deposed from his living, but his friends had saved his life by persuading him to give up his new opinions. His conscience was uneasy, however, and now that danger was at hand he himself petitioned the Parliament that he might be heard on the subject of religion, and being summoned before the Bishops' Convocation he was found guilty of being a lapsed heretic; the dreadful sentence was passed upon him, and after being degraded from the priesthood by the bishops stripping his robe off him in St. Paul's, he was taken out to Smithfield, and, before a vast crowd of onlookers, burnt to death.

The tidings of this new and horrible punishment

might well deter the Lollards from preaching as publicly as before, and one can readily believe that even the persecutors themselves could not at once get sufficiently hardened to the use of it, to resort to it often. For several years, the Lollards were harried with imprisonments, and fines, and whippings, and threats of worse things; but it was nine years before such another crowd assembled in Smithfield to see a man burnt to death. This second victim was a simple tradesman, one Badbie, a smith or a tailor, it is uncertain which; who, after being questioned by the archbishop for denying Transubstantiation, refused to abjure his opinions and was sentenced to the new way of death. Out into Smithfield they took him, and this time they tried a new plan, placing him in a huge cask surrounded with dry wood—they had not yet settled which was the best way of burning men to death. All around stood the people, and close in front, with the sheriffs and priests, was the Prince of Wales, the "Prince Hal" of Shakspeare's plays. It is in keeping with the frank jovial nature of the prince, that he offered Badbie his pardon if he would recant his opinions; and again, after the fire was kindled, the prince was so touched by his cry of agony that he had him taken out of the fire, "being with pitiful pain almost dead," and begged him to renounce his heresy, "promising him not only life, but also threepence a-day so long as he lived, to be paid out of the king's coffers. But he," continues the old chronicler, Hollinshed, "having recovered his spirits again, refused the prince's offer," and was put back into the hot, half-burned cask again, "from henceforth not to have any pardon or favour at all," and so he died the death.

It might have been hoped that the young prince, in

whom this seems to show some horror of such a method of converting heretics, would have discouraged it when he became king. But he, like his father, had to keep the priests and bishops on his side; moreover, the same impetuous temper which, when Badbie refused his "pardon and threepence a-day so long as he lived," made him order him back to death, "thenceforth not to have any pardon or favour at all," made him afterwards all the more bitter against these obstinate heretics, whom neither threats nor kindness could change. From this time, the persecution increased. The prisons were crowded with Lollards. So great was their number, that the Archbishop of Canterbury had to build an additional tower to his palace at Lambeth to hold them—"the Lollards' Tower," which still remains, with the iron rings in the walls, to which they used to be chained. Then burnings began to be more common—two in one year we read of, John Claydon and Richard Turwin, both of them London tradesmen; and a few years later, four priests were burnt at one time in Smithfield, and so the stake came to be regarded as the common doom for heretics.

Still the cause struggled on. For some time the Earl of Salisbury had favoured it, as, in its beginning, John of Gaunt had done. A little later, the leading man among the Lollards was Sir John Oldcastle, "the good Lord Cobham," as he was called by the common people. He seems to have deserved the title, for he had sincerely embraced the new opinions, and held to them for many years, till at last they brought him to his death. He was one of those who, years before, had helped in circulating the writings of Wyclif, having many copies made at his own charge, and himself supporting many of Wyclif's "simple priests." When the times of persecution came, Sir John was a powerful friend for the Lollards, sheltering many of them in his own castle in Kent. He had won renown in the French wars, and was one of Prince Hal's old friends, so that for a long time the bishops did not care to meddle with him. At last, however, they found their opportunity. Some threatening placards had been put up on the church doors in London, and rumour ascribed them to the Lollards, and Archbishop Arundel accused Sir John Oldcastle to the angry king. The king promised to speak with Oldcastle himself, thinking he could bring him round; but the sturdy old heretic was more than a match for the king, did not yield an inch, told the king that "as sure as God's word is true, the Pope is the great Antichrist foretold in Holy Writ;" and when the king grew impatient and angry, he went home to his castle, shut the gates, refused to have the summons of the archbishop served upon him, and only surrendered when his castle was besieged by the officers of the king. It seemed as if it must go hard with him now, for nothing could move him. Two whole days he stood up before the archbishop's court and argued his cause, but, at the close, he was convicted as an obstinate heretic, and condemned to be burnt. The king, however, on account of his old friendship, gave him fifty days' respite before the sentence should be carried out, and before that time had elapsed Sir John had escaped—some think the king wished him to do so—and was safe among the mountains of Wales.

A hard bitter time for the Lollards followed. There was discontent in the country, and plots were discovered, and they were attributed to Sir John Oldcastle and the Lollards. Now, it was rumoured that twenty-five thousand men were going to meet in St. Giles's Fields, and though only eighty were found there by the force sent out to meet them, thirty of these were first hung as traitors, and then burnt as heretics. Nothing was seen of Sir John Oldcastle, however; but some of these poor wretches were tortured to discover if he had anything to do with it, and in their agony they confessed that they had gathered to meet him; whereupon he was proclaimed a traitor, and a great price was set upon his head. For three years, however, he remained concealed, but then stricter search was made. There was a wild rumour that the Lollards had invited the Scots to invade England; the people were alarmed; and Lord Cobham was seen near London, and pursued and captured. There was no mercy for him now. He was sentenced to suffer both as a traitor and a heretic. Out in St. Giles's Fields the old man was hung alive in chains, over a slow fire, and so, brave to the last, with no sign of recanting, died.

Only one scene more in the Lollard story. The bishops could have their way now, and in 1428 they determined to wreak their hate on the memory of Wyclif. So, procuring a license from the Pope, they took up Wyclif's body from its resting-place in his old churchyard, and burned the mouldering remains on the little bridge at Lutterworth, and cast the ashes into the stream.

From this period, the Lollards gradually cease to occupy any place in the history of the time. Other interests took the attention of the nation. First the French wars, and then the long Wars of the Roses filled men's thoughts; there was little interest to spare for questions of sacraments and doctrines; the very name of Lollard silently passed out of use.

But the seed that Wyclif sowed was not dead. Many

a copy of Wyclif's homilies and Wyclif's Bible lay hidden away, up and down England, in the yeomen's farms and the burghers' closets, and through all those troubled times was silently doing its work, and preparing men for the great Reformation which was to come a hundred years later. As Fuller says of those burned and desecrated remains, cast into the stream at Lutterworth: "This brook did convey his ashes to the Avon, Avon into Severn, Severn into the narrow seas, they into the main ocean, and thus the ashes of Wyclif were the emblems of his doctrine which is now dispersed all the world over."

CHAPTER XVII.

THE BEGINNING OF THE REFORMATION.

For a hundred years after the time of Wyclif and the Lollards, there is not much that is specially noteworthy in the story of religious life in England. In the earlier part of this period, England was occupied by the great French wars, which resulted in the English being driven step by step from France. Then came the long Wars of the Roses. Trade went on, and in the necessities of the great nobles the cities kept bargaining for larger liberties. Meanwhile, the Church was ever gaining ground, for since Lollardry had been crushed, there was no reforming party worth considering, and both sides in the conflict would yield anything in order to win over the priesthood. Of course, this was an injury to religion. All through these hundred years religion was slowly declining, the monasteries were becoming more and more places of easy idle life, the clergy were growing more and more worldly, and yet the Church was gaining in wealth and power. Henry VII.'s reign was quite an era of church-building. It is curious to see how many of our old parish churches date their rebuilding at this period, just before the Reformation; many of the great monasteries were busy in the same way—restoring, beautifying, and rebuilding in greater magnificence than ever, or erecting noble bell-towers, some of which were destined never to be finished.

The reforming spirit, however, was not dead. There were signs which might have warned the clergy to put their house in order. Wyclif's writings were still kept as a hidden treasure in many a home. And, now and then, evidence of the work which these were doing, comes out in the story of Henry VII.'s reign, in ways which show what a leaven was moving among the people. We find one man arrested, for saying that there was as much virtue in a herb as in the image of the virgin, and another for saying that the image would make a good fire. In 1494, Widow Jane Boughton, over eighty years old, went bravely to the stake for holding Wyclif's doctrines, and died defying her persecutors and "crying to God to take her soul into his holy hands." In 1506, William Tylworth was burnt at Amersham, his little daughter being forced to set fire to the faggots with her own hands. Then Lawrence Guest was burnt at Salisbury "for the matter of the sacrament," and his wife and seven children were set before him, in his torment, to break down his fortitude—but in reality only confirmed it, so that he was faithful unto death. When such things as these were taking place, wise men might well have doubted whether the Church was really so strong and prosperous as it looked.

Many wise men did doubt; the greatest and the noblest of the time were troubled about the condition of the Church. One of the interesting things in the story of that period is, to see how some of the greater minds, in the Church itself, felt the urgent need of reform, and tried to bring it about without breaking away from the great Church of Rome. The first to expose ecclesiastical corruptions were not Protestants, but good Catholics. Fifty years before Henry VIII. destroyed the monasteries, Cardinal Morton, who was then Archbishop of Canterbury, procured authority to examine and reform them. He exposed their condition to a Synod of the clergy, and warned all priests and monks to amend their lives; but he was not strong enough really to grapple with the evil, and his protests ended in words. His successor, Archbishop Warham, tried the same thing, but with no better result. Then came Cardinal Wolsey; and he, too, was shrewd enough to see that the Church could not go on long as it was doing. He even had some great schemes of reformation; but what could be expected of a reformer who himself held in his own name an archbishopric, three bishoprics, and an abbacy? He suppressed a few of the worst religious houses, but he made no effectual change for the better in the real state of the Church and the clergy.

Some of the great scholars of the time, men of nobler mould than these, were animated by the same idea—of a higher and purer state of religion to be brought about *within* the great Catholic Church itself. It was a time of great activity in learning; its Renaissance, or "new birth," it is usually called. William Caxton had set up the first printing-press in England, in 1476. Books were multiplying with incredible swiftness. A whole new world of literature was opened to scholars. The great Erasmus was teaching at Cambridge, and holding up there the idea of a simpler religion, from which intelligent men should quietly drop the subtleties of the middle ages; but he was utterly opposed to any violent change. Colet, Dean of St. Paul's, another of these friends of the New

Learning, was one of the purest and most devoutly religious men of the age. He it was who founded St. Paul's school in London, putting over the doorway the image of the child Christ, and beseeching the scholars to "Lift up your little white hands for me which prayeth for you to God." But it is for his brave pleadings for religious reform, that he is most notable. Not only from his pulpit in St. Paul's, but in Convocation itself, he preached with the fiery earnestness of a prophet against the vices of his order, and appealed for purer life. "We are troubled with heretics," he cried, "but no heresy is so fatal as the vicious lives of the clergy." Strange as it may seem, it was this same eager desire for reform within the Catholic Church itself, which made the great and good Sir Thomas More, when he became chancellor to Henry VIII., more relentless in his persecutions of the Protestants than was his predecessor Wolsey. More was at once an earnest reformer, and a devout Catholic. He was horrified at the abuses and corruptions of the Church, but he believed that they might be cured from within; and his very belief in this made him the more impatient and intolerant of those who, by going to what he thought heretical extremes, seemed to him more likely to destroy the Church than to reform it. So, while he was urging through Parliament acts to restrain priests from holding more than one living, and forcing them to reside among their people, he was at the same time helping the bishops to imprison and burn heretics, and in some cases having them tortured in his own house. Yet in his "Utopia," describing his idea of a model kingdom, he puts it that every man should be allowed to be of what religion he would!

Fortunately for the subsequent religious life of England, the dream of these good men—of the Church being reformed, but still continuing subject to Rome—was impracticable. That connection with Rome was the root from which all the worst evils had sprung. Any reformation which left that unaltered, could only have been skin-deep and temporary. What was needed was, for the people of England to be left to work out their own religious life by themselves, just as they were working out their political liberty. It might be a slow work; it might be hindered by royal interference; it might be stained by disputes and persecutions among themselves,—but in the end the religious life of England could not fail. The beginning of any real reformation, that should have in it the seeds of wholesome development, had to be an utter breaking away from the Roman Catholic system.

The events which actually led to this beginning of the Reformation seem, certainly, small and ignoble enough. Henry VIII. desired a divorce from his queen, on the ground that, she having been the widow of his brother, the marriage had been, all along, contrary to the law of God. It is difficult to settle now, whether it was that his passionate nature was tired of the wife with whom he had lived for eighteen years, which is the general opinion, or whether it was that his superstitious fears had become really aroused by the death of child after child, as some believe. Possibly the lower and the higher feelings were mingled in him; but in the country at large the superstitious fear was the power which carried the people with him. The chief English statesmen of the time were alarmed by the fact that the king had no son to succeed him. The idea of another war of succession was a terror to the whole nation, and so, in spite of the respect felt for

Queen Catherine, Parliament and people desired the divorce. Such a divorce could only be granted by the Pope, and the Pope was at first inclined to consent. But soon difficulties arose. Year after year wore away in negotiations. The Pope did not absolutely refuse, but still hesitated and procrastinated. It was perfectly well known in England that this hesitation arose, not from any real religious scruple, but from fear of offending France and Germany; and at last Thomas Cromwell, the king's chief adviser, urged him to take the matter into his own hands; to break off from all connection with Rome; to declare himself, as king, Head of the Church as well as of the State, and to apply for the divorce to the Church-courts of England.

This counsel was at length adopted, and in the year 1534, the "Act of Supremacy" was passed. This important Act entirely separated the English Church from that of Rome, declared the king and his successors to be "the only Supreme head on earth of the Church of England," and set the religious life of England free from foreign interference, to work out by itself whatever it had in it to become.

It must have seemed at first, and to many of the most religious people in the country, a very poor beginning of reformation, to merely transfer the headship over the Church from a weak, hesitating, worldly Pope, to a strong, self-willed, and passionate king. To some it seemed a dreadful sacrilege. Sir Thomas More and Fisher, Bishop of Rochester, were among this number, and they would have no part in it, would not even take the new oath acknowledging the king's "supremacy." It was sad that men so good should have to suffer for obeying conscience, but this was no moment for Henry to hesitate,—if they were excused from the new oath, it could not be enforced upon any one, and then the separation from Rome would be practically a dead letter. They must give way, or die; so they died.

It was very soon seen that the change was not to be a dead letter, but a tremendous reality. The first effect of the separation from Rome was to place the religious life of England under a sharper despotism than ever. Act after Act gave the king more and more power. To him was practically given the choice of the bishops. Convocation could only meet by his permission, and its acts were null unless confirmed by him. No priest was allowed to preach without a special license from the Crown; the preacher so licensed was required to declare the royal will to the people, to preach against the false claims of "the Bishop of Rome," and publicly to uphold the king's supremacy.

This was change rather than reformation; but gradually the nobler religious spirit which had been leavening England for above a hundred years began to tell in the measures which this new, strong, native headship over the Church brought about. First came the liberty to all men to read the Bible in their own English tongue, "at their pleasure." That liberty, so long sought, so long denied, for which so many noble souls had suffered, was in itself a reformation, and has been the very root of all the subsequent noble religious growth and progress of England.

Then came the breaking up of that monastic system which had long been a dead and rotten thing, and had been the source of the worst scandals to religion. That many grievous wrongs were done in the suppressing of the monasteries, and a very poor use made of their vast property, is true enough; and yet, however badly it was done, it was the clearing away of a vast system of idle, useless life that was hindering instead of helping the religious life of the time.

The other element of what is called the Reformation, was the settlement of the doctrine and the services of the new "Church of England." At first there was but little reform in this respect. Henry had been a sincere Catholic to begin with—had even been entitled "Defender of the Faith" by the Pope, for writing a book against Luther,—and, through all the struggle, his opinions on religious doctrine had undergone little change. Yet, headstrong as he was, he could not altogether resist the changes that were going on around him. The English Bible had been already in wide circulation before it was permitted by law, and very many of the people and many even of the higher clergy, like Latimer, were abandoning some of the leading doctrines of the Romish Church. When Convocation drew up a petition to the king praying him to settle the articles of religion, they found sixty-seven errors which they said were becoming very prevalent, and required to be dealt with. They set forth the growing dislike of men to "the mass;" they quoted rough sayings of the common people, that the Host was nothing but a piece of bread, that it was as lawful to baptize in a tub of water at home as in the Church font, that the sacred oil of the extreme unction was no better than the Bishop of Rome's grease and butter; they specified even deeper heresies,—such as, that each man should confess his own sins to God, that purgatory was a delusion, that it was foolish and useless to pray to the saints, that priests might marry like other men, and that it was enough for any man to believe in Christ and repent of his sins,—these are a few of the grievous heresies which they asked to have dealt with and put down, and these show how far the Protestant tendencies were already carrying people.

Henry replied by issuing a series of articles which became for a time the authorized statement of what Englishmen must believe. As might be expected, they were not very much removed from Catholicism, but still they showed the changes that were coming over even those who still clung to the old ways. The new articles based men's faith broadly upon the Bible, though coupling with it the three creeds. They enjoined three sacraments, baptism, penance, and the Communion, instead of seven. The saints might be honoured and prayed to in modified degree; and it was lawful to pray for the dead, but not to think that "the Bishop of Rome's pardons" or "masses said before any image" would deliver them out of their pain in the world to come.

"It is yet but a mingle-mangle," said Latimer of all this; "a hotchpotch, I cannot tell what; partly Popery and partly true religion mingled together." And yet it was a great step forward; it was a great step even viewed as a system of doctrine; it was a still greater step as a sign that the Church of England had broken away from the authority of Rome, and that religious life and belief were henceforth to be settled by the king and the people together.

There were those, however, who were ready for a fuller reformation, who read their Bibles and thought for themselves, and who could no more believe a thing at the decree of the king than at the decree of the Pope. To these the new order of things brought a sore time; for this new "Head of the Church" was one who meant to be obeyed.

As long as Thomas Cromwell continued in power, indeed, the principles of the Reformation kept steadily making way, not indeed as fast as the more extreme Protestants wished, but quite as fast as the nation at large was prepared for. His influence was used to protect many whose opinions laid them open to persecuting statutes. Interpreted by that influence, the Reformation went on, in fact, beyond anything that was ordained by law. But the Chancellor used his great power too despotically. Gradually his opponents gained ground, and they used their advantage to force back the Church towards many of the old Roman Catholic ways. The famous Act of Six Articles was passed, which caused so much persecution that it was called the "whip with six lashes." It was a terrible step backwards. It restored the celibacy of the clergy and forced the priests who had married to put away their wives. It reaffirmed the sanctity of monastic vows, and the necessity of masses for the souls of the dead, and of Confession; and, worst of all, it sharply defined the Communion according to the extreme Catholic doctrine, of the bread and wine being absolutely changed into the very body and blood of Christ, and required every one to believe this under penalty of death at the stake. Cromwell tried to soften the carrying out of these provisions, but his own power was fast waning. In 1540 he perished on the scaffold, and his fall was followed by a new outburst of persecution. So all through the remainder of Henry's reign the axe and the faggot were busy. To be too Catholic and to be too Protestant were about equally dangerous, for Catholics were beheaded for denying the king's supremacy, and Protestants were burnt for disbelieving in the mass. Only two days after the fall of Cromwell, three Catholics and three Protestants were thus executed at the same time, at Smithfield. No man was safe; the king became in his last years moody and cruel. Political unsettlement was added to religious conflict. When the monasteries were dissolved, a fierce insurrection had broken out in the northern counties, called from its religious character, "The Pilgrimage of Grace," and when it was put down, abbots were hanged before their monasteries, and many of the nobles went to the block, while it left behind a seething and angry discontent with the new order of things.

It was a sore time for England, this beginning of the Reformation; yet it *was* a real beginning of it; and through all the strife and danger and perplexity and unsettlement, the mind of England was gradually working itself clear of the old superstitions which had so long oppressed it, and starting in that new course which was at last to bring better days, and to lead through religious toleration to religious liberty.

CHAPTER XVIII.

THE TRANSLATION OF THE BIBLE—WILLIAM TYNDALE.

Of all that was accomplished at the time of the Reformation, perhaps the most important thing was the giving the Bible to the people in the common English tongue, to be freely read by all. Indeed, throughout Europe, the battle of reformed religion was at first almost everywhere the battle for a free Bible. Whenever people began to read the Bible for themselves, it may not have led them to the truest idea of Christ's religion; we are only gradually getting back to that even now; but, at any rate, it taught them to follow Christ rather than to trust in the Masses and Absolutions of priests, and to think and act for themselves before God. So, wherever reformers have risen up to teach a nobler religion, one of the very first things they have attempted has been to give men the Bible in their own tongue; while, on the other hand, the constant effort of the priesthood has been to keep the people from reading the Bible for themselves.

We have seen how Wyclif busied himself with translating the Bible into the English tongue of his time, and how his friends and followers busied themselves in copying it out, until many hundred copies must have been scattered about among the homes of England. Through all the persecution of the Lollards, in which these Bibles were eagerly hunted up and burnt, this translation of

Wyclif's did very much to keep alive the reforming spirit. By the time of Henry VIII., however, its language was out of fashion—the language of an elder time; and printing had now been invented, so that something more than these old painfully-copied parchments was wanted. But just because books had now to be produced, not by copying, which could be done by lonely students in secret places, but by printing, which involved the use of a machinery difficult to hide, so it was become a harder thing to get an edition of English Bibles ready for circulation, in the teeth of penal laws and persecuting priests. It was done however, at length, and the story of its doing is the story of

WILLIAM TYNDALE.

All that we know of Tyndale's early life is that he was a Gloucestershire lad, born about 1480, and in time a student in Oxford University. Thence he went to Cambridge, where he, a priest now, and Master Bilney —whom we shall hear of again as the man who won Latimer over to the new religion—and others, earnestly busied themselves in studying the Scriptures and lecturing upon them. This branch of study had received a great impetus in those days; for, a few years before (1509), Erasmus had come to Cambridge, and interested many there in his great idea that Christendom wanted bringing back to the study of Christ as he lives for ever in the Gospels. To help in this work he set himself to bring out a scholarly edition of the Greek Testament, which should give a truer presentation of Christ's teachings than the imperfect Latin version, "the Vulgate," which alone was used by the Church. But it was not only for learned men that Erasmus did this. "I wish that even the weakest woman might read the Gospels and the Epistles of St. Paul," he wrote; "I long for the day when the husbandman shall sing portions of them to himself as he follows the plough, when the weaver shall hum them to the tune of his shuttle, when the traveller shall while away with their stories the weariness of his journey." This was the spirit in which his Greek Testament was brought out as a step towards the fuller work, and in this same spirit Tyndale opened his classes for the study of it at Cambridge. Such studies, however, were suspected in those days, and he had to abandon them. Then Tyndale went back into Gloucestershire, where he was for some time tutor in Sir John Walsh's household at Little Sodbury. One of the old-fashioned hospitable houses it was, and hither came oftentimes "abbots, deans, archdeacons, with divers other doctors and great beneficed men," making merry with the manor-house good cheer, and talking freely, as well-fed country priests were used to talk in those days, against the new notions and the folly of the evil men who put them forth. At last the poor tutor, of whom they would take little account in their talk, could hold his peace no longer, and dared to speak up, and argue, and even reprove them. At first they tried to put him down by argument, but that not being easy, by-and-by they would come no more to Sir John's, giving up their feasting there rather than take with it, what Fuller calls "the sour sauce" of Tyndale's reproofs. Then they began to defame him everywhere as a heretic, and at last he was summoned before the Bishop of Gloucester's court, where, he says, "the Chancellor threatened me grievously, and rated me as though I had been a dog." This did not silence him, however. The very opposition which he met with in setting forth what he felt was the very truth of Jesus Christ, only brought his labours to a clearer point; and when one of the priests at last said to him, "It were better for us to be without God's law than without the Pope's," Tyndale burst forth, "I defy the Pope and all his laws; and if God spare my life, ere many years I will cause the boy that driveth the plough to know more of the Scriptures than do all of you."

There spoke the purpose of his life. He went up to London, resolved to translate the Bible into common English; he tried to get help towards this from Tunstall, Bishop of London, but found that the bishops were very bitter against any such work. For half a year a London alderman, Humfrey Monmouth, kept him in his house, where he lived poorly and sparely, studying night and day at his great task. But it was too great a work for a lonely student to do all by himself, and as all the talk among these godly London merchants was of Martin Luther, and of the multitudes who were flocking to him at Wittemburg to learn of him, to him Tyndale made his way. He was helped on his way by a gift of ten pounds—a goodly sum in those times—from his friend, for which help, by the way, the alderman was afterwards imprisoned in the Tower. For a while Tyndale worked near Luther, busily translating the New Testament. Thence he went to Antwerp, where, joining with Frith (who was afterwards martyred), Barnes, and other trusty friends, they together set up a printing-press, to supply the Protestants of England with books which they dared not print in their own country. The first book which they set themselves to print was this New Testament that Tyndale had been translating. So wel' did they all work, that though the types and presses of that time were but clumsy contrivances compared with those of to-day, in less than two years they had ready the first edition of the New Testament ever printed in English. They printed three thousand of them, and, with great difficulty, these were smuggled into England in 1525, in two great bales, and were welcomed with great delight by the London Protestants, who formed an association of "Christian Brothers" for getting them sold and widely circulated. When it became known that these English Testaments were actually in the country, there was great stir among the authorities. Secret police were sent out, suspected houses were searched, many people were arrested. Tunstall, Bishop of London, finding that they did not come in fast enough, hit upon the plan of trying to buy them up; and as Tyndale was poor, and wanted to bring out a second edition with some important corrections, of course this exactly suited him. So his agents sold to the bishop, at a good price, about half of the edition, and these were solemnly burnt at Cheapside! Meanwhile, Tyndale and his companions were already busy with the proceeds, getting ready the better edition, which within a year was being still more largely distributed through England. Then Tyndale went on with the Old Testament, and this also was completed in 1530, and brought into England in spite of all the efforts of the Government.

In truth, Henry VIII. and his ministers were getting rather tired of such work. This dread of letting men read the Bible, at the very time that the king's party were constantly referring to it for the sake of strengthening themselves against the Papacy, was too plainly cowardly and mean to stand. When, in 1531, the bishops appealed to the king for severer powers against those who were circulating or reading Tyndale's Scriptures—the whole Scriptures were now to be had in separate portions, though not yet bound up as one Bible—they were obliged, for decency's sake, to take the ground that the translation was erroneous; and the fact that this was the only plea they put forward shows how opinion was gradually changing. Still more did the king's reply show this. If this translation was unsound, said he, let them then prepare a better one! For two years they did nothing. Then the king grew more urgent, and the bishops, in Convocation, went so far as to pass a resolution for a new translation; but that was all, they still *did* nothing. Finally, at Thomas Cromwell's instance, Miles Coverdale, a Cambridge scholar and a friend at once of Archbishop Cranmer and of Tyndale, went abroad to get something done. With Tyndale's help, he gathered his scattered versions of the various Scriptures into the first edition of the whole Bible, which was printed in 1535; and, the next year, this Bible, a great folio volume, with a dedication to the king and a frontispiece representing him handing it to the clergy and the people, was published in England with the royal sanction. Coverdale told afterwards, when preaching at St. Paul's Cross, that at first the bishops opposed this, saying, when the king asked their judgment of it, that "there were many faults in it. But he asked, upon that, if there were any *heresies* in it. They said they found none. 'Then,' said the king, 'in God's name let it go abroad among my people.'"

This is always called "Coverdale's Bible," but in truth it was Tyndale's, and to Tyndale belongs the real honour and glory of it.

And what of him, the brave, patient, earnest scholar,

who had so long lived in exile, praying and working for this one great object? Alas! he was to share the reward that was for so many of God's noblest servants in those days of darkness and struggle.

For some years he led a free, peaceful life in Antwerp, the refuge of persecuted Protestants. Secure under its liberties, Tyndale laboured on, the English merchants of the city caring for him, giving him a yearly allowance to live upon, which, "for the most part, he bestowed upon the poor." Two days a week "he reserved or hallowed to himself, which he named his pastime, Monday and Saturday," which days, Foxe tells, he spent in going about the poorer quarters of the city, "seeking out such poor men and women as were fled out of England," and comforting and relieving them. "The rest of the days of the week he gave wholly to his book, wherein he most diligently travailed. When the Sunday came, then went he to some one merchant's chamber or other, whither came many other merchants, and unto them would he read some one parcel of Scripture, the which proceeded so fruitfully, sweetly, and gently from him, that it was a heavenly comfort and joy to the audience."

This was the man whom the bishops hated and unceasingly tried to get into their hands; whose movements were watched and reported by foreign envoys, and whom paid spies tried to entrap from his shelter. At last one Phillips, an emissary of Gardiner, Bishop of Winchester (of whom we shall hear more in Mary's reign), enticed him beyond the city, and he was pounced upon by the officers of the Regent of Flanders, and put in prison. This was in the spring of 1535, just as the great work was passing through the press, and thenceforth Coverdale had to carry it on alone. For eighteen months Tyndale lay in prison, in the Castle of Vilvorde, near Brussels, and then the Emperor, Charles V., condemned him to die; and October 6, 1536, he died the martyr's death—strangled and then burnt—his last cry being, "Lord, open the eyes of the King of England!"

It would seem, by that cry, that he had not heard, there in his prison, that already the eyes of the King of England were opened, and that for some months now the English Bible, for which he had lived and for which he was dying, was being openly sold in London without hindrance.

This is the story of the translation of the Bible. There have been many other translations since, but they have all been little more than revisions of Tyndale's great work, which remains the basis of the English Bible as we still read it at the present day.

When once the permission to read the Bible was given, its circulation proceeded rapidly. The king issued an order that one should be set up in every parish church, where all men might read it. To this day there are some of these old Bibles to be found in old country churches, chained to a little stand, as they stood, according to that order, for any man "to look and read therein." So eagerly were the new Bibles bought, that within the next sixteen years, before the Reformation was arrested by Mary, it has been estimated that above a hundred thousand copies were scattered abroad over England.

Of course so wide a use had its inconveniences. It at once produced very great excitement. The new book was read by many who could not understand it. Men argued and brawled about it in the highways, and even in the taverns. Groups gathered around the chained volume as some skilled reader read it aloud, and vehement disputations often broke out among the hearers. But all this was only the inevitable result of the jealousy with which men had so long been kept from reading it at all, and through those years of wrangling and controversy the mind of the English nation was gradually working its way out of the old Darkness into the new Light.

CHAPTER XIX.

THE SUPPRESSION OF THE MONASTERIES.

THE story has been already told, how the monasteries which were dotted all over England came to be. In their early days they had been very noble institutions. Through ages of tumult and barbarism they had been witnesses for right and truth, upholders of the weak against oppression, the refuge for many noble men and women from the struggles and passions of the world. There, giving up everything that most people cared to live for, men and women devoted themselves to worshipping God, helping the poor, teaching the children of the people round, keeping open hospitality for travellers, and copying such books as they knew.

Gradually, however, their first piety had died out; gifts of money and lands made them rich, and the monasteries became resorts of idleness and self-indulgence, too often, of vice. The monks were perhaps not worse than the society around them, but they had won their position by being better, and as they gradually declined to the common level, men could not help asking why they should be allowed to go on, generation after generation, holding a great part of the wealth of the country and doing nothing for it.

Already, as early as the time of Wyclif, there had been a strong outcry among the people against the idle, useless lives of the monks and friars. Soon after Wyclif's death, so widespread had the indignation become, that the House of Commons urged King Henry IV. to take the estates of Abbots and Priors which were being wasted in pomp and luxury, instead of taxing the people; and the next king, Henry V., did suppress all the "Alien Monasteries"—those held by foreign orders of monks—in England. If the monks had been wise they would have felt that this was a warning not to be disregarded. But they were not wise. They went on as before. They grew more careless of their rules, more indolent, more worldly. The friars, who at first had shamed the elder orders by their poverty and zeal, soon became the worst of all.

So things went on for another hundred and fifty years after Wyclif's time, till the whole institution was like a rotten old tree. And yet it was a dangerous and difficult work to pull it down. It is difficult for us, now, to realize how these monasteries had become rooted in the common life of the people, almost like a part of the order of nature. They were everywhere. First and last, above six hundred and fifty regular monasteries were suppressed, which gives an average of more than twelve to each county. Many of these were magnificent piles of buildings—of which some idea may be formed by visiting such ruins as those of Fountains, Glastonbury, or Furness—which threw into the shade the mansions of the wealthiest nobles; while, at the other end of the scale, were small houses with only eight or ten monks and some small estate. All over England were these houses, and the monks lived among the gentry as pleasant companions. Usually they kept up some kind of school for the neighbourhood; they were generally easy landlords—indeed, they dared not be otherwise; and if they no longer did the poor any good religiously, they gave them plentiful alms, and had the good word of all the "sturdy beggars" throughout the land. And these "monasteries" were not all. There were nearly a hundred "colleges" of priests, and above a hundred "hospitals" which were really little groups of monks living together on endowed estates left for religious uses; and besides all these there were about two thousand four hundred "chantries"—little chapels, sometimes on bridges, sometimes in remote places where there was no regular church, often in corners of cathedrals or parish churches—and all these had monks attached to them—one or two to each—to sing masses for the souls of the founders. And all these institutions were in much the same condition—the *religious* life of them was gone.

What little religious work the monasteries seemed to be doing, was done, not by the religious services of the monks—nobody cared for these now, they were performed so carelessly and irregularly—but by relics and images. Every monastery had its odds and ends of bones or hair, finger-nails or scraps of clothing, preserved as precious relics of this Apostle or that Saint. Many had famous images of Christ or the Virgin Mary, which could bow, or move their eyes, and do wonderful things for those who brought handsome offerings in gold or jewels. So, crowds still gathered to the monasteries, here and there; and the common people had no particular feeling against them; and the nobles found them convenient schools for their sons, and pleasant resting-places on their journeys; and the beggars lived upon their doles of bread and beer; and the old buildings had a strong, prosperous look—almost to the end.

It must not be supposed that there were absolutely no exceptions to all this religious deadness. Here and there were monasteries well-conducted, and here and there we come upon monks who were bold, brave, true men. Such a monk was Friar Peto, who, when called to preach before the king, rebuked him sternly to his face, and warned him of the fate of Ahab; and such another was Friar Elstowe, who, the next Sunday, on a courtly chaplain taking occasion to attack Peto for what he had said, stood up in the roodloft in the stead of Peto, who was absent, and fearlessly replied to the chaplain, until the king thundered out to both of them to hold their peace. Next day Peto and Elstowe were taken before Lord Essex, who told them they both deserved to be put in a sack and thrown into the Thames. "Threaten these things to rich and dainty folk," answered Elstowe. "We heed them not, for, thanks be to God, we know the way to heaven to be as ready by water as by land, and therefore care not which way we go." Such, too, monks of the nobler sort, were the brethren of the Chartreuse—or "Charterhouse" as it came to be called, in London, one of the very few monasteries that, even in this later age, when so many were corrupt, cherished a religious life as pure and high as that of the early times. John Houghton its prior, at first bent to the storm, and with his monks took the oath required by the government, though in a meaning of their own. They were unhappy however at having yielded even so far, and took no trouble to conceal their abhorrence of the king's course; and so at length Houghton and two of his brother priors were called up again for closer question, and quietly but firmly declared themselves, and, five days after, died the dreadful death allotted for treason. The remaining monks of the Charterhouse were dispersed among other monasteries, and every effort made to force them to submit, but they could not do so. Nine died in prison, and three were executed. Had the monks generally been such men as these, no reformation had been needed. But these were the very rare exceptions; the system as a whole was dead, and had to be done away.

There is one thing more that must be remembered in reading the story of the suppression of the monasteries: it was not Protestantism which first discovered and pointed out how corrupt they were. For generations, every pious and good bishop had been troubled by their condition, but the bishops had no power over them, had not even power to visit and inspect them, monks and nuns being responsible only to the head of their own order and to the Pope. In Henry VII.'s time, the monasteries were so notoriously scandalous that Cardinal Morton, then the head of the English Church, procured special authority from the Pope to inspect them, and to punish those monks and nuns who were guilty of gross crimes, and his letters show what frightful abuses were common and known, though he was quite powerless to check them. Again, when Henry VIII. came to the throne, and while he was still a bitter enemy to the Reformation, Archbishop Warham tried to effect some amendment, but found it utterly beyond his power. Cardinal Wolsey took hold of the evil with a stronger hand, and with the authority of the Pope actually suppressed a number of the smaller monasteries which were so hopelessly bad that even he felt that nothing else could be done with them. But Wolsey was not a genuine reformer, and dared not really grapple with the evil.

It was Henry's great minister, Thomas Cromwell, who

first resolved that the monasteries should be thoroughly looked into and dealt with. In the year 1535 he appointed three men whom he could trust, as "Commissioners" to visit all religious houses, with considerable powers for making a beginning of reforms in them at once, and with directions to draw up a full report of their condition. There was great consternation throughout the monasteries, when the news of this commission spread abroad, greater still when the commissioners made their appearance here and there, looking into everything and insisting on ferreting out the truth. It seemed as if nothing could be kept from them. They *would* see the deeds of the abbey property, and have out all the facts about the large sums which the abbots had pocketed for renewing leases at fraudulently low rents. They would look at the altar ornaments and plate, and know what had become of this or that famous jewel that was missing, and where the gold vessels were hidden away which they were sure such an abbey must have. But most searching was their investigation into the characters of the monks. Perhaps they were too ready to believe all the bad stories that the village gossips told them, but enough scandals were evident and admitted, to make them ready to believe anything. It is impossible to describe in this book the state of vice that the commissioners found. The greater abbeys were the least corrupt, though there were few even of these that had not some of the inmates living in notorious profligacy. The smaller abbeys were, in many cases, sinks of iniquity beyond all telling. And everything went down into the visitors' report! Then, before they went away, they called all the monks or nuns together; all monks under twenty-four years old, and nuns under twenty-one they set free from their vows, and giving them forty shillings in money and a common dress in place of their monastic habit, allowed them to go out into the world again whither they pleased. To those who remained they gave strict warning to amend their lives, to occupy themselves in useful labour and study, to keep to simple fare as their rules enjoined, and to be charitable, but not to encourage "idle beggars and vagabonds, such as commonly use to resort to such places;" especially they directed that, every day, the abbot should read aloud to them, some portion of their foundation rules, so as to revive among them, if it were possible, something of the spirit of their founders.

For months, the commissioners, Legh and Layton, each with a few trusty servants, were going about from place to place, all over England. Then their report was complete, and early the next year it was presented to Parliament.

Great was the commotion and great the horror when the "Black Book," as it was called, was read. It was not a Parliament eager to destroy them, for, as has been shown, the monasteries were interwoven with the whole life of the time, and probably there was hardly a member but was connected with one or another of them; yet Latimer tells that when the reading of the report was ended, a cry arose from the Commons, "Down with them!" Indeed, there was nothing else for it. There might be hope for the larger monasteries, which were not quite so corrupt, and had at any rate kept up some responsible organization, but with few exceptions the case of the small ones was hopeless. Before Parliament separated an Act was passed dissolving all the smaller monasteries, those with less than two hundred pounds a year of income. The measure was only passed after long debate, for there was the great difficulty in the way—what to do with the property. The great families in the neighbourhood of the monasteries, whose ancestors had in many cases bestowed estates upon them, thought they ought to have them back. Others, again, contended that properties having been once given for religious uses ought not to put to be any other use, and wished to see the property transferred to colleges or churches. In the end, however, the property was "given to the king," for the use of the state. Three hundred and seventy-six monasteries fell under this Act. Those of the monks or nuns who wished to continue in the same life, were distributed among the larger monasteries which remained untouched; the others were sent out into the world, with some small allowance for their living—which, however, in the troubled times that followed, it is doubtful whether most of them received.

It might have been hoped that after such a warning the larger monasteries still left would amend their ways, and justify their continued existence. But there were many reasons why this was difficult. The suppression of the smaller monasteries had, for one thing, produced rather rage than repentance. Then, the fact was that the monastic life was out of harmony with the time. There was no need for such a life; monasteries were not now, as they once had been, the only refuge where men could have much chance of serving God earnestly. The living religion of the time was among the parish priests, and the godly laity. Monasteries were out of date; and as soon as the subject was once fairly faced, their abolition was only a question of time.

The actual cause of their final suppression was the great insurrection in the North of England, called the Pilgrimage of Grace. There had been for some time, a great deal of discontent among the people; for taxes were heavy, and there had been many changes in the laws, which the poor thought pressed hardly on them. Now, the suppression of all these monasteries threw back among the people thousands of sturdy beggars who could no longer live on the convent doles, and thousands of dislodged monks and friars, who had to work for their living, and were full of bitterness against the Government. These spread among the people the idea that the king intended ere long to do away with all parish churches, and to take their property as the property of so many of the monasteries had been taken. So, in the autumn of that year of the first suppression, thousands of men were flocking together, and Lincolnshire and Yorkshire, and indeed, nearly all the North of England rose to arms. All classes joined the insurrection. At the head were many of the noblest northern families; and the farmers came by whole parishes together, with their priests at their head, carrying the Church crosses instead of banners; and some of the abbeys sent bands of armed followers, and others helped with food and money and plate, and these priests and monks were the fiercest insurgents of all. There was no actual fighting, indeed, for the Government was not strong enough to crush the movement at once, and the leaders of the insurrection professed not to be making war against the king, but only to be seeking justice, and opposing the king's evil advisers; so the king temporized, made some concessions, promised a general pardon, and in a few weeks the great force dispersed again and the Pilgrimage of Grace was at an end. Unfortunately, however, some of those who had joined in it were not contented, thought the terms promised by the king would not be kept, and a few small risings took place here and there; then the Government, angry at these, withdrew the promised concessions and pardons from all, and punished all who had been concerned with a swift and heavy hand. To the monasteries that were still remaining this insurrection was fatal. It was seen that they were mere hotbeds of disloyalty, even where they were no longer haunts of vice. A number of the abbots and leading monks were hanged at once for treason, and their abbeys closed and confiscated. There was no law by which the rest might be suppressed, but there was no law to prevent them from voluntarily surrendering to the king, and the abbot and monks of many of the abbeys were only too glad to do this to escape closer examination into their proceedings during their insurrection. Ghastly hints were sometimes given. Abbot Paslew of Whalley was hanged before his monastery gate; and while the body still swung in chains, the Abbot of Furness was summoned thither, and with that terrible warning before him hastened to proffer the "voluntary" surrender of his abbey. So, abbey after abbey fell through those next two years, and then, in 1539, Parliament confirmed these surrenders, and empowered the king to suppress all that still remained; next year the monastic system was at an end in England.

It is very sad to think of the ruin that came over those beautiful buildings that had risen over every part of England during the previous four hundred years. Their new owners, to whom they had been given or sold by the king, quickly dismantled them—"picked out their eyes" as Fuller says—to prevent their ever being restored. A few of the great abbey churches, as at St. Albans, Tewkesbury, and Malvern, were spared and converted into parish churches. But most of them were left to utter ruin; the beautiful stained windows were plucked out and carried away; the marble sculptures were set up in barons' halls; the libraries were scattered about and destroyed, and the massive masonry was used as a common quarry by all the farmers round, who had a wall or a barn to build.

It is sad to think that all the vast property of these abbeys was even more wastefully misused than even the buildings themselves. A small part was indeed devoted to religious purposes. Five new bishoprics were made and endowed—Oxford, Peterborough, Bristol, Gloucester, and Chester,* and a few grammar schools were set up; but the great bulk of the abbey lands were either given away, or granted at very low prices to the needy nobles and courtiers whom it was important to keep on the side of the changes which were being carried out. So little did all this vast property add to the resources of the state, that, the very year after the final suppression of the monasteries, the king had to ask Parliament for a grant to meet the expenses he had incurred in forwarding the reformation of religion! One is induced at first, to wish that so much property had been continued for some religious use; but hardly any one who looks at what the Church of England has been since, and considers what a snare and source of corruption its vast wealth has been to it, will be disposed to wish that the Reformation had left it still richer!

* Another, Westminster, was also constituted at the same time, but was suppressed again in the next reign.

CHAPTER XX.

LATIMER, BISHOP AND MARTYR.

Let us leave the general course of our history, and look at one of the noblest and most memorable of the men of that Reformation-time—one who began with being a devout and humble believer in the old faith; who caught the spirit of the Reformation and became one of its leading men; whose life tells us much of the common life of the time, and who, in his death brings vividly before us what Protestants had to undergo in the terrible Catholic reaction under Queen Mary.

We first see Hugh Latimer as a child, growing up on the little farm, at Thurcaston in Leicestershire, where he was born, in 1490. Years afterwards, in one of his sermons, into which he was constantly bringing recollections of the men and things he had known, he gives a pleasant picture of the old English yeoman life. "My father," he said, "was a yeoman, and had no lands of his own, only he had a farm of three pounds or four pounds by the year at the uttermost, and hereupon he tilled as much as kept half a dozen men. He had a walk for a hundred sheep, and my mother milked thirty kine. He was able [well to do] and did find the king a harness [suit of armour] with himself and his horse. I can remember that I buckled on his harness when he went to Blackheath field. He kept me to school, or else I had not been able to preach before the king's majesty now. He married my sisters with five pounds a-piece, so that he brought them up in godliness and fear of God. He kept hospitality for his poorer neighbours, and some alms he gave to the poor, and all this he did of the said farm." And he adds: "In my time, my poor father was as diligent to teach me to shoot, as to learn me any other thing; and so, I think, other men did their children. He taught me how to draw; how to lay my body in my bow. I had my bows bought me according to my age and strength, as I increased in them so my bows were made bigger; for men never shoot well, except they be brought up in it."

In such a simple sturdy country life, the lad grew up, able by and by to lay the whole strength of his being to shooting nobler arrows than those cloth yard shafts.

Then as he grew to manhood, he was sent to Cambridge University. It was a great time at Cambridge, for the minds of men everywhere were eager with the new learning which printing had opened to them; and Erasmus had just come to Cambridge, and the colleges were alive with dicussions about religion and philosophy. The youth had heard little of such discussions in the quiet Leicestershire home, where he had grown up with the old reverence for the Church and the Pope, and at first he was shocked at the freedom with which such topics were handled, for, says he "I myself was as obstinate a Papist as any in England;" and indeed, when he took his bachelor's degree, his "whole oration was against Philip Melancthon," who was just then coming into note as Luther's ablest helper. But there was "one Master Bilney" who came to his study, talked quietly to him, and showed him things differently, and he adds in his quaint way, "from that time forward, I began to smell the word of God, and forsook the school doctors and such fooleries." He was an important accession to the little band of earnest men who were feeling their way towards the new light; for he was already becoming known as a forcible, direct preacher, and the students always eagerly crowded to hear him. It is told of this time, how one day the Bishop of Ely "came secretly and suddenly" with a company to hear him, timing his entrance when Latimer was "well entered into his sermon" so that he should have no time to prepare some less heretical discourse than usual, to suit the bishop's ears. But Latimer stopped, when he saw the new comers; waited till they were all seated, and then said "It is meet that a new auditory requireth a new theme" and straightway began to preach on the Office of a Bishop, setting forth "the pattern" of what bishops ought to be, in a way which, though he did not say so, was a terrible rebuke to the worldly prelate before him. The bishop, "being a very wise and polotique worldly man," thanked Latimer afterwards, and then went away and complained to Cardinal Wolsey that he preached "very seditious doctrine." So Wolsey sent for Latimer and made him rehearse what it was that had angered the bishop; but when he had heard it through, instead of blaming him he told him he should preach it to the bishop's beard, and sent him home with a license to preach throughout England.

It was not only in preaching and teaching that Latimer was busy, in these years at Cambridge. With Bilney and the rest of the little company of reformers, he busied himself in active works of doing good, visiting the sick and the prisoners in the gaol. They were regarded with suspicion by the authorities, and at length Bilney and several others were summoned before a court of bishops, to be examined about their heresies. Bilney gave way to the threats of the court, and made the sign of recantation, and he being the leader, the rest were merely admonished and let go. 'But Bilney could not bear the self-reproach of having been unfaithful in the hour of trial, and in a little while preached the reformed doctrines more strongly and openly than before, and was seized and tried by the Bishop of Norwich, and went humbly and bravely to his death. Then Latimer became the head of the reforming party, though, his earnestness being directed more against the corruptions and abuses of the church than against its doctrines, he was not, for a time, exposed to quite so much danger as some others. When the question of the king's divorce came up, he stood for the King and against the Pope, as did many other Englishmen who did not care much for the question of ecclesiastical law, knowing the Pope's refusal was only the result of political intrigue. Then the king heard of him, sent for him to Windsor, and made him one of his chaplains. But Latimer was ill-fitted for the part of a courtier. His plain, homely dress and ways, and most of all his utter fearlessness, and outspokenness against all wrong in high or low, were too much for such a position, and by and by the king gave him a little country living down in Wiltshire. But during this time he did one of the bravest acts of his life. The persecution was just springing up against the reading of the English Testaments that Tyndal had managed to smuggle into London, and Latimer wrote an earnest and indignant remonstrance to the king, against this persecution, ending with the entreaty "Wherefore

Gracious King, remember yourself; have pity upon your soul; and think that the day is even at hand when you shall give account for your office, and of the blood that hath been shed by your sword." Bold words for a poor priest to write to the headstrong and irritable Henry VIII.; but perhaps his very courage was his safety, for the king was one who knew a man when he saw him, and though he did not stop the persecutions, he answered the letter with unusual kindness, and always remained Latimer's friend.

And now, as the course of the Government towards reformation became more decided, Latimer came into more public notice by his preaching. Before that time preaching had been very poor, and indeed had almost died out. There were few even of the bishops that preached. All the sermons that men had known in the old times were disquisitions about monkish legends and marvels. Of late the reforming clergy had began to preach long scholarly arguments on points of doctrine. Latimer's preaching was a new thing in the land. He talked about religion in a plain, straightforward way; in the speech of the field and the street; seasoning his discourse with anecdotes, droll sayings, and homely, direct exhortations and applications that no one could help listening to—and all with such a vehement earnestness that he seemed like one of the old prophets. Thus, preaching before the king's court, he turns round upon the Lord Chancellor and tells him that the saying is abroad that "it is money that is heard." But "heare poore men's suits yourself," he cries, "I require you in God's behalf; and put it not to the learning of these velvet coats, these upskippes"—"upstarts" as we should say. And another time: "Regard no person; fear no man; mark this saying, thou proud judge! Hell will be full of these judges if they repent not and amend." As for the bishops, he lashed them again and again, unsparingly. "I would ask you a strange question," he cried out suddenly, as he was preaching once at St. Paul's Cross with a number of bishops round him, "Who is the most diligent prelate in all England? that passeth the rest in doing of his office? I will tell you! It is the devil!" "Of all the pack of them that have cure, the devil shall go for my money, for he ordereth his business. Therefore, you unpreaching prelates, learn of the devil to be diligent in your office; if you will not learn of God and good men, for shame learn of the devil." Nor did he spare the king himself, but with the king also, it was all before his face he spoke. "I should have been a very dolt" he said, once, when he was accused of fostering sedition by this plain speaking, "I should have been a very dolt to have preached so at the borders of your realm, as I have preached before your grace."

Thus all through the changing policy of Henry VIII. Latimer spoke his word. Now the king wanted him away, and sent him down to his little country living at West Kingston in Wiltshire. He went, nothing loth; threw himself into his simple parish work among the poor, went hither and thither preaching with the license he had to preach throughout the kingdom. So indefatigable was he, that the clergy took the alarm and he was summoned again before the Court of Bishops, and this time it had like to have gone hard with him, but he appealed to the king, and Henry sent word to convocation not to press the matter further.

Then came a turn of the tide. Thomas Cromwell was at the head of affairs; the Reformation was moving on; the monasteries were about to be inspected and dealt with. The abler men who were on the side of progress were wanted in the front, and Latimer was (in 1535) made Bishop of Worcester. For a few years this gave him great power in the reforming direction. He was just as active as he had been in his little Wiltshire parish, putting godly preaching ministers into the livings; preaching himself, up and down his diocese; clearing out the great wooden image of the Virgin Mary from his cathedral and sending it up to London to make, with some others which he named in his letter, "a jolly muster in Smithfield." Sometimes sterner work fell to his share. When Friar Forest was condemned to be burnt Latimer was sent for by Cromwell to preach the sermon, and there, close to the faggots, all ready to be lighted, by which the condemned Catholic was placed, Latimer plied him with the usual Protestant arguments, and then in closing, pointing to the pardon waiting for him if he would recant, asked him if he would live or die. "I will die" answered the monk; "do your worst upon me. Seven years ago you durst not for your life have preached such words as these. Burn me, hang me, do what you will, I will be true henceforth to my faith." And true he was. It was a stern age, and the Protestants had been steeled by seeing so many of their brethren perish, yet we sorrow to find Latimer having part—though it seems, reluctantly—in such evil work.

A few years more and another turn of the tide came. The Reformation was going too far! Men were brawling about texts and doctrines, in the taverns and at the street corners. The most violent language and action were used by ignorant declaimers, against doctrines that the reformers themselves were only gradually abandoning. A reaction took place, and a list of articles was set forth by the Government, by which everybody must be made to stand. The real presence, the celibacy of the priesthood, the inviolability of the monastic vows, private masses, and confession were re-affirmed, and "the Law of the Six Articles"—really including all the worst features of Catholicism—was passed, with terrible penalties attached to it for all who would not submit. Latimer at once resigned his bishopric and was glad to retire into private life, but the king was angry at his thus showing his disapproval of the articles, and though he would not have him persecuted he would not allow him to go free. He was put in ward with the Bishop of Chichester, one of the more Catholic bishops, and kept in a sort of half-imprisonment—allowed, however, to see his friends. After a year or so, Latimer was at liberty, and for some time lived quietly in the country, but the Catholic party who during the later years of Henry VIII. were several times in the ascendancy, were ever on the watch to injure him; and having come up to London for medical advice, he was seized, and imprisoned in the Tower, where he lay till the death of the king the following year.

The beginning of the new reign saw the Protestant party more hopeful and triumphant than they had ever yet been, for the young king was a zealous Protestant, and a nobleman of the same party had been appointed Regent by the dying king. The people loved Latimer, and the Government would have replaced him in his old bishopric at Worcester. But Latimer, though only about fifty-six years of age was already a feeble and bent old man, through the intense labours of his former life, and the hardships of imprisonment telling upon a body which had long been in poor health. So he would meddle no more in public affairs, but lived in a room of Lambeth Palace, with his old friend Archbishop Cranmer, and passed his days in preaching, and in studying, and in doing kind offices for the poor. He got such a name for kindness that he could not walk in the garden with his book but some one would be sure to come with some tale of need, in which his influence was wanted. Preaching was still his great work, however; and, as he often preached before the court, the power of his pointed humour, his irony, his fearlessness in rebuke, helped to strengthen the principles of the young king, and to keep the nobles more true to the cause of the Reformation.

The close of Latimer's life belongs to the later time of the reaction into Catholicism under Queen Mary, the fuller story of which has to be told in the next chapter. Men hoped that Mary, though herself a strong Catholic, would leave religious matters as her brother had settled them; but there was no ground for such a hope, and in six weeks after she came to the throne Latimer with Cranmer and many others of the leading reformers were in prison. Latimer knew only too well what would be the end of it. As he passed the burning place at Smithfield he said, "this place has long groaned for me." But he kept his old cheery temper. He was left in the cold prison, without fire, as the sharp winter came on. "Tell your master," he said to his gaoler, "that if he does not look better to me I shall perhaps escape him." The governor came in a rage to know what he meant. "Why, truly," said the prisoner, "you look that I should be burnt, but, as it is, I am more likely to be starved with cold." Awhile after, he was taken to Oxford, lodged in the common gaol there; lay there above a year, feeble and sickly, and broken down with suffering and hardship. They pretended to give him a trial, appointed a time for a public disputation between Cranmer, Ridley and himself, on the one side, and some of the leading Catholics on the other. But Latimer would not argue; he knew that the time for argument was past; indeed, he was too weak, so ill that he could not swallow food; he simply declared what he held the truth, refused to recant, and as he heard the terrible sentence pronounced on them of death at the stake, he said, "I thank God most heartily that he hath prolonged my life to the end that I may glorify him by this kind of death."

They were not to die yet, however. For nearly a year and a half longer they were all kept in prison, and every effort was made to induce them to recant, but all in vain. And so at length came the morning, October 16, 1555, when Latimer was led forth out of Oxford gaol to die, with his younger companion Ridley. The bent and feeble old man hobbled along in his old frieze coat, crying to his comrade, "Have after you as fast as I can follow," and so they came to the open space beyond Balliol College. Then Ridley embraced his friend and they kneeled down there and prayed together, and then, stripping off their outer clothes and giving little remembrances to their friends, they were ready for the fire. "Before," says Foxe, speaking of Latimer, "he appeared a withered and crooked old man," but as the keeper pulled off his dress and left him standing in his shroud, "he now stood bolt upright, as comely a father as one would wish to see." Mercifully a friend hung a bag of gunpowder round the neck of each of them and then they were chained back to back to the post, and the fire was brought. "Play the man, Master Ridley," said Latimer as the gorse below the faggots kindled and crackled; "We shall this day light such a candle by God's grace in England, as I trust shall never be put out," and as the flames rose up he bathed his hands in them, as it were, until they reached the powder, and he died.

CHAPTER XXI.

THE CATHOLIC REACTION UNDER MARY.

THE Reformation begun by Henry VIII., was continued under Edward VI. and during this second reign, was carried both too fast and too far. To a large extent the people did not go with it. Of course it was right for those who held even the most extreme Protestant doctrines to carry them out in their own worship. The wrong thing was the attempt to carry them out in the worship of the whole nation, and to force all people to believe them. The only true plan is for all people to worship God in their own way and to hold what views of religion seem to them true, and for the Government not to help any or hinder any. But Englishmen had not come to any such idea as yet. They found a great Church existing, and the whole nation was considered as belonging to it, and each thought that the Church ought to be altered and ordered according to the views of his own party, but that the whole nation should still be forced to conform to it. So, for generations the story of the religious life of England is the story of the struggles between an advancing party and a receding party, each in turn getting the upper hand, and each, when uppermost, trying to force everybody into the one way. People only gradually learned the lesson of religious toleration, and they have not quite learned, even yet, the true lesson of religious equality.

The Reformation was carried much further in Edward VI.'s time than it had been by Henry VIII. The Latin mass was done away, and the services of the English Book of Common Prayer were drawn up and used in its place; the stone altars were removed and wooden communion tables set up in the churches; forty-two articles of religion were drawn up, embodying the doctrines of the extreme Protestants, and many other changes introduced for which in Henry VIII.'s time men would have been hung or burnt. Such changes from the old accustomed ways would have caused discontent among the people, even if the general government had been good. But it was not good. The boy-king's advisers were a set of greedy nobles, and the people were harassed and oppressed. The old refuge of the poor in the abbey doles had been done away, and no other means of relief had been created in their place. The law was weak against wrong-doers; the coin was debased; learning was decaying and the colleges were empty; and crowds of labouring men were out of employment. Those who hated the new doctrines had an easy task in persuading the people that all this state of things was the punishment of heaven for the wicked changes which had been made in religion and in the Church.

Mary's accession to the throne, therefore, was welcomed with joy by the nation at large. There had been an attempt at first to set up as queen, the Protestant Lady Jane Grey, a great granddaughter of Henry VII., but it was an utter failure. People did not care about the technicalities of her royal descent, nor about what Edward VI. had done to try to change the succession on his death-bed. They felt that Mary was the rightful heir to Henry VIII.'s throne, and she entered

London amid general rejoicing; Protestants generally rejoiced with the rest. They knew, indeed, that Mary was a Catholic, and they expected that she would continue so; but she had told the council that she had no intention of interfering with the existing settlement of things, and the utmost that any feared was that she would refuse to allow the later and more extreme changes that had been made, on the ground that Edward VI. had not lived to be of age so as to confirm them. No one had any idea that she would undo all that had been done during the two previous reigns, and institute the fiercest persecution that was ever known in England.

But the nation was not long left in doubt. Mary was of an intense though narrow nature, cultivated and learned for her age; fearless, self-willed, and a sincere, bigoted Catholic. At her side were Bonner, Bishop of London, and Gardiner, Bishop of Winchester, who under the extreme Protestantism of the previous reign had been deprived of their bishoprics and imprisoned, and who were eager with priestly hate to persecute in their turn. The first changes, however, needed little prompting from the court; the people turned back to the old accustomed ways in religion with an eager unthinking reaction before which the thoughtful arguments of the Protestants were utterly powerless. The bishops who had been deprived of their sees went back to them. The clergy who had married wives under the recent laws, were driven out again. The English prayer books were torn up and the old Latin mass restored. A great blow from their own side completed the discouragement of the Protestants. The Duke of Northumberland had been, during the late reign, the most forward and influential of the Protestant leaders. Now, condemned to die for treason in trying to set Lady Jane Grey on the throne, he turned round and declared himself a Catholic, and on the scaffold protested that his rebellion had been owing to the false teachers who had led him to err from the faith. The Protestants were stunned by this desertion; even in London, where the first attempt to revive the Mass had nearly cost the priest his life, all opposition now seemed to have collapsed, and everywhere the people and the churches fell back into the old Catholic ways.

But this was not enough for Queen Mary. She wanted that the nation should return not only to Catholic belief, but to its subjection under Rome. For this, however, the people had no wish. The old English dislike of home-interference by a foreign Pope was as strong as ever. Among the higher classes there was an additional reason for fearing it, in the expectation that the Pope would require the abbey lands to be restored! The day for this to be possible, however, was gone for ever. Not only the Protestant families that had been enriched out of the abbey property, but Catholic nobles who had quietly resumed their own former chantry grants, and Catholic tradesmen who had bought the confiscated property, and Catholic farmers who had built their houses or barns out of the carved stonework of the dismantled monasteries—all dreaded the possibility of such a calling to account. Added to this was a feeling that all this desire to be reunited with Rome was connected with a plan which was on foot for marrying the queen to Philip II. of Spain; and the English people did not like Spain or the Spanish family, with its iron despotism and its fierce persecuting ways. However, Mary, who was eagerly set upon marrying Philip, and her priestly counsellors, who cared little about the marriage but very much about restoring Popery, together carried all before them. Spanish gold corrupted the Parliament, until it repealed the law which prevented a papal legate from entering the kingdom, and then Mary had Cardinal Pole beside her to strengthen her course. More gold among reluctant members, and the marriage with Philip was agreed to, though the nation still disliked it so much that the citizens looked on in sullen silence as the Spanish envoy entered London, and the boys pelted him with snowballs! It is the first steps in such a backward course which are the hardest. Parliament having gone so far, the rest of Mary's work was easier, and just one year after her accession, London saw the reconciliation of England with Rome accomplished in a grand and solemn ceremonial. After high mass in Westminster Abbey, the Lords and Commons gathered at Whitehall, and there, before the queen and her Spanish husband, they all kneeled humbly down while Cardinal Pole gave them absolution for the sin of heresy and schism, and formally received the nation back into the fold of Rome.

It remained to enforce this as a reality upon the people. Mary had been obliged to agree that no steps should be taken to compel the restoration of the abbey lands, but no one had stipulated against the revival of persecution! Yet many hesitated. Persecution—of the fiercer sort, at any rate—was no longer looked on as it once had been. The old laws for burning heretics had been abolished eight years before, and the worst that Catholics had had to fear in Edward VI.'s time was imprisonment and fine. So, the first bill for the revival of the old persecuting statutes was thrown out, and for two sessions Parliament continued firm in this refusal. At last, however, it gave way, and acts were passed reviving the old Lollard statutes of a hundred and fifty years before, and also restoring the bishops' courts with a power which made them into nothing less than the Inquisition.

Then began the most terrible persecution which this England of ours has ever known. The bishops seemed to spring upon their victims like wild beasts. The act only came into operation on the 20th January, 1555, and by the 4th of February the fire was lighted. The first victim was John Rogers, one of Tyndale's old fellow-labourers in translating the Bible, and since that one of the clergy of St. Paul's. With him they seized good old Bishop Hooper, and sent him down to Gloucester, where he had been bishop, to be burned. He was much beloved there, both by rich and poor, and friends came about him the day before his execution, weeping and beseeching him to save his life by recanting, but he would not; and when, as he stood at the stake, they set a box before him with his pardon in it, he only cried, "Away with it!" Through a long three quarters of an hour of agony—for it was a wild, wet morning, and the faggots would only burn slowly—he did not flinch; only once he cried, "For God's sake, good people, let me have more fire," and then at last, "Lord Jesus, receive my spirit," while the people looked on, horror-struck, and yet glad that their good old bishop was so steadfast.

The same day, Rowland Taylor was burned on the common at Hadleigh, in Suffolk, where he had been vicar. Like John Rogers and others, he was not allowed to have his wife come to see him, the priestly judges denying that he was lawfully married; but when she knew that he was to be taken to his own parish to suffer, she waited with her children through the night at a place where he must pass, and besought the sheriff, who was more merciful than the priest had been, for leave to speak with him; so there, in the darkness, he took one little daughter in his arms, and with his wife he kneeled down and prayed. Then he rose up and kissed her, and said, "Farewell, dear wife; be of good comfort, for I am easy in my conscience." And so they parted; and all the way "Dr. Taylor was merry and cheerful as one that accounted himself going to a most pleasant banquet or bridal." As they neared Hadleigh, the sheriff asked him how he was. "God be praised, Master Sheriff, never better; for now I know I am almost at home." Hadleigh streets were crowded as they led him through, people having come from all the country round; and when they saw him, with his "reverend and ancient face" and "long white beard," which they knew so well, they burst out weeping; and yet it was something nobler than mere pity that they felt, for they would not have their old friend turn coward. "God save thee, good Dr. Taylor!" they cried; "God strengthen thee and help thee!" And so he was taken to the stake on Aldham Common, and he would have spoken to the people, but he was not allowed, so he prayed, and then "went to the stake and kissed it, and set himself into a pitch-barrel which they had set for him, and so stood with his back upright against the stake, with his hands folded together, and his eyes looking up, and so let himself be burned;" and all he said was, when one of the sheriff's men threw a faggot in his face, making a ghastly wound, "Friend, I have harm enough; what needeth that?"

So the work went on. The persecutors had begun

with men of high standing, but the people were to be taught that, down to the poorest labourer, all must shape their faith as Mary and the priests laid it down, or else die the death. Five days only after Rogers' death in Smithfield had given people warning what to look for, three labouring men—a weaver, a butcher, and a barber—with an apprentice lad and two others, were condemned by Bonner. The Bishop of London asked one of them, Tomkins, a weaver, if he could bear the fire. "Try me," said he, and he put his hand in the flame of a candle that was standing by, and held it there without flinching. A few weeks later he and his companions, sent here and there, to this or that town or village where it was thought their burning would create most terror, all died, faithful to the end. More followed them. Within three months more than fifty men and women had thus been put to death. In the autumn came the martyrdom of Ridley and Latimer, already told, and, before the year was out, some twenty more. The next year the victims numbered eighty-nine, of whom was Archbishop Cranmer, who at first recanted, but afterwards recovered courage, and when they brought him into St. Mary's Church at Oxford to make his recantation public, renounced it, and sorrowfully confessed his weakness in having made it. And when he came to the fire, he stretched forth his right arm, saying, "This was the hand that wrote it, therefore it shall suffer first punishment," and held it steadily in the flame, "and never stirred nor cried."

Still the work went on. It seemed as if Bonner and his fellows were trying in desperation to make the scenes more horrible; at first people were put to death one at a time, here and there, but now they began to burn them in groups. In that third year, two men and five women were burned together at Maidstone; and the next day seven more, of whom four were women, at Canterbury; and two days later ten at once, four of them women, died at Lewes—eighty-eight in all, this year, besides many who happily escaped the fiercer doom by dying in the filthy and crowded gaols.

The effect of all this, however, was to create not terror, but horror and sympathy. The bishops overshot their mark. These poor men and women, burned among their neighbours in market-places or on village greens, did for Protestantism what no preaching could have done. The people wept for them, and yet even through their tears urged them to die faithful. As time went on, fierce execrations were heard here and there. Some of the bishops would have no part in the work, so that in the north of England we hear of very few burnings. Bonner was reproached by some in his own party, that in one year he had lost the hearts of twenty thousand people who before had been good Catholics. Even the ambassadors from France and Spain were struck by seeing that the effect upon the popular mind was the opposite of what was intended, and urged milder measures. But still the queen would be seized with some new fancy that her troubles came of God's anger at heresy being not yet stamped out, and still Bonner and Pole seemed to get more eager in the work; and even when, at last, the populace in London showed their horror of such doings so unmistakably that he dared not risk any more executions in London, Bonner took a batch of heretics, and, after trying them privately in his own palace, burnt them in the night time at Brentford.

This was nearly the end, however. Three months more, and Mary lay dying. The thing that most troubled her on her death-bed was that she had lost Calais. Had she only realized the effect of her reign, she would have felt still sadder to think that she had lost England—lost it utterly to that very Catholic cause she had most wanted to serve. For, the result of her reign was to attach England to Protestantism with a deep, eager fervour unknown before. The Reformation under Henry VIII. and Edward VI. had been mainly the doing of a certain class of statesmen, and of a certain class of thinkers. It was the work of Mary's bloody reign to unite the nation as a whole in it, to arouse an intense and general hatred of Rome, and to make Protestantism no longer the movement of a political party, but the passionate conviction of the great body of the people.

CHAPTER XXII.

ELIZABETH. THE FIRST "ACT OF UNIFORMITY."

THE death of Queen Mary was like the removal of a heavy weight from the heart of England. All parties, except a few of the extremest Catholics, were sick and ashamed of her reign. Those who were not horrified by its persecutions, were humiliated by its political weakness, which had ended in the loss of Calais. The church bells were rung and bonfires lighted, as the tidings spread through the country; and Elizabeth was proclaimed Queen amidst a universal outburst of joy.

The rejoicing for Elizabeth was the more general because it was known that, though a Protestant, she was not an extreme Protestant. People felt sure that Protestantism would be restored, but no one was afraid of the burnings of the last reign being renewed. At her entrance into London the citizens presented her with an English Bible, and she promised "diligently to read therein." All Protestants rejoiced, but they did not attempt any such eager and fierce reaction as that with which, when the Catholics had come into power with Mary, they had immediately begun to trample down their opponents. No violent changes were made. Mary's Catholic bishops were admitted to pay honour to their new Sovereign, and she spoke fairly to them, and gave her hand to them to kiss—to all except Bonner, from whom she could not help shrinking with a movement of disgust that was noticed by those who stood by. The first sign of the change was, that all persons who were in prison for religious offences were set at liberty; and those who had taken refuge in Germany and Switzerland to escape persecution, were recalled. The Latin mass, which had been one of the first things restored by Mary, was not abolished, but it was ordered that some of the most important parts, such as the Lord's Prayer, and the Commandments, should be read in English. As to the reunion with Rome, which had been accomplished with so much ceremony, it was not formally repealed, but simply became a dead letter, and was heard of no more.

Gradually, however, further changes had to be made. Those who were really, and by conviction, Protestants —though still probably not above a third of the whole people—were much more in earnest than they had been; and those who had been exiles at Frankfort, or Geneva, had brought back with them a vehement horror of everything Popish, that would not be satisfied with such slight reforms as the reading of a few prayers in English. Moreover, these Protestants, though not the more numerous, were the abler party, and the party whom Elizabeth could most rely upon in her difficulties with France and Spain; and so gradually the government took more distinctly the character of Protestantism. The laws for burning heretics, under which so many had suffered, were once more, and this time for ever, repealed; the monasteries, to restore a few of which Mary had almost beggared the treasury, were again suppressed; and the Supremacy Act was passed, once more enacting that the chief jurisdiction over the Church, just as over the State, should rest with the Crown. Elizabeth, indeed, refused to be called "the

Head of the Church," but all through her reign she kept the power unmistakably in her own hands, threatening bishops to unfrock them if they opposed her, interrupting preachers who offended her, and sometimes driving her more moderate councillors nearly distracted by her despotic and self-willed measures.

After the passing of the act for the Royal Supremacy, came the act which most of all touched the religious future of England—the Act of Uniformity. Elizabeth, as has been said, was by no means an extreme Protestant, and in outward matters she liked many of the Catholic forms and ways. What she most desired was, to settle the Church in a fashion that should bring the different religious parties together, and cause there to be but one Church in England, as in the olden times—only, that a Church no longer ruled by the Pope. The day for the Latin mass had gone by, and the Protestants were clamouring for King Edward's Prayer-book again; but if that prayer-book must be restored, it might at least be made less offensive to the older party. This was accordingly done. That is the reason why there has been, from time to time, and is, even at the present day, so much disputing as to what is the real doctrine of the Prayer-book. It was left indistinct on purpose, with words and phrases that would meet the view of each party, and enable all but the extremest in each to think that it substantially expressed their own views. Thus altered, it was adopted by Parliament, and the Act of Uniformity was passed, requiring all clergymen to use it, on pain of being deprived of their livings.

This "Act of Uniformitv" deserves special notice,

for it is, in reality, one of the great landmarks of the religious life of England. Up to this time the endeavour had been to make all people *think* alike. The great crime was *heresy*. Now the endeavour became, to try to make all people *conform* to one way of worship; the great crime henceforth is *nonconformity*. We shall not hear much more about heresy, but we shall hear a great deal about Nonconformity. Elizabeth's councillors admitted that men must think as they liked, but they had not yet learned the further lesson, that men must be left free to carry out their different thoughts, in different forms of worship and different churches, and that Government must not interfere with these at all. It seemed to them that it was the part of a true Government to make this one national Church, which had come down from the past, such that, though there might still be great differences of opinion among the people, all might, at least, attend it, and join in its services—"conform" as it was called. And, indeed, it seemed so to all parties in that day; even the extremest Protestants thought there ought to be but one Church, only that that one ought to be ordered their way. Of course the attempt to make men conform to one worship, proved, in the end, just as impracticable as that to make them to believe one doctrine.

The attempt, however, was as fairly and moderately made, in the Church services now settled by Elizabeth and her councillors, as it could possibly have been by any party in those times; and on the whole it was well received. The extreme Protestants, indeed—the men who had been working with Calvin at Geneva—were very angry, regarding the concessions made to enable Catholics to remain in the Church as a tampering with deadly popish error. And the bishops, who had been the special agents of Mary's Romish restoration, would not give way. This refusal of the bishops was not very dangerous, for they expected that Philip of Spain would, in a little while, interfere, and force England back into the old subjection to Rome, and meanwhile there was no fear of death, for the persecuting laws had been repealed; so they professed themselves ready for martyrdom, and made a great show of their firmness. The only martyrdom they had to suffer was to be put in ward at the house of some trusty friend of the Government; and, for the worst of them, a mild imprisonment in the Tower, with their own attendants to wait on them. One curious difficulty arose out of this obstinacy on the part of the bishops. How were successors to them to be consecrated? It had always been supposed that a certain supernatural grace was needed to make a bishop; and the Church of Rome claimed to derive this grace by direct and unbroken succession from the apostles. This was called "apostolical succession," and the English Church protested that, in separating from Rome in Henry VIII.'s time, this apostolical succession had been preserved, the bishops having then mostly kept with the Reformed Church. Now, however, the whole body of bishops stood out against the changed order of the Church, with only one exception, and he notoriously the worst of the set. The Catholics were in exultation, for it seemed as if the newly settled Church would have to start without bishops, or at least without regularly consecrated bishops. However, it was found that among the men who had returned from exile, were several who had been bishops in Edward's time, and who therefore were, without dispute, in the line of the true succession. So the difficulty was got over, and by these revived bishops new men were consecrated for the vacant sees. It has always continued, however, to be one of the great questions in dispute between the Romish and Anglican Churches, whether the true apostolic succession was or was not brought into the line of the English Church by this way of getting over the difficulty. While, however, the most extreme, alike Protestants and Catholics, stood aloof from this new settlement of the Church, it was gradually accepted by the country at large. Here and there, especially in the North, where the population was more scattered and more ignorant, men stood stoutly for the old ways, and the Prayer-book aroused bitter opposition. There was many a country squire's house in Lancashire and Yorkshire where they kept private chapel and had mass in the old fashion. Here and there, too, the clergy, while not actually refusing the Prayer-book, used it as little as they could, and some even shut up their churches to avoid using it. Out of the nine thousand and more clergymen throughout the country, there were, however, less than two hundred who finally refused and gave up their livings. So the new service came into general use, and when, four years later, the "Thirty-nine Articles" were added, those who had yielded so far might well feel that these were not worth making a new stand against. Meanwhile there was no active persecution going on to stir men up to strong partizanship. For the first dozen years of Elizabeth's reign, those who still stood out as Catholics had a comparatively easy time of it. Their worship was prohibited by law, but the penalties were not great, and, for the most part, little notice was taken by the magistrates. There were well-known Catholics in the court itself, and here and there, all over the country, were Catholic families, who kept up their own worship, and protected their poorer neighbours who clung to the same faith, and the worst that happened to them was to be occasionally fined for "Recusancy," that is, for not attending their parish church. All this gradually produced its effect. Many who would have avowed themselves Catholics to the death had they been threatened with martyrdom, gradually fell into the common way when let alone. As the disloyal clergy died out, or removed, they were replaced by good Protestants. The wavering and the lukewarm fell into the general tone of feeling. The consequence was, that by the time Elizabeth had been twenty years on the throne, the mass of the nation had gradually settled into this new and moderate Protestantism.

While this blending of the different religions was very satisfactory to those who wished to see England strong and independent, there was one party who regarded it with hatred and aversion. The extreme Romanists, who had helped the reunion of England with Rome in Mary's time, could not give up the hope that a similar reunion would some day take place again. From the beginning of Elizabeth's reign they were a party of irreconcilables, perpetually plotting and intriguing with the Pope, or with the Catholic powers of Spain and France. While, therefore, large numbers of those who, at the beginning of Elizabeth's reign were nominally Catholics, kept gradually blending in the new Protestantism, those who resisted the tendency became more than ever a separate party, more closely tied to Rome, and more narrow and bigoted and unpatriotic in their Catholicism. Thus, gradually, the Catholics came to be a very difficult party to deal with. They professed to be noways different from other Englishmen, except in religion; but in reality their religious difference carried with it something very much more serious. They owned a foreign head—the Pope, and allegiance to the Pope meant, in those days, the acknowledgment of his power to depose princes. We are so safe in these quiet later days from any danger arising from this claim, that we can afford to smile at it; and it is apt to seem dreadful to us that in the later half of Elizabeth's reign so many of the Jesuits and of the "Seminary Priests" should have been put to death on any such ground. But it was no trivial matter in those days. England stood alone in Europe, surrounded by bitter enemies, and every one of those enemies making Catholicism the pretext of attack. When Elizabeth had been twelve years on the throne, the Pope issued a solemn Bull, excommunicating and deposing her, and absolving all subjects from their allegiance. How real the effect of this was, became visible in the plots and intrigues which were continually going on around! How terrible was even the possibility of those plots and intrigues succeeding, there were many things to show. The very year after this bull of excommunication, the Catholics of France rose upon the Protestant Huguenots, on St. Bartholomew's Day, and in two days seventy-two thousand of them were massacred. The Pope blessed the deed, and had a medal struck in honour of it! Think how such tidings would thrill through England, where it was but thirteen years since the burnings of Smithfield, the story of which, in "Foxe's Book of Martyrs," had just been chained up for the people to read in every parish church. And, year after year, events kept happening, which never allowed this feeling of danger to sleep. Now a Papal expedition landed in Ireland to head an insurrection; now French troops were in Scotland; now there were rumours of a great Armada collecting, with which Spain was to restore the Papacy in England; again, word came of a Catholic fanatic having assassinated the Prince of Orange, the leader of the Dutch Protestants; and soon it was known that the Pope had promised his blessing to any one who should remove Elizabeth in like manner. It is not to be wondered at, that gradually the queen and her ministers came to regard the Catholics as a party whose principles were a constant source of danger, and that she was at last goaded out of her more tolerant policy into one of persecution. Yet, even then, the persecution was not aimed at simple Catholics, but against those who were the notorious emissaries of Rome. Catholic seminaries of English priests at Douay, Rheims, and Rome, were beginning to pour in scores of priests and Jesuits into England, who went up and down the country in disguise, gathering the Catholics together, insisting on their keeping utterly apart from the church services, doing their utmost to keep them a separate class in the nation, and encouraging them with mysterious hints of a time near at hand, when the present state of things would come to an end. They always professed that their mission was purely religious; in reality it was a constant and insidious work of treason. At last the Government found that its whole strength must be put forth against these men. Elizabeth and her council acted very reluctantly. They dreaded the idea of reviving the persecutions of Mary's reign. When Father Campian and two other priests were brought to the gallows, pardon was offered them if they would only say in plain words, that the Pope had no right to depose the Queen of England. But they would not say it, for they did not mean it, and whatever their faults, cowardice was not one of them. When at length the Government did take up the struggle against this treason, which disguised itself in the cloak of religion, they used no half-measures. The persecution was not, indeed, like that of Mary's reign. There was no burning. There was no harrying to death of poor labouring men and women. It was the Jesuits and the priests from these foreign seminaries—"all persons pretending to any power of absolving subjects from their allegiance"—who were aimed at. But for them there was no mercy. The persecution was lasting and very pitiless. And it brought out, as persecution always does, all the nobler elements of character. The hunted priests became heroes; when they were caught and hung, they were reverenced as martyrs. England might treat them as traitors, but to them, and more and more to their fellow-Catholics, their cause seemed the very cause of God. As, one after another, they were taken from the hiding-places in the old Catholic manor-houses, others came forward to take up their work. The story of those years has many a noble and touching incident in it, and however much we may abhor their cause, we cannot help admiring their constancy and courage in it. It was not, indeed, for their religion that they were persecuted, but it was for their religion that they endured.

For the time the Catholic movement was beaten down; and when the long-dreaded danger came in the shape of the Spanish Armada, the fervour of patriotic feeling which swept throughout all classes, and in which the old Catholic families of England stood loyally shoulder to shoulder with the rest of the people, showed how exaggerated had been the fear that those Catholic missioners were really endangering England. Politically, their mission had done nothing; but religiously its work remained. Those who continued Catholics were henceforth more separate from the Protestants than ever. The dream of all the English people being united in one national church was for ever at an end.

CHAPTER XXIII.

JOHN KNOX AND THE REFORMATION IN SCOTLAND.

We must now take a look at the story of the Reformation in Scotland, and that story may be almost told in the life of one great man who was the very soul of it—John Knox.

The Reformation in Scotland did not take place till five-and-twenty years after Henry VIII. had begun it in England. The same under-current of feeling, against priests and monks and the corruptions and mummeries of the Church, had, indeed, long been stirring among the Scottish people as among the English. But the one strong passion of the Scotch was antipathy to England. What England did, that Scotland was pretty sure not to do. So when King Henry took up the Reformation, it was in vain that he tried to persuade his nephew, the young Scotch king, James V., to join him in his cause. James might laugh at his companion Sir David Lindsay's satires on the priests, but he could not govern without them, and his ablest state-adviser was Cardinal Beaton, the Archbishop of St. Andrews. So, the year when Henry was putting down the monasteries, and giving men an open Bible, James was marrying a French Catholic princess, heaping favours upon the clergy, and signing death-warrants for the poor Protestant heretics whom Cardinal Beaton was hurrying to the stake. And so, for twenty years and more, the rising Protestant feeling of Scotland was pent up, and gathering to ever greater intensity. In England, as we have seen, the Reformation was imperfect, because it was pushed on as a political movement, before the people were fully ready for it. In Scotland, political considerations kept it back; but for that very reason, when at last it did come it was much more a passionate outburst of popular life, and far more thorough and sweeping in its changes.

There is little to be told about the youth of the man who, more than any other, led and shaped that Reformation in Scotland. John Knox was born in 1505, near Haddington, of a family of yeomen who had been for generations retainers of the great Earls of Bothwell. Like many of those who afterwards became Reformers, he was trained for the priesthood—first a scholar at Haddington Grammar School, and then a student at Glasgow University, where he soon became known for his skill in argument, and whence he went as a young priest to be a preacher at St. Andrews. Then we lose sight of him for a dozen years or more, during which time the eager influences of the Reformation, which were stirring all through Europe, must have taken hold of him, though we are not told how. What we do know is, that when he was about thirty-seven years of age, and brave Protestants from Geneva were moving to and fro among the common people of Scotland, preaching the Reformed doctrines, Knox finally cast in his lot with them and was degraded from his priest's orders. Ablest among these preachers was one George Wishart, and it is as his companion that we first get a clear sight of John Knox, who, as he went from place to place in the Lothians preaching in the fields, waited upon him and carried a huge two-handed sword for his master's defence. When Wishart was at last seized by Cardinal Beaton, Knox wanted to go with him and share his fate, but Wishart would not let him, said that "one was enough for a sacrifice," and bade him "gang hame to your bairns." It seemed as if now the movement for reformation could no longer be held in; for when Beaton took the brave preacher to St. Andrews, and there, in front of the episcopal castle, had him burnt alive, the public execration was terrible, and before six months were gone a band of Protestant lairds seized the castle and put the Cardinal to death, hanging his body from the very battlements where he had sat gloating over his victim's agony. But the final outbreak was not to be yet, for Henry VIII. took the assassins under his protection, and made St. Andrews the centre of a reforming movement; and the English patronage caused a Catholic reaction among the people. Thus the Reformation was again put back; St. Andrews was taken; Reformers and assassins were sent together to the French galleys, and among those so sent was John Knox.

A fruitful time that—in the cruel and hopeless lot of a galley-slave—for meditating on the blessings of Catholicism. It did what such sufferings always do to true men—burnt-in his principles. Two weary years he bent over the oar, but he did not lose hope; he felt it as if borne into his soul by the spirit of God, that he should yet preach, even in St. Andrews, and the brave heart failed not. Two long, weary years he wore the chains of a galley-slave, and then came one of the changes of that uncertain time, and the Protestant prisoners were free, and among them John Knox.

Scotland was not open to him then (1549), but he went to England, where Edward VI. was completing the work begun by his father, Henry VIII.; and in England he lived four years, working hand in hand with Cranmer and Latimer and the English Protestants, and hoping for an opening to return to his own country.

No opening came, however. And when Edward died, and Mary's bloody reign began, like other Reformers, who had not some plain necessity to remain, Knox took refuge on the Continent. He was loth to fly, but he was persuaded to it, he says, "partly by advice, partly by tears." He was but a year married, so one can understand where the tears came from. For six years he lived abroad, now at Dieppe, now at Frankfort; for three years a pastor under Calvin at Geneva; and once making a flying visit to Scotland, where, for a few months, he went preaching to and fro among the people with fiery eloquence.

When, at last, Elizabeth came to the throne, putting new spirit and hope into all the Protestants of Europe, Knox could no longer resist the impulse which urged him back to his native land. He would have gone through England, but Elizabeth would not allow him. The fact was, a few years before, in his horror at the rule of Mary in England, and of the French Queen-Regent in Scotland, he had written a book called "The First Blast of the Trumpet against the Monstrous Regimen of Women," to prove that for women to bear rule was an abomination before the Lord. When Elizabeth came to the throne, he saw that there was another side to the subject, and begged her forgiveness, allowing that she was an exception to the rule. Elizabeth, however, declined to be an exception, and never forgave him, never would let him set his foot in England; and so he had to wait till he could find a vessel sailing direct to Scotland.

With this return, in 1559, begins the open conflict of the Reformation in Scotland, and the great work which made John Knox famous. For years the Reforming party had been silently growing, and had become increasingly dangerous to meddle with. They had formed themselves into a league called "The Congregation of the Lord," and the nobles joining which, were called "The Lords of the Congregation;" but no outbreak had taken place, no great movement had yet been made, to change the religion of the country. On the other hand were Mary of Guise, the Queen-Regent, with the clergy and the Catholic nobles—temporizing, afraid of an outbreak, now making concessions, and now taking them back.

When John Knox landed he was an outlaw, and the Government was still Catholic. He had been a stranger to Scotland for twelve years, except during the few months' visit of four years before. But he was not forgotten. Men remembered him as the friend and comrade of the martyred Wishart; they told of his fiery preaching at St. Andrews, and they recalled his sufferings for the Lord's cause in the French galleys. A strong mind was wanted for the struggle that was coming on, and John Knox came to the front simply by his natural fitness. Almost at once he became the representative man of the Scottish Reformation. With the Lords of the Congregation, though only a plain commoner, he became the directing spirit. Crowds flocked to hear him everywhere, as he preached, denouncing the idolatry of the mass, and the trickeries and cruelties of the priest-led Government. The

Queen-Regent, alarmed at the excitement, summoned all the Reformed preachers to answer for their conduct at Stirling. They went, but in their train went thousands of armed men, and no one dared meddle with them. A few days more, and the inevitable explosion came. Knox was preaching at Perth, and after his sermon, while the excited crowd still stood about the church, a priest began to say Mass. A lad among the crowd called it "idolatry," and the priest struck him. The people crowded round, a stone was thrown and the great crucifix fell broken to the ground. In a moment the popular feeling broke out; the church was gutted, torn robes, broken images, and shivered glass strewed the floor. There was a cry, "To the Grey Friars!" and that cry was the beginning of the end, the death-knell of monasticism in Scotland. "It was the work of a rascal multitude who cared nothing for religion," wrote Knox, afterwards, of the burning of that Grey Friars' convent, with which the destruction of the monasteries began; but others told of a saying of his—"Pull down the nests and the rooks will fly away!" which is quite as likely to have been the hot word of the hour. Any way they *were* pulled down. The churches were saved for the Reformed worship, but the abbeys were destroyed far more completely than in England. So the Reformation went on. The people were carried away with the enthusiasm of it. The nobles fell away from the Queen-Regent; she had to sit quietly, while, the summer through, without a blow struck or a life sacrificed, the whole fabric of Catholicism was being cleared away. She fell ill ot mortification and died, and within a year of Knox's landing, a free Parliament was summoned to Edinburgh, and the abolition of the old religion, with the establishment of the Reformed Kirk of Scotland, was solemnly decreed by law.

That Reformed Kirk was very different to the Church as the Reformers in England settled it. Henry VIII. cared little for doctrinal reform; what he wanted was to be himself head of the Church. Elizabeth hated Knox and abhorred Calvinism. There was no chance of setting up in England such a kingdom, based on religion, with a presbytery of rigid divines to keep the Government in order, as Calvin taught men to consider the true idea of a State. But in Scotland it was the Reforming ministers, with Knox at their head, who were the real power of the Reformation, for men distrusted the "Lords of the Congregation;" and so the Scottish Kirk was shaped out after Calvin's model, with its bare, unmusical, unadorned worship, and a rigid, minute censorship over every part of life.

Of that Reformed Kirk, John Knox had to be not only the architect but the defender. No sooner did the Reformers get into power, than division, ambition, corruption, began to creep in. The "Lords of the Congregation" cared for little except enriching themselves with the Abbey lands, and would only give up the most beggarly fragments of the Church property to support the Reformed worship. While they were quarrelling and intriguing, and before the Reformation had been extablished a year, the young Mary, "Queen of Scots," came to Edinburgh; with her beautiful face, her winning ways, and a subtle purpose to use every art to bring Scotland back to the Pope, and a Catholic reaction was beginning, and the whole work of the Reformation was in danger.

Mary's first steps showed her ability. She issued a proclamation against Catholics trying to change the

Protestantism which was now established by law, and then pleaded that surely she might be tolerated in herself having "mass" for the present in her own chapel royal. It seemed so reasonable a request that the council could not refuse it, but Knox mistrusted it, and said that "that one mass was more terrible to him than ten thousand armed men." Mary invited the Puritan lords to her presence, and her gracious, winning French ways disarmed all opposition, and she had them all at her feet. She tried the same ways with Knox himself, sent for him, and again and again had interviews with him. These interviews are among the most characteristic passages in his life, for at the first of them he took his measure of the queen, and saw that, underneath her soft ways, the cause he loved had a fearless, crafty, and bitter foe. So she tried her blandishments in vain. Always gravely, sometimes severely, he held his ground. She talked to him about his book, and by-and-by brought the conversation to the point "whether subjects might resist their sovereign." Said Knox, "If a father go mad and attempt to kill his children, surely his children may tie his hands and take his sword from him." She sat silent awhile, and then said, "My subjects, then, are to obey you and not me." "Nay," said the preacher, "let us both submit to God; kings should be the foster-fathers of the Kirk, and queens its nursing mothers." "You are not the Kirk that I will nurse," she rejoined; and one who was present tells that she wept, but that he thought it was for vexation, not for sorrow. Knox has been much blamed for his sternness with the queen, but unjustly. There was no word of rudeness, but he saw that she was an enemy to the cause which to him was more than life, and he would use no flattering speech. And so for all the seven years of compromise and intrigue before Mary was finally in safe keeping in Loch Leven Castle, Knox was the one strong man who kept the Reformation from falling to pieces. It was a difficult task. The Reformation was the creed of the towns and of the trading classes, but very few of the nobles cared for it now that the Church property was all disposed of; and as for the clans, the only things they believed in were plunder, and fidelity to their chieftain, whatever side he chose to take. But Knox never gave way, never lost heart. Above all suspicion of any desire for personal gain; clear-sighted through the tricks of statesmen; firm when the middle class would have given way disheartened; undaunted when the nobles would have cajoled or threatened him into joining in their temporizing policy; ever ready to infuse courage into men by his preaching—which, the English ambassador wrote home, "stirred him more than six hundred trumpets"—he it was who kept Scotland to the Reformation.

Thus the years wore on till, with Mary's fall, the Catholic cause was disgraced beyond recovery, and Protestantism once more stood firm, with the Earl of Murray, the noblest of the Protestant leaders, at the head of the kingdom. Knox felt now as if his work was accomplished. He was an old man, his health was failing. He thought of retiring to Geneva, where he had left a flock whom he ever remembered fondly. But he went to St. Andrews instead. The scene of his earliest labours found him a home in his old age. In 1570 he had a paralytic stroke; and, though he partially recovered, he could no longer walk without help. But even then he still tottered to the church, and, lifted up the pulpit steps by his old secretary, "godly Richard

Bannatyne," he would dwell on the old themes, and as he preached the passion of feeling rose, until, as one who used to hear him tells, "He was like to ding the pulpit in blads and fly out of it."

And even yet the old man's work was not quite done. There was to be one memorable flashing up before the flame expired. In the closing days of August, in the last year of his life (1572), there came a dreadful whisper through England and Scotland, which made men's flesh creep with horror, which seemed too dreadful to be true, only that there was nothing too dreadful to be true of Popery as it was *then*—a whisper that shaped itself, as the tidings became clearer and fuller, into the awful story of the massacre of the Protestants throughout France, on St. Bartholomew's day. It may be imagined how that story stirred John Knox! It stirred the whole people; Catholics and Protestants were horror-struck alike. If Knox's work was only partly done before, this completed it. There were no more waverers in the Reformation.

So much was John Knox stirred, that when, in the following month, the Convention of Estates met at Edinburgh, he roused himself, and though now in the extreme of feebleness, dragged himself to Edinburgh. And there, before the assembled Parliament, with lords and ambassadors gathered about him as he preached, he bore one last testimony for the great cause for which he had lived, and denounced the awful crime with a prophet-like power that sent the French Ambassador home in anger, and thrilled through the heart of Scotland.

It was the last flashing up of that wonderful life. In a few days Knox was again seized with paralysis, and the end was evidently drawing near. It was a memorable death-bed. Thither came the elders of the Congregation, to receive his last charge against any compromise with evil. Thither came the Regent, and noble after noble. Even some fine lady came and began to praise him. "Hush, hush," said the dying man, "flesh is ower proud and needs no means to esteem the self." With many a word of bright fearless piety and faith, the hours passed, and the end drew on. They asked him if he was in pain. "It is no painful pain," he said, "but such as will end the battle." And when night came, they gathered about him in his chamber, and he listened as they had their long evening worship together; and then, with a long-drawn sigh, he said, "Now, it is come!" and the battle *was* ended, and the spirit passed away.

CHAPTER XXIV.

THE PROTESTANTS OF PROTESTANTISM; PURITANISM STRUGGLING.

It is the purpose of this book, not to give the history of what is called "the Church of England," or of any one Church, but to trace out the story of the most earnest religious life of this country. Sometimes that earnest religious life is met with in one Church, sometimes in another. It was among the monks till the monasteries became rich and powerful. It was among the Protestants while Protestantism was struggling under Henry VIII. and persecuted through Queen Mary's reign of terror. But when Queen Elizabeth established that compromise between Protestantism and Catholicism which she hoped would make it possible for Catholics to remain with "the Church of England," a great deal of the most earnest religious life of the people found itself ill at ease. So, for a long time now, we shall find our deepest interest not in that Church of compromise, and those who managed to "conform" to it, but in those who could *not* conform, in the various movements of "nonconformist" life.

The first of these movements of the religious life which was too strong and earnest to be kept within the bounds of the Church as Elizabeth established it, was Puritanism. For a hundred years, Puritanism, in one or other of its various forms, was the most living power in English religion.

For the origin of Puritanism we must look to those bands of English Protestants who, during Mary's persecution, found refuge on the continent. Their Protestant feeling grew rapidly stronger, when it had nothing to check it, and when it came into contact with Protestantism abroad. At Frankfort they kept very much to the old lines to which they had got during Edward VI.'s time; but those who went to Geneva became much more extreme. Under the overmastering influence of John Calvin, they laid aside Edward VI.'s Prayer-book as too like the mass-book, from which, indeed, much of it was taken; they learned to think that there should be no order of bishops above other ministers, and they began to love a much barer and simpler worship.

When, on the accession of Elizabeth, these men thronged back to England, enthusiastic for the new power which they expected Protestantism would now have, it was a grievous disappointment to find, not only that there was to be no going forward, but that there was to be an actual going back. King Edward's Prayer-book had been too Popish for them, and now, even more of the old mass-book was put back into it, in order to make it acceptable to the Catholics; while, instead of their idea of Christ being recognized as the only head of the Church, with his ministers ruling for him as Calvin and the presbyters ruled at Geneva, they found that this new Protestantism to which all were to conform only freed the Church from the headship of a distant and feeble Pope, to put it under that of a queen who was close at hand, and very powerful, and very wilful. "They came threadbare home," said Strype, of these exiles, "bringing nothing with them but much experience as well as learning;" and "those who would comply with the queen's establishment" did well enough; but for the rest it was a hard time, and it got harder as the years went on.

At first these more extreme Protestants were not much interfered with. The country was in too pressing danger from foreign foes for loyal Englishmen to be much meddled with, and even in the days of their sorest persecution the Puritans never wavered in their loyalty. The Act of Uniformity was not very rigorously enforced. These Genevan exiles were among the most learned of the clergy, and men of high pure lives; and where the churches were in their hands, it was a real religious work that was done by them. Mr. Froude, in his History of England, gives, from some MSS. in the Rolls House, an interesting example of such a work at Northampton, where the clergy and the people, with the Bishop of Peterborough at their head, seem to have all worked harmoniously together, in the spirit of this earnest Evangelical Protestantism. On Sundays and holy days, the usual services were read from the Prayer-book. In the morning there was a sermon: in the afternoon, when prayers were over, "the youth" were instructed in Calvin's catechism. On Tuesdays and Thursdays, a "Lecture of Scripture" was read, with a few prayers from the Liturgy, and afterwards there was a general meeting of the congregation, with the mayor presiding, when cases of quarrelling, blaspheming, drunkenness, and other sins of evil living, were brought forward and "disciplined." On Saturdays, the ministers of the different neighbourhoods assembled for conference, and once a quarter all the clergy of the county met for mutual survey of their own general behaviour. Communion was held four times a year, and the clergyman of each parish visited from house to house, during the previous fortnight, to prepare his people for it. "The table was in the body of the church, at the far end of the middle aisle," and while the people were partaking of the service, "a minister in the pulpit read to them comfortable Scriptures of the Passion." It is interesting, too, to find, that their doctrinal position was very broad. As their "confession of faith," they simply set up the Scriptures and the Apostles' Creed, and "did condemn as a tyrannous yoke whatever men had set up of their own invention to make articles of faith, or bind men's consciences to their laws and statutes."

It might have been well if this intenser Protestantism had always acted as moderately, and been left as quietly to work out its life in its own way, as in this case. But in those times this was almost impossible. Men were too eagerly excited on these great questions. Fiery enthusiasts like Thomas Cartwright, who, after sitting at Calvin's feet, had come home to be a professor at Cambridge, denounced Prayer-book and surplice and the sign of the cross, and—what endangered their cause still more —thundered against the rule of the bishops and any tolerance to the Catholics. Such men were among the greatest hindrances to Elizabeth's endeavour to keep the Catholics in the Church, and as she got stronger on her throne she resolved to put down these obstructives, and to make the bishops enforce the Act of Uniformity. The bishops besought and protested, for they knew that these "precise Protestants," as some called them—or "Puritans," as others called them—would be very hard to compel; but Elizabeth was angry, and persisted. The result was that numbers of the most useful and beloved ministers were silenced and imprisoned, or wandered about in poverty and suffering; and at last it became plain to them that they could not lead the Church their way, and that they must separate from it. Still, it was not for some years that they could make up their minds to form any separate organization. Private houses were still open to them, and they ministered as they found opportunity. In London, especially, they had large numbers of followers and sympathizers; and in many a merchant's parlour they met, and held their services, and talked of the true Church-order as they thought they saw it set forth in Scripture —a church with no proud bishops lording it over the people by the queen's will, but only a presbytery of godly presbyters or elders, ruling in the name of Christ, the only head.

At last, however, it seemed necessary for their own fellowship and mutual help to set up some true Church-order among themselves, even if they might not see it set up in the Church at large. It was at Wandsworth, near London, that, on the 20th of November, 1572 —the massacre of St. Bartholomew just before might well make them feel that they must delay no longer— a number of ministers and gentlemen from Middlesex and Surrey secretly met and banded themselves into a "presbytery," drawing up their rules in a little register called "the orders of Wandsworth." "This," says Neal, "was the first presbytery formed in England," and was the beginning of English Presbyterianism. The bishops got wind of the new society, and the Court of High Commission tried every way to discover and get hold of its members, but in vain, nor could they prevent other presbyteries being set up in neighbouring counties. In a few years such Presbyterian *classes*, as they were called, were established in Warwickshire and Northamptonshire, and not long after in Lancashire and Cheshire.

This was not the only form that the Puritan movement took. Robert Brown, a clergyman, not only attacked the system of the Church of England, but protested against the attempt to set up any general Church, whether ruled by bishops or presbyteries, and maintained that each little society of Christians formed a complete Church in itself. Those who thought with him, therefore, simply formed themselves into separate congregations, each managing its own affairs, whence they came a little later to be known by the noble and historic name of "Independents;" but at first they were only called "Brownists."

Here and there, too, were little groups of these Puritans, whose strongest objection to the Church was its doctrine and practice of the baptism of infants, and these formed the beginning of the Baptist body. In connection with these, it is worth remembering that two of their brethren, Anabaptist refugees from Holland, were burnt for heresy in 1575—the real cause of their suffering being, however, that Elizabeth was in one of her angry moods, owing to the Spanish Ambassador having written home sneeringly of the religious confusion which Protestantism was causing, declaring that England was a paradise for heretics. Old John Foxe, the author of the Book of Martyrs, wrote a very earnest letter to the queen remonstrating against such a punishment, and begging that the piles and flames of Smithfield might not be revived. But it was in vain, and they were burned "in great horrour, crying and roaring," as Stowe tells.

Brownists, Baptists, or Presbyterians, however, all were alike hateful to the Government; but all, and, most of all, the Presbyterians, made way. Archbishop Parker died, and under his successor, Grindal, it seemed at first as if they were likely to have an easier time, for Grindal was a good and tolerant man; he wanted to see the Church freed from its corruptions, and he would not be the mere tool Elizabeth wanted, and wrote to her advising milder measures; but Elizabeth's only answer was an order from the Star Chamber confining him to his house, and suspending him from his bishopric. Then came Archbishop Whitgift, who took up her work of persecuting Puritans with an eagerness which so outraged the feeling of the nation, that Parliament attempted to interfere. They even began to debate some bills for lessening the power of the Church, but they were quickly stopped by a sharp message from the queen, rebuking such meddling with her prerogative.

Still Puritanism kept making way. It made way until Sir Walter Raleigh could declare in Parliament that there were twenty thousand "Separatists" in Norfolk, Essex, and the neighbourhood of London. It made way until even into Parliament came petition after petition praying for a reform of Church abuses; and in 1584 bills were introduced into the Commons (though not passed) not only condemning various abuses, but proposing "to appoint a presbytery or eldership in each parish, together with the minister, to determine the spiritual business of the parish."* Two years later another effort was made, and a bill offered which would have taken the jurisdiction of the Church out of the hands of the Episcopal courts, and placed it in "an assembly of ministers and elders in every shire." All the demands of the Puritans were not so reasonable. At the same time, Neal tells us, others were dispersing over the country a pamphlet calling upon Parliament to put down "all cathedral churches, where the service of God is grievously abused by piping with organs, singing,

* Neal's History of the Puritans, vol. i. p. 398.

ringing and trowling of psalms, with the squeaking of chaunting choristers disguised, as are all the rest, in white surplices, some in corner caps and filthy copes, imitating the fashion and manner of Antichrist—the Pope."

Reasonable or unreasonable, however, the demands of the Presbyterian party were fruitless. The queen ordered both bill and petition out of the House, and roughly told the Commons that "she was settled in her religion, and would not begin again." The members who had spoken for the bill were sent to the Tower; the clergy who attempted such reforms were fined, suspended, imprisoned; and the printers of such dangerous pamphlets, when caught, had their presses broken and their hands cut off.

Some took refuge abroad. It was now that a little flock of "the Lord's free people" in Lincolnshire, harassed by the persecution which their conventicle meetings drew upon them, fled to Amsterdam with their pastor, John Robinson; from which little flock went forth, a few years later, the Pilgrim Fathers, in the *May Flower*, to found a "New England" in America.

Those who went abroad, however, were but a few compared to those who remained, and all through Elizabeth's reign the Puritan party kept increasing.

Elizabeth's death set the Puritans hoping for a peaceful reform in the Church, for the next heir to the throne, James, the King of Scotland, had always been a Presbyterian. But this hope was disappointed. James was a Stuart and loved power, and had never liked the control which the rigid Scotch Calvinists had held over him. So, he was delighted with the submissiveness and courtly reverence of the English bishops, which was as pleasant to him as it was new. He threw himself at once, therefore, on to the Church side; nay, he even went beyond his predecessors. He upheld the divine right of bishops, as they had upheld the divine right of kings. He persecuted the Puritans with the spiteful hostility of a mean and narrow mind; he could not appreciate their conscientious difficulties, he only remembered how much he had disliked their power over him when he was in Scotland. "I will make them conform," said James, "or I will harry them out of the land."

So it was, all through the reign of James, and so it continued to be when Charles I. became King. Archbishop Laud was then at the head of the Church, and bent all the force of his intense but narrow mind to exalt the Church of England and crush out these Puritan societies, which he would not admit to be churches at all. Darker and darker days settled down upon the Puritans; but through all, their spirit kept rising into that stern enthusiasm for a purer Church and a juster Government, which in a few years was to bear fruit in civil war and revolution.

CHAPTER XXV.

PURITANISM IN POWER.

We are coming, now, to a time when Puritanism, after being so long trampled down and persecuted, was at length to rise and become the ruling power of England. Little by little the tyrannies of Charles I., his disregard of law, and his shameful violation of every promise and agreement, drove the people to resistance. At first, they tried to resist by legal means; they withstood his demands in Parliament, and would grant no taxes till he had consented to the Petition of Right. Then he angrily dissolved them and attempted to rule without any Parliament.

"None have gone about to break Parliaments, but in the end Parliaments have broken them," said Sir John Eliot, who stands with Pym and Hampden as one of the leading patriots of that great struggle. For eleven years Charles ruled without a Parliament and then at last the end came. The "Long Parliament," as it came to be called in after years, was summoned in 1641, and at once the feeling of the people, so long crushed down, came to a head. These were no demagogues or conspirators who met together, but the strong, thoughtful men of England. Many of them were Puritans—men who had seen what the power of Laud and the bishops meant; who had seen people pilloried, and their ears and noses slit, for refusing to worship God in churches where the service was, to them, little better than the Catholic mass. So, as soon as they met they began to take steps not only to reform the Government, but to curb the power of the bishops. One member said, that if there were to be such tyranny, better have a pope at Rome than a patriarch at Lambeth. About the first thing they did was to take away from the bishops their votes in Parliament, a measure in favour of which, it is worth remembering, a petition signed by 700 clergymen was presented. Then the courts of High Commission and the Star Chamber, which had been the instruments of Laud's terrible persecutions, were abolished, and Laud himself was sent a prisoner to the Tower. There was no idea of destroying the Church, and many of the members who voted for these measures were themselves moderate churchmen. But political and religious events were soon hurrying on beyond the power of moderate men to control them. Even while these measures were still in debate, the king had withdrawn from London, and the conflict between the Royalists and the Parliamentarians had begun.

With a stern, God-fearing purpose, the Parliament took in hand the work of "saving the kingdom," regarding the king as having thus practically abdicated his position. From the moment when it was seen that Parliament was for religious reform, petitions came pouring in, complaining of the immoralities of the clergy; and a committee was appointed to inquire into these, and went through the country, expelling many for their irregularities. In the confusion of the time Episcopalianism went to the wall. The bishops and leading clergy took the side of the king, and as the king's side lost ground, the churches became occupied more and more by clergymen who sympathized with the struggles of the people, and with the Puritanism which was the religious inspiration of that struggle. For two years there was no uniform order of worship. Men did what was right in their own eyes. Where the spirit of the clergy and of the people was already mostly on the Puritan side, the white surplice and the Prayer-book were laid aside, and the services were conducted according to the Geneva form, which was very much the order used in Nonconformist chapels to this day. Where the Royalist gentry had the upper hand, there the parson kept on wearing his robes, and read the liturgy, and prayed for the king; while, in places where feeling was divided, there was many an unseemly wrangle, as first one party and then the other got the upper hand. Thus at Ribchester, in Lancashire, we read how the old incumbent had been turned out—"sequestrated" as it was called—by the commissioners, for "insufficiency and being scandalory in life and conversation;" but he held his place, and tried to keep it when his successor came; stood up in the pulpit and made a bold and pathetic appeal to the congregation, but in the end was taken into custody, roughly handled, and sent to Preston. At Wigan, on the other hand, the Cavalier gentry, returning victorious from Bolton fight, pulled down the pulpit in Hindley chapel, played cards in the pews, and taking the Bible with them, tore it up as they went, sticking the leaves on posts and trees and crying "this is the Roundheads' Bible." Gradually, however, as the strife grew fiercer, the Puritans, with whom was certainly the strongest religious earnestness of the people, gained the upper hand, and when in 1643 the Parliament called an assembly of clergy to settle the government and worship of the Church of England, there were very few to say a word for Episcopacy.

The assembly thus created by Parliament, commonly called "the Westminster Assembly of Divines," was one of the most remarkable religious gatherings ever held in England. To it were summoned the ablest and most revered clergymen in England, those of various opinions who were most known for their religious earnestness and scholarship. It was hardly to be expected that those who had thrown themselves very strongly on to the king's side and against the Parliament should be summoned, and so there were but a few of the old Episcopalian party who appeared, but eight or ten were invited, among whom were Archbishop Usher and three bishops. About as many more were Independents, who by this time had outgrown the contempt which at first had nicknamed them Brownists, and were becoming a large and important element in Puritanism. The most part, however, were Presbyterians. Almost all were Calvinists in doctrine, their chief differences being as to Church government, on which the Independents stood strongly for each congregation managing its own affairs, as a complete Church by itself in the Scripture meaning, objecting to being ruled by a presbytery almost as much as by the bishops. What the Assembly had first to consider, however, was the settling of some uniform order for worship and religious teaching, so that for a while their differences did not come out very strongly; and, working in the spirit of the deepest religious earnestness, they brought out a "Directory of Public Worship," instead of the Book of Common Prayer, and also two manuals of doctrine which are called the Westminster Confession and the Westminster

Catechism. At length they came to the question of Church government, and then the discussions were long and sharp. The great majority, however, were Presbyterians, and moreover the cause of Presbyterianism had been strongly enforced by the alliance with the Scotch. The Parliamentarians found that to carry through the struggle on which they had entered, they must make common cause with the Puritans of the North; and in Scotland the Puritans were all Presbyterians, and their Presbyterianism was of a far sterner and more rigid kind than what went by the same name in England. This alliance fanned the flame of religious fervour to a greater enthusiasm than ever before, and it was a memorable day when, in St. Margaret's church, Westminster, the commissioners representing the Scottish people joined with the English Parliament and the Westminster Assembly in the "Solemn League and Covenant," pledging themselves to unite the three kingdoms in one religion, and to extirpate popery, prelacy, superstition, schism and profaneness. For the moment, Presbyterianism carried all before it, and, if the matter had straightway been carried through the Assembly and to Parliament, it would probably have been established as the universal order of the Church throughout the country. But in a year or two the enthusiasm for it had a little cooled. The fact was, that through the times of persecution, even those who had learned from Geneva to look upon Church-government by presbyteries as the divinely right thing, had been unable to carry the system out, and their little scattered bands had really all been acting for themselves, and managed their own discipline and other affairs, very much as the Independents advocated. So that, though they carried their Presbyterian scheme to Parliament, and Parliament at last formally sanctioned Presbyterianism as the order which should be set up throughout all the churches of England, it never was so set up; there was no general attempt to carry out the law. It was carried out fully in London, and in Lancashire. In Lancashire, for instance, each district had its "*classis*" or "Classical Presbytery," to which all the ministers of that district belonged. The "Manchester *classis*," used to meet in the old library at Cheetham's College. At these meetings all cases of heresy, sabbath-breaking, disputes, scandalous living, either on the part of ministers or laymen, were brought up and dealt with. All these separate *classes* were united in one "Provincial Assembly," a relic of which still exists in the annual Provincial Assembly still held by those congregations of Lancashire and Cheshire which were formed at a later time, when the Presbyterian clergy had been ejected from the church.

Though, however, Presbyterianism, as a form of Church government, kept losing favour from the time that men began to find out what it was really like, Puritanism, as a religious spirit, became more and more powerful. It became the one strong force of the time, to which everything else had to give way. The Puritans held the idea that they ought to make the earth into the Kingdom of God, by establishing the rule of professing Christians and utterly repressing all evil. Unfortunately, they did not recognize all that human nature requires. They were men of a stern mould, who had grown up through hard and bitter times; life had been a very grave and solemn thing to them, and they could not see how it ought to be otherwise to any. Sport and play seemed to them vain and foolish trifling; sports which had anything to do with the old saints' days, or the old religious festivals, were worse than foolish—were popish and idolatrous. No more May-day festivals for villagers! No more Christmas games! No more rush carts or morris-dancers! Music, except in psalmody, was a sin,—theatre-going, an abomination to the Lord! All the lighter and brighter side of life was checked and frowned upon. Sunday, beforetime in England as all over Europe, had been a festival day, when men went to church in the morning, and afterwards spent the day in games and sports. The Reformation on the continent did not alter this. Luther and Calvin both wished Sunday to be a pleasant holiday; Calvin used to play bowls on Sunday afternoon. But in England, much reading of the Old Testament by the Puritans had led them to think that the Sunday should be kept after the fashion of the Jewish Sabbath; and unfortunately they took as their model, not the Sabbath as Moses left it, which, though very rigid in forbidding work, was otherwise a happy social day, but the sabbath as the Pharisees had spoiled it by their small and frivolous requirements. So, it is to the Puritans we owe that severe and rigid sabbatarianism which long made Sunday a day of gloom and weariness, and which still keeps it from being the happy and refreshing day that it might be. Sundays and week-days alike, Puritanism tried to keep human life wound up to a constant interest in religious subjects and enjoyment of religious exercises. The attempt resulted in a few years of strangely serious and earnest life, throughout the whole people; then in a great deal of discontent and hypocrisy; and at last in a violent reaction to the opposite extreme, in which it seemed for the time as if all the good had been swept away.

Gradually Puritanism became almost universal in the

Church. Many of the Episcopalian clergy had joined in the struggle for the king, and others were found plotting for him, and all these were turned out as "Malignants." Others were deprived of their livings by the examining commissioners sent round by Parliament: many no doubt justly, for the country parsons had many of them been a drinking, card-playing set—many probably, very unjustly, merely because they did not come up to the standard of Puritan strictness in manners, or because they would not take the "Solemn League and Covenant," or use the "Directory of Public Worship." Some of the men who were "sequestered" from their livings were men of fine learning or holy character. Such was Archbishop Usher, and such also Jeremy Taylor, author of "Holy Living and Holy Dying;" and there were hundreds of others who suffered really for conscience sake. It was made a crime even to read the Prayer-book. Puritanism in power became almost as persecuting and intolerant as the Episcopacy it displaced.

It is very sad to think that the Puritans had learned no better than this, in the long sufferings through which they had themselves passed. Yet it must be said in justice to them, that, even when their power was at its height, they never went to such lengths of cruelty as they and their fathers had suffered through the times of prelates like Whitgift and Laud. The very law under which so many of the royalist clergy were deprived of their livings, directed that they should still have one-fifth of the income as pension, though it is to be feared that in the confusion of the time many of them never actually received it. It must also be remembered that, in those days, religious liberty was not understood by any party. Each party thought that the State ought to maintain the truth, and to prevent error being publicly advocated; and each was quite sure that its own views were the truth. The Presbyterians upheld, in theory, the divine right of presbyteries, just as the prelatists believed in the divine right of bishops. Only the Independents, who were a small and struggling party, upheld toleration; but it was generally regarded as a weak compromising of principle on their part. The Presbyterians nicknamed toleration "the Great Diana of the Independents," and in the first years of power, they always protested vehemently against it.

Yet, in practice, and especially as time went on, there really was a great deal of toleration. The churches contained men of very different opinions. Episcopacy was for the time gone out of sight, but there were many ministers still in their livings who had been in from the days of the bishops, and who preferred the Prayer-book, though they cared more for religion than for forms, and were willing to use the Puritan way, rather than give up their ministry. Some were Independents, a few were Baptists. The most part were classed as Presbyterians, but, even of these, a large number were men who cared very little—and less every day—for Presbyterian forms of government, and who, through association with their fellow clergymen of various views, were growing more moderate and tolerant every year.

The most marked progress in this toleration occurred when Cromwell came into power. Cromwell was an Independent, and one of the few men of that age who really understood religious liberty. He insisted that the State, in choosing men to serve it, must take no notice of their opinions; and when he became the head of England, he used his great power to prevent any party from persecuting the others. He wanted strong, true men in the churches, and endeavoured to secure that none others should be put in by appointing a committee of "Triers," as they were called, to examine all candidates for pulpits. These Triers "admitted any that were able serious preachers, and lived a godly life, of what opinion soever they were that was tolerable." The consequence was that, through those later years of Puritan power, the religious life of England was more quiet and dignified, more earnestly occupied in true religious work, than it had been for generations. Pious and learned divines occupied the principal churches in London and the larger towns, while, scattered throughout the country parishes, were numbers of earnest and faithful men of lesser note; and in many districts these were all associated together, not indeed in formal "presbyteries," but in friendly conferences. Thus the venerated Richard Baxter got the ministers of Worcestershire—Episcopalian, Presbyterian, and Independent—to work harmoniously together, meeting in conference with one another for study and prayer and mutual advice. Baxter was one of the Presbyterians who had learned the true spirit of religious liberty, and when he was appointed one of a committee to settle what must be regarded as the fundamentals of Christianity, he proposed the Apostles' Creed, the Lord's Prayer, and the Ten Commandments as containing all that was needful to salvation. It was objected by some that this might include Papists and Socinians. "So much the better," said he, "and the fitter to be matter of concord." There were few men indeed as liberal as this in those days; but in Christian character, Baxter was but a fair example of the Puritan clergy who had come to be scattered over England. The Church of England never stood so high in piety and learning and good works as during those later years when "Puritanism" was "in power."

CHAPTER XXVI.

THE RESTORATION, AND BLACK BARTHOLOMEW'S DAY.

It was a sad day for England when Cromwell died. Whatever his faults, he was one of the best rulers this country has ever had. He had made the nation more prosperous at home, and more respected abroad, than it had ever been before. But when he died there was no one either wise enough or strong enough to carry on his work. The army and the Parliament began to quarrel. The country fell into confusion. The only party who knew what they wanted, and had a strong clear purpose, was that of the old Royalists. They wanted the exiled son of the late king back, and as this seemed the only chance of a settled Government, many moderate men of other parties began to join with them.

Charles Stuart—Charles II.—had long been waiting on the continent, for an opportunity to return. He was a selfish, profligate man, utterly untrustworthy, caring for nothing but wine and cards, and any kind of wicked pleasure. If he had anything of religion, it was only that kind of superstition which often keeps hold of bad men, and about enough of it to make him send for a Catholic priest on his death-bed. In order to win back his father's throne, he was willing to make any professions, and to declare himself of whatever religion would best help his cause.

The Presbyterians were, at this time, about the strongest body in the country, and there was no doubt that if they joined with the old Church and King party, the king would be restored. The Presbyterians were the more disposed to this because they were jealous of the Independents; moreover, they had gradually become much more moderate in their views. They had come to see that many of the things which had once seemed horrible to them as "rags of Popery" were really not so bad as they had thought. They would no longer have objected to the Prayer-book if some alterations were made in it; they could even see something to be said in favour of an order of bishops; only, if there were to be bishops again, they thought they ought not to have so much power as formerly, and that some share in governing the Church should be left with the clergy themselves, meeting together in their presbyteries or conferences.

All this, the king's party professed themselves ready to agree to if the Presbyterians would help in bringing back the king; and Charles, who was at Breda, a little town in Holland, waiting to be sent for, issued a Declaration in order to help on the movement in his favour, in which he used these words: "We do declare a liberty to tender consciences, and that no man shall be disquieted or called in question for differences of opinion on matters of religion which do not disturb the peace of the kingdom; and we shall be ready to consent to such an Act of Parliament as, upon mature consideration, shall be offered to us for the full granting that indulgence." This declaration gave great delight to the Presbyterians, and when it was read in Parliament there was a great shout of joy throughout the House, and the two Houses at once invited the king to return.

On the 29th of May, 1660, the restored king entered London, the bells ringing, the streets strewed with flowers, fountains flowing with wine, music playing, and the ways crowded with people shouting with irrepressible joy. None were more joyful than the moderate Puritans. Six of their leading ministers had gone with the deputation from Parliament, to attend Charles on his journey home, and he was very gracious to them, and spared no promises, and did all he could to make them believe he was a sincere Protestant. On one occasion he kept them waiting in an ante-room, while he said his prayers aloud and with the door open, so that his piety might not be lost upon them; whereupon one of them, old Mr. Case, "lifted up his hands to heaven, and blessed God who had given them a praying King."

For a while the mask was kept on. It was only a mask from the beginning. The very day after his restoration, the king had said to one of his courtiers that "Presbyterianism was no religion for a gentleman." He did not like its strict, sober ways. It was not safe to break with it yet, however, and a few of the leading Presbyterians were offered bishoprics, at once to give them confidence, and to bring them more completely over to the king's side. To their honour it must be told that they all, except one, declined; they would wait, they said, till the declaration of Breda became law.

The affairs of the Church of England at this time were in a curious condition. All was in a state of uncertainty. A large number of the churches throughout the country were held by clergymen of the Puritan sort. Some of these had been put in in place of Episcopalian ministers, who had been deprived of their livings for siding with the king, for refusing to give up the use of the Prayer-book, or for ignorance or unfitness; but the most part had been put in, gradually, during the Commonwealth times, as the older race of ministers had kept passing away. As soon as the Restoration took place, all of the old clergy who had been turned out, and who were still alive, began to come back. No resistance was made to their doing so; indeed Baxter and the leading Puritans had themselves promoted their restoration, and before the end of the year there was hardly a single claimant who had not been replaced. All this strengthened the old Church party, and increased the feeling among the people in favour of reviving the old Church usages. But still there was great variety in the ways of conducting the services. The restored clergymen were very zealous for the Prayer-book, and all the old forms. The Puritan part of the clergy, however, for the most part, still used free prayer. Disputes arose about this, and about Baptism and the Lord's Supper, and so it seemed necessary that there should be some regular settlement of all such matters.

The Puritan clergy, of whom the most part were the moderate Presbyterians, of course took for granted that this settlement would be one which would carry out Charles's promises at Breda. They did not want to have the nation divided into separate Churches, only that such a moderate settlement should be made, as would leave some liberty to ministers and people, and so enable all to keep together. This was also what the best of Charles's advisers wished and intended, and accordingly they brought a bill into Parliament for carrying it out, and tried hard to pass it.

They could not do it, however. A new Parliament

was entering on its labours, the most bigoted ever known. The old High Churchmen were becoming bolder every day. They were resolved on no settlement except one which should drive all the old Puritan clergy out of the Church. They proposed a conference between the bishops and some of the leading Presbyterians, to consult about the proposed altering of the Prayer-book. It was only a sham, however. What they really wanted to do was to find out the points which were absolute stumbling-blocks to the Puritans, that these might be especially retained! "Now we know their minds," said Sheldon, Bishop of London, "we'll make them all knaves if they conform." And so the Prayer-book was made a little more Popish than it had been before; and then they got the celebrated "Act of Uniformity" passed, which obliged every clergyman or schoolmaster not only to use the Prayer-book, but to declare his "unfeigned assent and consent" to everything contained in it!

This act was passed in May, 1662, and was to come into force on the next 24th of August, the feast of St. Bartholomew, as it was called. This day was chosen because it came just before Michaelmas, when the payment of the yearly tithes was due, so that those who refused to conform would lose their whole year's income!

Three months remained, during which the Puritan party among the clergy had to decide on their course. It was a hard and bitter choice for them. Many of them would not have objected to *read* the Prayer-book, but to declare their "unfeigned assent and consent to everything contained in it" was what they dared not do. "I bless God it is so good," said one, "but yet it might be better." There was another difficulty, too.

The act required all clergymen, who would remain in the Church, to be ordained by a bishop; now most of the Puritan clergy had been ordained according to the Presbyterian fashion, by the prayers and laying-on of the hands of their brother ministers; and, to be ordained over again would be a sort of declaration that this ordination, under which they had many of them been ministering for years, was nothing, and that they had not been real ministers; and they did not believe this, and dared not act as if they did.

So the time passed, and the day of "Black Bartholomew," as it was called, drew on. The Church party were full of triumph. The Puritans were very troubled; many and long were their conferences together, and their meetings for prayer, to decide whether they could stay in the Church or whether they must go out.

"I am afraid," said Lord Manchester, "that the terms are so hard that many of the ministers will not comply."

Said Bishop Sheldon, "*I am afraid they will!*"

Great was the temptation; sore the struggle of conscience. Many a story has come down to us, of how the ministers met the crisis with a cheery, trustful heart. Mr. Edward Lawrence, of Baschurch, in Shropshire, pointing to his wife and ten children, said that he had "eleven strong arguments against nonconformity," but he answered them by his faith in God. Being asked how he meant to maintain them all, he cheerfully replied, "They must all live upon the 6th chapter of Matthew!" Nathaniel Heywood, of Ormskirk Church, who, like his brother Oliver, was one of the gentlest-hearted men of the time, was earnestly pressed by his parishioners, who loved him dearly, to conform, and remain with them. "Ah, Mr. Heywood, we would gladly have you preach still in the church." "Yes," said he, "and I would as gladly preach as you can desire it, if I could do it with a safe conscience." "Oh, sir, many a man, now-a-days, makes a great gash in his conscience; cannot you make *a little nick* in yours?"

But those Puritans were not men who could make even "little nicks" in their consciences.

So when at last St. Bartholomew's day came, with hardly an exception they went out from the Church. Many a country parson went forth from his little glebe and parsonage not knowing whither he went or what was to become of him. Most of them were university men, scholars of Oxford or Cambridge. Among them were many of the noblest preachers and most learned divines of the time. In almost every large town in England, the worthiest and most popular clergymen were found among the number of those who were thus silenced. Some had been offered high positions in the Church if they would conform, but very, very few yielded. It is called "the ejection of the two thousand," because in all there were nearly two thousand clergymen who on that day were thus cast out of the Church.

But if they were cast out of the Church of England, they felt that they were not cast out of the Church of Christ. They had been called to the ministry, and they must go on ministering, and if they could not minister to men inside the churches, they must do so outside. They dared not lay down their ministry, and so they preached to such as would hear them, in private houses, and fields, and any place where even a faithful few would gather together.

This only made the Church and King party more angry. The Church was suffering injury. There were not half enough clergymen, of any good standing, to fill the vacant pulpits, and so all sorts of ignorant, incapable men were hastily put in, and the best of the people everywhere would not go to hear them. These ejected ministers must be silenced; and so began a fierce and bitter persecution against them, and all who sided with them. First the "Conventicle Act" was passed, making it a crime for people to refuse to attend their parish church, and making it another crime for more than five persons to be found together at any religious service, except that established by the law. But still the ejected clergy would not cease their ministry, and their faithful people held to them. They had to meet in secret; informers were always on the watch to find out their meeting-places; their worship was constantly being disturbed and broken up by constables and soldiers, but they held on their way. Then another and worse act was passed: "The Five Mile Act," it was called. This made it a crime for any Nonconformist clergyman even to be found within five miles of any place where he had been a minister, or to come within five miles of any city or borough at all, under a penalty of forty pounds fine and six months imprisonment! Yet even this did not deter them; many a touching story has come down to us of the sufferings of those times, and of the brave way in which the ministers still went on with a work which they believed was all the more needed because of the darkness and wickedness of the time. Thus Mr. Chantrye, ejected from Weford, in Staffordshire, took "a small farm in a mean corner of Derbyshire," and "used all opportunities of preaching, encountering many dangers and hardships, going in the twilight to escape the informers, with a Bible in his pocket, and a fork over his shoulder." Such a man, too, was Mr. Ince, a Wiltshire clergyman—"Praying Ince," he was called

—a good scholar and with "an admirable gift of prayer." Not long after the ejection, Mr. Grove, a country gentleman in another part of Wiltshire, sent for his parish clergyman to pray by his wife, who was very ill; but the messenger found the parson just going out hunting, and came back with the message that "he would come when the hunt was over." The gentleman was angry at such an answer; on which the servant said, "Sir, our shepherd, if you will send for him, can pray very well; we have often heard him at prayers in the field." So the shepherd was sent for, and being asked if he ever prayed, replied, "God forbid that I should live one day without prayer;" and by-and-by he prayed by the sick lady with such fervour and beauty of language as astonished the household. But their astonishment ceased when they found that it was "Praying Ince," who, having been ejected from the Church, had taken to the humble employment of tending sheep. "Sir, you shall be *my shepherd,*" said Mr. Grove, and he made a home for him and built a chapel for him, where he preached to the day of his death.

But it was only a few whose places were so remote, or whose friends were so powerful, as to secure them from attack. Fewer still were those who, like old Mr. Angier, of Denton, near Manchester, did not conform, and yet quietly stayed in their churches, and were not meddled with. Even the constables would not take Mr. Angier, when they were ordered to do so, he was so beloved. When they were obliged to search for him on some warrant, they would look another way and profess they could not see him. "He is an old man," they said, "and cannot live long, let him alone while he does live." It was very few who had so easy a lot; almost all suffered great hardships. Numbers were imprisoned

—not ministers only, but those who had harboured them or who were found at their meetings. John James, a Nottinghamshire vicar, was imprisoned at Newark for six years, and could obtain no release unless he promised to give up preaching, which he constantly refused. John Bunyan, not an ejected minister, but a faithful Baptist preacher, was put in prison under the Conventicle Act. They offered him, too, liberty if he would give up preaching: "If you let me out to-day, I will preach to-morrow," said he, and so for twelve long, weary years he lay in Bedford Gaol, strengthening his soul with those visions which he shaped into that immortal work "The Pilgrim's Progress." It may be imagined how many suffered, when it is remembered that during the reign of Charles II. nearly eight thousand Nonconformists *died* in prison.

And what of the Church, whose leaders and bishops wrought these cruel and shameful persecutions? Was it the stronger for having got rid of these men? The very opposite; it continued to be "the Church of England" in name, but the best religious life of England was no longer in its ranks. Not for a century and a half did the Church recover from the self-inflicted blow which cast out its ablest, most devoted, and most scholarly divines. In its high places there were, indeed, here and there, men of learning and character; but throughout the country generally the clergy were as a rule neither learned nor pious, the churches were suffered to fall out of repair, the services were careless and slovenly; the upper classes became scoffing and indifferent, and the mass of the common people were left neglected and untaught, with few to care for their souls.

CHAPTER XXVII.

GEORGE FOX AND THE SOCIETY OF FRIENDS.

Besides the contest which, through these times we have been telling of, was going on between the Episcopalians and the Puritans, there was another religious movement gradually growing up, different from either of these,—opposed and persecuted by both. This was the religious movement which began with the wandering preacher George Fox, and which grew into the Society of Friends, or, as they came to be commonly called, "The Quakers."

George Fox was born in 1624, the year before Charles I. came to the throne; and he was growing up to manhood all through the troubled time of that king's reign, while the storms were gathering which at last burst forth in the civil wars. It was not much that he knew of all this, however. He was growing up in a little out-of-the-way village of Leicestershire—Fenny Drayton—where his father was "by profession a weaver," a well-to-do craft in those days. Something more than a skilful workman, however, was his father—a man of strong, upright character; the neighbours called him "righteous Christer"—Christopher—a man who in one of the cities would have been a leading Puritan, but there, in the little Leicestershire village, he and his wife simply went to the village church, and brought up their son after the same staid, godly fashion. A quiet, grave child, that son grew to be; not caring much for games and sports; loving to listen to older people, loving especially to listen to their talk about religion, and taking it all in into that wondering little head of his, and believing it — yes, believing it, and thinking of it, and wondering how those who talked so much about it could be so foolish and worldly as he often saw them; and sometimes saying to himself (as he wrote afterwards in his journal), "If ever I come to be a man, surely I shall not do so, nor be so wanton." His companions laughed at his grave, sober ways, yet they respected him, too; and when, by-and-by, he was apprenticed to a shoemaker, his master found him so utterly trustworthy, and so true and unbending in his word, that the saying began to go about, "If George says 'verily' there is no altering him."

Gradually these serious thoughts and ways of his —so different from those of the people about him— brought him into trouble. He was more and more grieved at what seemed to him the lightness and carelessness of men's lives. He felt as if he were living in the midst of hollowness and hypocrisy, and at last, one day, when he was about nineteen years old, he was so shocked by seeing two relations of his, who were "professors," as he calls them—that is, professors of religion—setting to for a drinking bout, that he left them and went home, and walked about all night, "crying and praying to the Lord" about it. And it seemed to him that the Lord said to him, "Thou seest how young people go together into vanity and old people into the earth; thou must forsake all, both young and old, and keep out of all, and be a stranger unto all." So, "at the command of God," he adds, "the ninth day of the seventh month, 1643, I left my relations, and broke off all familiarity or fellowship with young or old."

For years after this, life was very hard and lonely and sorrowful to him. He saw what he should not do, but he did not see what he should do. His soul was full of great thoughts of something better and nobler than the common religion, which seemed so poor and worldly; but he was only a village youth, and it is not wonderful that he could not work out his restless thoughts into any clear system, or see any open way before him. He wandered about from place to place—Northampton, London, various parts of Warwickshire—seeking out people here and there whom he could hear of as very religious, and likely to help him through his difficulties. In his perplexity he went to several clergymen, but he was out of their depth. They made light of his troubles. One advised him to take tobacco and sing psalms. "Tobacco," he says in his grave way, "was a thing I did not love, and psalms I was not in a state to sing; I could not sing." Another, an "ancient priest," advised blood-letting; and another, as they were talking together, suddenly burst into a rage because Fox happened to set his foot on a flower-border, "and stormed as if his house had been on fire." So the young man turned away from them. Miserable comforters were they all; he felt that there was nothing for him but just to walk alone with God and his Bible.

After two years of lonely, wandering life, he began to see a little light. It came to his soul that all these outward forms, and ceremonies, and professions that people were setting up, and making so much ado about as "religion," were nothing in themselves; that priestly education and ordination was nothing—did not really make a man any nearer to God; that God simply wanted the hearts and souls of all men to be turned to Him, and the worship of their own thought and feeling. And with the sense of this there arose within him a great loathing of all the formalism, and priestcraft, and outward observances of the Churches, which seemed to him mere delusions, making men fancy themselves religious when they were not, and hiding the true life from them. But he did not find peace yet. It is one thing to see the light, quite another to be in it, and another, again, to know how to show it to others. So he writes: "My troubles continued, and I was often under great temptations; I fasted much and walked abroad in solitary places many days; and often took my Bible, and went and sat in hollow trees and lonesome places till night came on, and frequently in the night walked mournfully about by myself, for I was a man of sorrows in the times of the first workings of the Lord in me." It was a time like Christ's temptations in the wilderness, or Paul's three years in Arabia, before they went forth to their great life-mission. But to him, as to them, came, at last, light and peace and an open way; for when he had found all hope in men vain, and had got bewildered by that long studying of the whole vast Bible, a voice seemed to come to him which said, "There is one, even Christ Jesus, that can speak to thy condition." "And when I heard it," he says, "my heart did leap for joy." Fixing his mind upon Christ, all things began to be clearer to him; he saw the grand, simple truth of a religion of spirit and life; and he saw, too, in his Master's wandering life, just the light he was needing, as to what he must do to bring his fellow-men to the same grand thoughts and truths.

It was at Dukinfield, near Manchester, in 1647, that he began to speak openly to men of what was in his heart. It was a curious thing, the rising up—right into the midst of the struggling parties of that stormy time—of this man, who had had no part with any of them; who cared nothing for them; who had been living, all through the civil war, almost like one in a dream, and now came out among the people almost like one from another world.

His very appearance added to the strangeness and wonder. In those days, when he was wandering away from men, and shrinking with a sort of horror from the fashions of the world, he had made himself a strong, rough suit of leather, and this for many years was his dress. Very white and clean indeed was the linen under that rough leather suit, for he hated all uncleanness either of soul or body; and very calm and clear were his eyes, that seemed to search into men's souls, and quailed before no danger, and sometimes lighted up with wonderful tenderness. A tall, burly man he was, too, of great strength; one who, when he bore meekly the insults and blows of his persecutors, plainly did not do so from any inability to hold his own—indeed, such a fine, noble-looking man, that one of the Parliament leaders once offered to make him captain of a troop of horse, if he would join them.

Such was the man who in 1647 began to go among some of the Puritan meetings in Dukinfield and Manchester, everywhere speaking these new thoughts which he felt upon him from the Lord. It was the year that Charles I. was finally in the power of the Parliamentary party, and Puritanism, puffed up by success, was beginning to degenerate into a formalism little better than that of the Episcopalianism it was crushing out. Puritan or Prelatist, it was all one to George Fox. The long laboured prayers of the Puritan "professors" seemed to him as empty as the forms of the Prayer-book. It was all outward—form, letter, show—to him! And it seemed to him as if it was the same all life through. Men did not really mean anything by their bowing and scraping and complimenting to one another, any more than they did by their bowing and posturing and high-flown language towards God. Everywhere he saw vanity and worldliness, pretence and injustice. It seemed laid upon him that he must testify against it all. He went to courts of justice, and stood up and warned the magistrates to do justly; he went to fairs and markets, and lifted up his voice against wakes and feasts and plays, and also against people's cozening and cheating. "I was moved also to cry against all sorts of music, and against the mountebanks playing tricks on their stages, for they burdened the pure life and stirred up men's minds to vanity." He testified against great things and small, bade men not swear, but keep to "yea" and "nay," and this in courts of justice as everywhere else; he spoke against lip-honour —that men should give up using titles of compliment, and keep to plain "thee" and "thou;" "for surely," he said, "the way men address God should be enough from one to another."

But all this was merely the side-work of his life, flowing from his great central thought of true, pure life in the light of the Spirit of God. That was his great thought, and that he preached most of all; he wanted men to give up all their forms, and come face to face with the Spirit of God, and so worship Him and live to Him. Therefore he spoke most bitterly of all against all priestcraft. God is in your hearts, he said to men; he is not only in the Bible. It is only the ever-living Word that can open your hearts to understand that dead word; it is only the Spirit that wrote the Bible that can really teach you how to read the Bible. So all religious feeling attaching to outward things seemed to him mere superstition. Why should men call the Sabbath a holy day? All days ought to be holy. Why should four stone walls be called a church? "The Church," said he, "is the assembly of faithful souls, wherever they are." The idea of the mere building being regarded as holy seemed to him horrible. He would only call the churches "steeple houses;" when he entered one of them it was to speak his word as soon as the preacher had done. When he came, once, in sight of Lichfield, the spectacle of its three spires visible all together, was too much for him, and he took off his shoes and strode through the town, crying, "Woe to the bloody city of Lichfield." But it was not often he made such mistakes as this; for the most part there was a dignity and weight about him which won him a hearing, and often made a very deep impression.

Gradually followers gathered to him; little groups of people here and there accepted his teachings—began to look to him as their leader. He did not want to found a sect; and as for a church—the Church was the whole body of Christ's faithful people everywhere; so those who joined him would not take any name as a sect or church. They simply called themselves "friends;" they used no form of worship, but met together, to wait upon the Lord with one another; believing that his Spirit was always with them, and that, if anything was to be said, He would put it into their hearts to say it. Till then they would sit silent.

Of course such ways soon led him into trouble. The

Puritans were angry at having the same sort of things said against them, that they had been used to say against the Episcopalians. The ministers denounced him and attacked him almost everywhere. At first they tried arguments. But Fox was not one who believed in the inner light merely because he knew nothing of any other. He was a shrewd, ready man, and he knew the Scriptures from beginning to end; it used to be said that if the Bible were to be lost, George Fox could write it all down over again. So in his quiet way he quoted text after text, and turned the arguments of his opponents inside out, and showed their foolishness to the people about, till they grew mad at him, and fierce persecution began. As soon as it was discovered that he would not take an oath, they found that they had at once a ready way of putting him in prison. Thus the Puritans kept imprisoning him for refusing to swear allegiance to the Commonwealth; again and again he suffered in this way: in Nottingham Castle, in 1648; then, two years later, at Derby, for six months, at the end of which time they tried to force him to enter the army; but he refused, and so they thrust him into prison again, this time into a place called the Dungeon, among thirty felons, where they kept him another half-year. Then, two years later, in 1653, he was imprisoned at Carlisle, in a foul, horrible hole, where, a little while before, a woman had been almost eaten to death by vermin, for prisons were very different places in those days from what they are now. On his release he went on with his work as before, and after a couple of years' hard wandering life, he was again imprisoned in Launceston gaol, for eight long months. After this came a quieter time for him; for he was taken before Cromwell, and Cromwell had a long conversation with him, and saw that this was no seditious recusant; indeed, so struck was he with his fearless faithfulness—for Fox spoke plainly to him, and bade him hearken to God's voice—that when Fox was going, Cromwell caught him by the hand, and with tears in his eyes, said, "Come again to my house, for if thou and I were but an hour of a day together, we should be nearer one to the other." Cromwell sent after him, to bid him dine with the officers of the household, but Fox answered, "Let the Protector know I would not eat a bit of his bread, nor drink a sup of his drink." At which the Protector said: "Now I see that there is a people risen up that I cannot win either with gifts, honours, offices, or places, but all other sects and people I can!" During Cromwell's life he was persecuted no more, but with the restoration of Charles II. his dangers and sufferings began again, and he who had been imprisoned for refusing to take an oath of allegiance to the Commonwealth, was now imprisoned for refusing to take one to the king. In 1664 he was imprisoned in Lancaster Castle, in a half-ruined room where the rain and cold came in all through the winter, so that his body was swelled and racked with rheumatism; and after two years of this he was removed to Scarborough Castle, where he lingered out a third year before he was set at liberty. But, through all, his spirit was never changed. He was offered liberty if he would not preach. "I must do as the Lord shall bid me," he answered. When he came out he went again among his societies, and the sufferings he had gone through only made his preaching more effective. His followers caught his spirit, and no persecutions could intimidate them. In one respect they stand out different from any others of the reformers who from time to time have suffered persecution. They carried out their forbidden worship openly. The Puritans were strong and noble men, and when their evil day came they still held to their Puritanism; but they studied concealment, set watches against being disturbed, met in by-places where they might be most safe. But the Quakers never did this; they would have no subterfuges, no disguises! They made no secret of where their meetings were to be, and at the time there they assembled. Constables and informers might be all about the place, it made no difference; they went in, sat down to their quiet worship; if any one had a word to say he said it. The magistrates tried closing the places, locked the doors, put a band of soldiers to guard them. The Friends simply gathered in the street in front, held their meetings there; went on exactly as if nothing had happened. They might all be taken off to prison, still it made no difference; others would be there next meeting day. The only hindrance they ever offered was that once or twice, when a whole meeting was thus arrested under a warrant "to carry them to prison," on the order being given to "march," they quietly declined, saying that the warrant was to "carry them" to prison, and their captors might do as they liked, but "they were not free to walk."

This same spirit of rigid and perfectly fearless conscientiousness characterized Fox and his followers throughout. Perfectly fearless, perfectly true, neither threats nor favours could move him. Even his persecutors knew they could depend on his word, and more than once, when he had been summonsed, and refused to give bail, they took his word that he would deliver himself up at the time for trial, "if he was free to do so," and let him go.

Is it wonderful that such principles, preached with

such noble devotion to truth and duty, rapidly made way? By the year 1665, when Fox had been preaching for eighteen years, the Society of Friends numbered 80,000, and in another ten years it had spread more widely still, and its founder had visited America, and travelled through Holland and Germany, preaching his doctrine of the inward light, and everywhere founding Meetings.

Fox himself did not pass away till he had seen his people past all the days of persecution. Then, in 1690, his iron frame broken down by the sufferings and labours of his life, though only 67 years of age, he spoke for the last time in the Gracechurch Street Meeting, and going home, lay down to rise no more. They asked him how he felt himself. "Never heed," was his brave reply, "the Lord's power is over all weakness and death." And with his mind clear and peaceful, he lay through three days waiting, and then passed on into the light.

CHAPTER XXVIII.

THE SCOTTISH COVENANTERS.

While the English Nonconformists, and the Society of Friends, were painfully working out their right to worship God in their own way, holding their meetings, going to prison, suffering in many bitter ways, Scotland was the scene of struggles and sufferings even more terrible. In all the eventful history of religious heroism, there is no nobler story than that which is associated with the name of the Covenanters.

To understand thoroughly all that the word "Covenant" stood for, and how it came to be such a supreme, life-and-death matter with those who are known as "the Covenanters," we must keep in mind the character of the Scottish Reformation. While, in England, the Reformation was largely forced on by the political action of the king and the Government, in Scotland it was kept back for a quarter of a century, but then burst forth as the irresistible movement of the people; and instead of resulting in a compromise, such as the Episcopalianism which Henry VIII. set up, it went at once to the extreme of Puritanism, in the setting up of the simple Presbyterian Kirk. This was, as we have seen, in 1560, and almost the whole century and a half which followed was taken up by a struggle between the people who were eager to uphold this simple Presbyterian Kirk, and the rulers and aristocracy who were continually wanting to draw back a little towards Popery and have a Church like that of England, with a liturgy and bishops. This eager popular struggle led to the idea of the whole nation joining together in a solemn "Covenant" to uphold the Protestant religion; and great was the joy throughout the country, when the young king, James—afterwards James I. of England—on mounting the Scottish Throne, in 1580, though still only a boy of twelve years old, agreed to join with his whole people in such a great solemn pledge. This was called "the National Covenant," but was in reality only the first of several covenants.

James's Protestantism was only a flash, and very soon he went on, as the great nobles had been doing, claiming more and more authority in religious matters, and setting up the bishops again over the ministers. So things went on, till the Spanish Armada and the Catholic plots on the continent frightened the king into a new fit of Protestantism, in which he turned completely round, declared himself a Presbyterian, abolished the bishops, said that the Church-service was only "an ill-mumbled mass in English," and for the second time, in 1596, took the National Covenant amid the rejoicings of the people.

It was only a short-lived rejoicing. In a few years Elizabeth died; and as soon as James became King of England, he threw himself on to the side of the English bishops, and set to work to try, little by little, to make the Scottish Church the same as that in England—and the Covenant was heard no more of for a generation. It was a generation of darkness, discouragement, and decay for the Kirk. All through the reign of James I., all through the reign of Charles I., the insidious process went on. Bishops were set up again, and more and more authority was given to them. From time to time, a little more of the old religion was restored. Now it was ordered that Christmas day and Easter day, which the Puritans had disused because of the superstitions connected with them, must be observed in all the churches. Now it was that people must take the Communion kneeling. These may seem little things now, but they were not little to the people of that day. In one sense they were little—no one of them alone was sufficient to rouse the country into revolt, and so they only wearied the people out. There was no great man, such as Knox had been, to withstand the pressure. Religion decayed, and as it decayed, the Kirk became less and less strong for resistance. Yet, still the heart of the nation was sound. Here and there, the Puritan feeling burst out into enthusiastic revivals, which spread through the country, and drew out the people to great field meetings and preachings, the beginning of those gatherings, by hill, and moor, and glen, which afterwards became such a power in Scotland. And so the attachment to the plain Puritan worship was kept alive—pent up indeed, but not crushed out—and when at length Charles I., emboldened by his previous success, went on to enforce the use of the English Church-service and the Book of Common Prayer throughout Scotland, then the popular feeling burst forth. It was no mere minister's question this time. This was a matter which came home to every man, woman, or child who ever went to the Kirk. The excitement produced was intense. When the day came for its first reading in Edinburgh, an immense crowd gathered in the High Church of St. Giles, and as the Dean began to read out of the Prayer-book, an old woman — Janet Geddes—cried out, "Villain, wilt thou read the mass at my lug?" and taking up the three-legged stool she had brought with her to sit upon—for there were no pews in those days—she flung it at his head. In a moment there was an uproar, and the uproar became a riot, and the riot became a rebellion. In all the country round, the people rose, often headed by women. By thousands upon thousands they gathered to Stirling, where the Scottish Privy Council was assembled, and there they resolved upon a new National Covenant. This was a *National* Covenant indeed. Never before had the whole nation been so united. On an appointed day, the Covenant, written on an immense parchment, was unrolled in the old Greyfriars Church at Edinburgh, and spread out upon a tombstone; and hour after hour the people crowded in to sign it. Some signed it in their blood. The parchment got so full, that many could only get in their initials, and still they crowded in; and what was done in Edinburgh was repeated throughout Scotland.

From this time the movement went steadily on. The Puritan feeling in England gradually came up with that of Scotland, owing to the deceit and oppression of the king; and when at last the English Parliament took up arms and the Civil War began, the Puritans of the sister kingdoms made common cause, and the "Solemn League and Covenant" was adopted for the whole country. One September day in 1643, both Houses of Parliament met in St. Margaret's Church, Westminster, and with them the Scottish Commissioners, and also the great "Westminster Assembly of Divines;" and after a solemn service the

Covenant was read, and the whole great assemblage stood up, uncovered, and lifting their hands towards heaven, swore to it; and then it was sent to Scotland, and subscribed with enthusiasm throughout the kingdom.

What was this "Solemn League and Covenant?" It was, simply, a pledge that those who took it would endeavour to bring about unity of religion and Church-discipline, throughout England, Scotland, and Ireland; and then it went on: "and that we shall, in like manner, without respect of persons, endeavour the extirpation of popery, prelacy, superstition, heresy, schism, profaneness, and whatsoever shall be found to the contrary of sound doctrine, and the power of godliness, lest we partake in other men's sins, and thereby be in danger to receive of their plagues, and so that the Lord may be one, and his name one, in the three kingdoms."

One cannot read this document in the present day without astonishment. To us it seems contrary to every principle of religious liberty. What right have Protestants to make "Solemn Leagues" for the extirpation of either Catholicism or Episcopalianism? But in those days few people had any idea of religious liberty. All thought that it was the duty of the State to maintain true religion, and to put down what was false. The Covenant seemed, to the most earnest men of that time, a great charter of union for securing the freedom and maintenance of what they felt was the true religion, which had been long and sorely persecuted; so they signed it with great enthusiasm.

In English history, indeed, this Covenant plays hardly any part. It was taken sincerely at the time, but more as a political than a religious movement. By-and-by the Puritans of England quarrelled with those of Scotland, and the Covenant, like any other treaty, was regarded as at an end, and was quickly dropped and forgotten.

But it was not forgotten in Scotland. To the Scottish people it was the crowning victory of a century of special struggle, and it seemed to them the seal of providence, set upon a great act of national self-consecration to the Lord's true religion. All through the Commonwealth times, "the Covenant" continued to be the watchword of Puritan Scotland. When the Scottish people took the part of the young Charles Stuart and tried to restore him, they would not stir a step till he had signed the Covenant. And when the restoration actually took place, and Charles II. forgot all his pledges and promises, and began to enforce an Episcopal Church with the Prayer-book throughout Scotland, "the Covenant" became the banner of resistance, and the story of that resistance is the story of those who are known in history as "the Covenanters."

There was not very much resistance. Twenty years before, when Charles I. had attempted to make the Scottish Kirk like the Church of England, the whole country had resisted. But times were changed now, when Charles II. tried the same thing. Puritanism now was fronting, not a king at variance with his people and tottering to his fall, but a king in all the flush of an enthusiastic restoration. The English Puritans could help them no longer; they were themselves crushed and persecuted. Moreover, the Scottish nobles were on the king's side, and the mob went with the nobles; and neither with mob nor nobles lay the deep earnestness of Scottish religion. So there was no power of general resistance in the country. The

Covenant was publicly torn up by the common hangman, and Scotland sullenly submitted.

But there were some who could not submit. Throughout the Western Lowlands was a race of yeomanry and peasantry, very different both from the wild Highland clans and the fickle mob of the great cities. Upon these men religion had taken a strong fervent hold. In many other parts of Scotland there were some ministers and people who could not conform to the new service, but throughout these Western Lowlands this attitude was, either openly or secretly, almost universal. So, when the day of submission was past, and four hundred of the bravest and most honest ministers throughout Scotland had been cast out from their livings, they found shelter among these western farms and cottages, and kept up the same kind of irregular services, here and there, wherever they could, as the English Puritans were doing. The churches were closed against them, but they began those field-preachings which soon became celebrated. At these meetings the one great topic was the Covenant. It seemed an awful thing to them that this sacred engagement, undertaken alike by the Government and the Churches, should now be treated as so much waste paper; and so the Covenant, and its permanent obligation, became the watchword of their cause.

Very sad and tragic is the story of their struggle for that cause. The English Nonconformists, as we have already seen, were very hardly and bitterly dealt with—harassed with fine and imprisonment for harbouring their ministers and listening to their services. But in those remote Northern parts of the Island, matters were managed with a much rougher and heavier hand. Bands of soldiers were quartered here and there in the disaffected districts, generally under some of the "soldiers of fortune" whom the late wars had trained, and who were ready to serve in any cause which would pay them. These men were turned loose among the farms, levying fines on all who did not attend church, quartering their men on all who did not pay their fines promptly, and inflicting every kind of oppression and exaction they liked upon the people, entirely unchecked. Yet still the fervour of the people only increased. The harder their lot, the more need they had of encouragement and prayer. They only valued their field-preachings the more. They only set the tenderer love upon the faithful ministers—many of them gentle, scholarly men—who, though hunted from place to place, still kept true to their flocks. They only sang the stern old Puritan hymns with a stronger enthusiasm, and hugged closer to their hearts the thought of that Covenant which all others might forsake, but which they felt they must hold by even to the death.

Then the king and his bishops took sterner measures. The Covenanters were swept into the gaols by scores and hundreds. Out in the German Ocean, many miles from the Scottish coast, rises the Bass Rock, a bare, desolate place, only fit for the haunt of sea-birds. That Bass Rock was the Covenanters' prison. There, in low, small dungeons, open to the wild ocean storms, many of them passed weary, suffering years. And meanwhile the fines were pressed more hardly—£50,000 in one year was squeezed out of the farmers and peasantry of Ayrshire alone—and women were whipped for giving food and shelter to the ministers, and boys were branded and shipped to Barbadoes as slaves, and gradually the people were goaded into desperation.

Bear in mind the kind of people these were. It

was but a few generations since the old border feuds had raged through all this Lowland country, and still every farmstead had its old matchlock or broadsword hanging over the fireplace, and its traditions of the border raids and battles in which, before the Union, it had done sturdy service. Soon the weapons began to be taken to the field-preachings; for though there was no purpose of resistance, still the soldiers, if they should come upon them, were fierce and brutal, neither woman nor child was safe from them, it would be better to be armed! Once armed, it was only too easy a step to fighting. A few fugitives from one of these field-meetings were resting in a village, when word was brought in that some of the soldiers had bound an old man and were about to torture him with fire because he would not pay some church fine. The countrymen rushed out to rescue him; there was a scuffle and a fight, and they were taken prisoners. But the news spread, and the whole country-side was up, and the gathering crowds took sixteen of the soldiers prisoners, then surprised their head-quarters, and then went, aimless and angry, towards Edinburgh, gathering strength as they went, till there were three thousand men in arms. But what could come of it? They had no plan, no leader, no supplies. The Government troops were pressing on them, and as they got nearer the capital the people dared not help them. They could only draw away again towards Galloway, and when the forces overtook them, they could only fight in brave desperate groups until the dark November night came down, and such as were left could scatter among the hills. Such was the battle of Pentland, and of course it only made matters worse every way. In many of these men, it deepened the desperation and bitter sense of wrong into a spirit of fierce revenge. It was in such a mood that a group of them, Balfour of Burley at their head, fell in with Archbishop Sharp on Magus Muir. Archbishop Sharp was the very head of all the persecution, and, moreover, he was a renegade. So in their rage, old man as he was, they dragged him from his coach and murdered him. It was a horrible deed, and a deed that only brought the arm of oppression upon them more pitilessly than ever, and that upon thousands who would have cut their hands off before they would have done such a thing. Only the fiercer grew the persecution. Eight thousand of the wild lawless Highlanders were sent among the Lowlands, at free quarters there, and no one to inquire into their doings, and any man who was suspected of having been at Pentland was at their mercy, to cut down or torture.

So the years went on—year after year, till a whole generation had grown up in this beaten, hunted life; till those who had been carried as little babes in arms to the first field-meetings, to be baptized, were growing into manhood; and still no light, no hope! Yet they held to the old cause. The original meaning, indeed, of "the Covenant" was almost forgotten, but it meant to them the cause of their fathers' faithfulness to the simple Puritan worship, and all the suffering they had gone through for it only made it dearer. Every family had some story of cruel outrage, of hairbreadth escape. Who could forsake a cause so consecrated? They could not even lack for preachers. As, one by one, the hunted ministers were taken and tortured and put to death; or, as, worn out with cold and wet and exposure in the caves which often were their only shelter, they sickened and died, brave youths kept stepping into their places, and preached and prayed with a fervour that seemed to those who heard the very spirit of prophecy.

Once more, too, as the years rolled on, the old Puritan fire flashed up in unpremeditated resistance. In the twentieth year of this persecution, a great body of Covenanters, interrupted at their worship amid the Drumclog moors, drove Claverhouse and his dragoons back into the morass, forced their leader to fly, and won the single Covenanting victory; but only, after a brief three weeks of hope, to be utterly routed at Bothwell Bridge, with twelve hundred prisoners huddled in the Old Greyfriars Churchyard at Edinburgh, some to be hung, and nearly three hundred sold abroad for slaves. Their victory did them no good. It is not such things which gild the story of the Covenanters with its undying glory. It only brought upon them fiercer, more unrelenting persecution. James declared that there would be no peace till the Lowlands were turned into a hunting-field. The whole country was given up to Claverhouse, now, to work his will. The Covenanters drew off into still lonelier solitudes, but only to be followed there also, and hunted down even with bloodhounds. No one was safe. The two years, 1684 and 1685, came to be called "Killing time," so ruthless was the bloodshed. Often there was not even any form of trial. Claverhouse and his dragoons went whither they would, and put to people whatever test they chose, and, if they hesitated, shot them. To be seen walking quickly was enough for suspicion; to be found with a Bible was proof! Now it was that John Brown, the Ayrshire carrier, was shot. A quiet, inoffensive man he was, against whose peaceableness there was not a whisper, but it was known that more than once ministers had found shelter in his little cottage on the moorside. One morning the dragoons came upon him as he was cutting turf, and they seized him, and led him down the hill to where, before his door, stood his wife, with a little child in her arms, and near her time with another. John knew that his hour was come, and he kneeled down and prayed—prayed so like one inspired that even the troopers wavered, and hesitated to obey the word to fire—and Claverhouse shot him down himself. "What do you think of your husband now?" cried he, in his fury, to the poor wife, as she knelt there with her husband's shattered head in her lap. Said she, "I aye thocht muckle of him, sir, but I never thocht sae muckle of him as I do this day."

It was only ten days after this that two women—an old widow, Margaret McLachlan, and a young maiden, Margaret Wilson—were drowned in the Solway Frith for the same cause. Their tormentors bound them to the fishing-stakes below high-water mark, the old woman nearer to the sea, that her sufferings might terrify the younger one. Did you ever watch the tide come in, and try to mark its rising, so slowly, but with such dreadful certainty? So they watched it, but they prayed and sang, till the waves choked their voices. Then the persecutors gave the girl another chance; they unbound her, offered her her life if she would abjure the Covenant. "Never!" she cried, and so they tied her there again and watched her drown.

Thus might one story be added to another of the brave way in which poor labouring men went to their death; of the noble words often spoken in those dying moments; of youths of nineteen or twenty refusing to pull their bonnets over their faces when the soldiers levelled their muskets at them, saying they had done nothing to be ashamed of and could look them in the face. Amid such crimes that long, dire eight-and-twenty years of persecution was drawing to its climax and its close.

One great crime was yet to come, which thrilled Scotland through and through. Among the last of the preachers who had not yet been hunted down was James Renwick. A few years before, in 1681, he had been at Edinburgh University, a youth of fine scholarship and almost of genius, teaching for his support while he studied, when he saw David Cargill, one of the Covenanting preachers, executed. The sight touched Renwick's heart. He was but nineteen years old, and the persecution was at its direst, but he threw himself into the cause, and became one of its most celebrated preachers. Young, active, fired with a lofty enthusiasm, gifted with eloquent, persuasive speech, he seemed to the discouraged people like a new prophet raised up for them by the Lord. The Government set a price upon his head. A dozen times over he was specially searched for, but through his activity and the love of his people he escaped. Six years, however, of such hardships and sufferings broke him down, till at last he could neither ride nor walk, and could only get from his hiding-places to the meetings by being carried in men's arms. He was in this state when he was discovered in Edinburgh and seized. The authorities were in a comparatively merciful mood, and his youth, and his weak, worn frame, evidently not far from death, excited pity. If he would have made any concession he would have been spared. But he would not. He did not want life. He closes the last letter he wrote: "Death to me is as a bed to the weary." He went to the gallows in the Grassmarket, saying, "The bridegroom is coming, I am ready, I am ready;" then he sang the 103rd Psalm and prayed, while the soldiers tried to drown his testimony with the roll of drums, and with words of triumphant trust he died the martyr's death.

This was in February, 1688, and he was the last victim. The cup of King James's tyrannies was full. Already the people of England were awaking from their long stupor; murmurs of discontent were everywhere; even the most loyal of his subjects were alienated; his throne was tottering. Within six months the Revolution broke out, the king was flying for his life, and the accession of the Prince of Orange, as William III., put an end alike to the sufferings of the English Nonconformists, and to the still greater sufferings of the Scottish Covenanters.

Then it was that the effect of all this heroism was seen. Their sufferings had not been in vain. They had seemed to be struggling for the extreme principles of one small party, but the real issue was not "the Covenant," which by this time had almost disappeared from the living interest of men; it was the duty and right of men to follow conscience and worship God in their own way. Thus, though Scotland as a whole had looked sullenly on while they suffered, it was really the battle of all Scotland they were fighting—the battle for the simple worship which the whole people loved. So when, at last, the Stuart despotism was overthrown, the whole Church system which had been forced upon the land fell with it, and the Kirk of Scotland was once more established in the same simplicity which Knox had taught, and which the people had never ceased to love.

CHAPTER XXIX.

THE ACT OF TOLERATION.

For a little while, just previous to the Revolution, it seemed as if the religious differences and sufferings which had so long distracted England were about to be healed. A great common peril was drawing together all Protestant Christians. James II. was a Catholic, and the one purpose for which he was always scheming was, to re-establish Popery. He tried to win over each party in turn to favour his policy. First he revived the persecution of the Nonconformists, hoping thus to conciliate the Church into letting him carry out his schemes. Then, finding that this would not do, and that the clergy stood firmly for Protestantism, he turned round and endeavoured to get the Nonconformists on his side by issuing "Declarations of Indulgence" (in 1687 and 1688), doing away all the persecuting laws by his own authority, and offering all people the free exercise of their religion. These declarations were a great temptation to the Nonconformists, who had for so many years been suffering bitterly; yet they knew that they were illegal—that the king was assuming a power to which he had no right, and by which the country had already grievously suffered—and so for the most part they refused to accept them. For a moment all parties stood together. When the king ordered the illegal "Declaration" to be read in the churches, the Nonconformist divines of London united in beseeching the clergy to refuse, and "the Seven Bishops" went to the Tower sooner than publish it. No more was heard about persecution. The old nicknames against the Puritans were no longer heard. It began to be discovered that on the most important points Churchmen and Dissenters were not so far apart as they had seemed, and the clergy began to talk quite cordially about their "Nonconforming brethren," and to regret the persecution they had so long suffered, which they were now very eager to lay upon the king. On all sides the talk was about toleration and comprehension. There must be no more imprisoning for conscience' sake; and by a little widening of the Church, it might surely be made broad enough to hold all parties! For a moment it seemed as if it would, at last, be possible for all Protestant Christians to be united in one great National Church.

But the Revolution took place. James II. fled from the country in a way which enabled those who had preached the very highest doctrine of Divine Right to declare that the throne was vacant; and Mary, James's daughter, with her husband, William, Prince of Orange, came to the throne. At once the Nonconformists were full of hope and joy, for they thought that the time they had waited for so long was come, and that at last the way was to be opened for them to return into the Church from which they, or their fathers, had been driven out in 1662.

But with the flight of James the fears of Churchmen took wings also, and with their fears a large portion of their liberality. When William and Mary were safely established on the throne, the clergy began to think they had been too hasty in fraternizing with the Dissenters, and the points of difference began to look large and serious again. Some of the nobler Churchmen, to their credit be it told, tried to carry out the understanding for a union, and Lord Nottingham, one of the most conscientious and honoured statesmen of the day, introduced into Parliament, at the same time, a "Comprehension" Bill "for the uniting of their Majesties' Protestant subjects," and also a "Toleration" Bill. The Comprehension Bill, if it had passed, would have enabled any minister who had been ordained according to the Presbyterian manner to become a clergyman of the Church of England, without being ordained over again by a bishop, on making a simple declaration of approval of "the doctrine and worship and government of the Church of England as by law established;" and, moreover, it left several things, such as the sign of the cross in baptism and the wearing of the white surplice, to the choice of the minister. The king was warmly in favour of the bill, for he longed to see all the people, of this new kingdom he had undertaken to rule, heartily united, and, indeed, he hated intolerance in any form. But, in spite of all that some of the noblest men in the country could do, it did not become law. The fact is, the time for it was gone by. The ordinary country clergy could not give up the prejudices which had kept them separate and often hostile to the Dissenters, and the High Churchmen were not willing to let go anything of the forms and ceremonies, which they cared for far more than for the doctrines, of the Church. Nor were the Dissenters themselves very eager for Comprehension, when they began to look at it closely, and to realize what it would mean to them. The Nonconformist ministers had too long enjoyed a noble independence to like the idea of becoming subject again to the rule of bishops; and their flocks had held so well together in spite of all the persecution they had endured, that, the moment they were free to act and organize themselves, they stood forth as strong united religious societies, and did not relish the prospect of disbanding and being scattered among the parish churches, and losing their beloved preachers, who might be sent to distant livings or curacies. So the Comprehension Bill went slackly; nobody was really very anxious for it; and though the House of Lords passed it, when it came down to the Commons it was opposed and hindered, and, by-and-by, laid aside on the pretext of waiting till the clergy had given their opinion about it; and so no more was heard of it.

The Act of Toleration, however, was passed by both Houses with very little opposition. This Act, which is one of the great landmarks in the Story of Religion in England, received the Royal assent May 24th, 1689. It is justly regarded as the "Great Charter" of the religious liberty of England; and in its practical effect it did lay the foundation of that religious liberty under which all the different forms of religion have ever since gone on their own way with very little interference, and with hardly anything that could be called persecution. Yet it is curious to note how very limited was the "Toleration" really permitted by this great Act. It did not lay down any principle of general toleration for religious differences. It did not even repeal a single one of the persecuting laws, by which people had been previously compelled to attend church or punished for heresy. It merely provided that these laws should not be enforced against such Dissenters as would take the oath of allegiance, and make certain declarations against the power of the Pope and some of the leading Romanist doctrines. It permitted them also to assemble in their meeting-houses, but not with the door locked (which was a wise law, and no real hardship), nor were they to be exempted from paying tithes and other church-dues. To the ministers the toleration was still more restricted. They had not only to take the oath and make the declarations above mentioned, but, before they could obtain a license to preach, they must also subscribe to thirty-five out of the "thirty-nine Articles" of the Church of England! The Articles to which they were not obliged to subscribe were those which assert the Church's power "to decree rites and ceremonies" (part of the 20th), the soundness of the Book of Homilies (35th), and of the service for consecrating bishops and ministers (36th), and the Article (34th) on "the Traditions of the Church." Special clauses were also introduced to meet the cases of Quakers and Baptists. It was, however, specially declared that *the benefit of the Act shall not extend to persons denying the doctrine of the Trinity.*

With the larger ideas of religious toleration and even of religious equality which we have at the present day, it seems very strange that the Catholics and the Unitarians should be so carefully excluded from this new settlement of religious affairs. With regard to the Catholics, however, it must be remembered that Catholicism was still, as in Elizabeth's reign, much more than a mere form of religious opinion. It stood in those days for every evil of religious and political despotism. The times were still too fresh in the mind of England of the burnings of Smithfield, of the Armada, and of the massacre of St. Bartholomew, for the nation to tolerate Catholicism. Moreover, if the

English people could have been willing to forget these things, they had been kept in mind of them by the stealthy efforts which James II. had been making towards the re-establishment of Popery, which efforts had only been defeated by a revolution. It was hard for the English Catholics, many of whom were loyal and good men, but they had themselves, or, at all events, their leaders, to thank for it.

As for the clause against those who denied the Trinity, it did not hurt anybody, while it satisfied many timid people, and enabled the bill to pass more easily. At that time very few persons in England had got as far as Unitarianism. Presbyterians, Independents, Baptists, Quakers, all held more or less to the general orthodoxy of the Reformation, though it was already beginning to shade off into vaguer forms. When, only a very few years later, the question of Unitarianism began to be much debated, the practice of general toleration had become too firmly established for anything to be attempted against those who took the Unitarian side. So the clause leaving them still subject to the old persecuting laws remained from the first almost a dead letter, though it was not actually removed from the statute-book till more than a century afterwards, in 1813.

As may well be supposed, the Act of Toleration was welcomed with great rejoicings by the Nonconformists. It is true their liberty was not perfect. The Episcopal Church was still to be the Church established by law, and they still had to pay for its support, and a man could not be a Mayor or a Member of Parliament except he would take the Sacrament at church. But, after such hardships and sufferings as those they had gone through, it was a great point gained to be able to build their own meeting-houses, and carry on their worship as they thought right. Besides, the Toleration Act really meant a great deal more than was actually said in it. It practically meant, that all forms of religion not dangerous to the State were to be allowed henceforth to exist peaceably, side by side.

Thus, at length, the churches had rest. It was not yet perfect rest, indeed, either for the Church or for the Dissenters. The Church clergy were divided by the question of whether it was lawful for them to swear allegiance to William III. From the time of the Restoration they had preached up the doctrine of the divine right of kings, preached it even to the extent of holding that, under no circumstances, even of the greatest oppression, could a people be justified in resisting their rightful sovereign. This was all very well, as long as the king was the faithful friend of the Church; but when James II. began to intrigue in favour of Popery, and the whole nation saw the necessity of a change, they found their doctrines of "Divine Right" and "Passive Obedience" terribly in their way. Fortunately for them, the king's flight helped them over the difficulty by leaving the throne practically vacant; but they were obliged still to maintain that he was, by divine right, King of England, and the utmost they could yield was that a regency might be appointed to act for him. William III. would not be a "regent," however; and his accession to the throne placed them in great difficulty, and when Parliament went on to require the clergy, like all other public officers, to swear allegiance to the new king and queen, on pain of losing their places, they could no longer evade the question. By far the larger proportion of the clergy throughout the country submitted, and took the oath; but they did not like it, and as a class became bitter opponents of the Government. All, however, were not of so pliable a temper, and Archbishop Sancroft, with eight bishops and about four hundred of the clergy, refused the oath, and were accordingly deprived of their livings. These are called, in the history of the time, the "Nonjurors." One cannot help pitying these men, among whom were some of the strongest and most honest men in the Church, but it must be remembered that it was not on any question of religion that they were ejected, but simply for refusing to William as "king" the allegiance they were willing to give him if called merely "regent." One is sorry to think of good old Bishop Ken, the author of the favourite evening hymn, "Glory to thee, my God, this night,"* having to leave the quiet abode at Wells, where his piety and goodness had endeared him to all classes. He found a home, however, at Longleat, the seat of Lord Weymouth, and there spent a peaceful and happy old age. The Nonjuring clergy generally, however, were not of his gentle spirit. All through the reign of William they kept up a bitter opposition, furnished James in his exile with many of his ablest partisans, and, with Sancroft at their head, maintained that they were still the only true Church of England, and that the bishops and clergy who had taken their places, and even all who recognized them, were usurpers and schismatics. They got James to nominate two of their number as bishops, so as to keep up the apostolical succession when the original Nonjurors passed away, and thus for generations they managed to drag on a feeble but pretentious existence, as a sect. Without churches; soon without congregations; with only a political scruple, not

* Or, as he originally wrote it, "*All praise* to thee, &c."

a religious principle, to unite them, they lingered on as a little group of irreconcilables through the last century, "and at length," says Macaulay, "in 1805, the last bishop of that society which had proudly claimed to be the only true Church of England, dropped unnoticed into the grave."

The places of these Nonjurors were filled by William with men of learning and goodness, such as Tillotson, who was made Archbishop of Canterbury, and Burnet, Bishop of Salisbury, who wrote a very interesting "History of his own Times." The king hoped that these bishops would elevate the character of the Church, but the clergy continued so bitter against the Government, and against the bishops it appointed, that they had very little power, and the Church of England kept declining in character and influence. Once, the bitterness of the clergy, against the new order of things introduced by the Revolution and the Toleration Act, broke out into a fierce violence, which showed that the builders of the Dissenting meeting-houses had not without reason placed them in out-of-the-way alleys and corners, where they might attract less attention, and be in less danger of attack. In 1710, what were called the Sacheverell riots broke out in London, excited by the preaching of Dr. Sacheverell, a London clergyman who vehemently attacked the Act of Toleration, the favours shown to Dissenters, and the principles of the Revolution. By this time a good deal of reaction had taken place in the country; a foreign war was going on; the people were suffering and discontented, and only too ready to listen to those who laid the blame on the new order of things; so that Sacheverell's fierce harangues were like a spark to a train of gunpowder, and the mob of London, gathering in angry crowds, proceeded to plunder and burn the Dissenting chapels. In many large towns the same thing was repeated at intervals; in Manchester especially, in 1714, the rioters burned the meeting-house in Acres Field (now Cross Street Chapel), and then marched out triumphantly to several of the neighbouring villages, destroying the meeting-houses at Monton, Blackley, and several other places. These were mere temporary outbreaks, however. The country at large was resolute both for the political liberty and the religious toleration, which had been brought in by the Revolution and William III. Parliament voted large sums for rebuilding the ruined meeting-houses, and gradually the churches settled down into the peace and quiet of the eighteenth century.

CHAPTER XXX.

THE OLD DISSENT.

VERY joyful were the Nonconformists throughout the country at the passing of the Act of Toleration. If it did not give them all that they would have liked, it gave them a liberty and a security which seemed almost like the kingdom of heaven, compared with the sufferings and persecutions which they had had to endure for nearly thirty years. At once they began to take a strong, open place before the world. Henceforth Dissent was to stand as a recognized and important element in the social and religious life of England.

The first thing the Dissenters had to do was to build churches for their worship. There were already a good many scattered over England. The Baptists had some chapels very early—that at Broadmead, Bristol, dates from 1640. A few of the churches, also, which had been built by Puritans during the Commonwealth times, had, of course, not been "consecrated," and could not be touched by the Act of Uniformity, but remained in the hands of the old Puritan owners or trustees, and continued to be used, when the times allowed it, for the plain Nonconforming service. Such were the chapels at Stannington, near Sheffield, at Bramhope, at Morley, and "the antient chapel of Toxteth Park," near Liverpool. Then, a few chapels—"meeting-houses," as they were at first called—had been erected during lulls in the persecution, such as the great chapel at Mill Hill, Leeds, built in 1672, and the first dissenting chapel in Sheffield, built in 1678. But most of the little bands of Nonconformists who had been holding together through those troubled times, had only been meeting in private houses. Now, however, the time had arrived when they could come out from their secret meeting-places, and openly take the position of religious congregations. What Joseph Hunter, the antiquarian, calls "the chapel-building era" began. Within twenty years the country was dotted over with about a thousand of these plain, homely structures. Their founders were still timid, as, indeed, they might well be after all that they had suffered, and feared to make very much display, or to come too prominently before the eyes of the people. So, the sites of these new chapels were generally chosen in back streets, or up some narrow court or alley, where they might not attract too much notice, and where, if evil times should come, they might be in rather less danger. Plain brick buildings, for the most part, were those of the Toleration era, and most of them have long since been replaced by more showy Gothic "churches"; yet in their time they were looked on as comely and even beautiful, by people who had often been glad to gather in a small back room or the barn of some remote farm-house; and very proudly and thankfully those staid old Nonconformists must have taken their little children by the hand to watch the building, and must have praised God in their household worship that at last they could dwell, as they loved to say, "every man under his own vine and fig-tree, none making them afraid."

A grave, strong, thoughtful race of people were these

of "the Old Dissent." This was natural after all that they had gone through. Not many of the very poor held with them. The mobs of the large towns were usually Jacobite; shouted for Church and King with the Tory squires and rectors. But some of the best of the noble county families still held with the Puritan side, as did the strength of the trading classes, and numbers of the substantial farmers and yeomen. Oliver Heywood, in the days of persecution, going from end to end of the West Riding, on his preaching journeys, could almost everywhere find some well-to-do family who, in spite of fines and threats, and sometimes even imprisonment, still sheltered any Nonconformist minister coming their way, and could gather a congregation at a few hours' notice in the barn, or house-place, or old hall. In London, so universally were the merchants and tradesmen Dissenters, that many of the halls of the great trading guilds or companies were turned into meeting-houses, and, furnished with pulpit and pews, formed the earliest Dissenting chapels.

They had no lack of means, in the large towns, at any rate. The same thoughtful, conscientious, resolute character which in those days made and kept men Dissenters, was the kind of character to make them enterprising, and trusted, and successful in business. Moreover, shut out from positions of public office or honour, and having much of the old Puritan disapprobation of sports and amusements, they naturally threw their whole energy into business.

The ministers of these congregations of the Old Dissent were a learned, dignified body of men. Some of the older of them had been of the number of the ejected clergy of 1662; others were sons of these, or men who had been trained and ordained by them. The Universities of Oxford and Cambridge were closed against them, but some went abroad to Holland, and others studied in the Scottish Universities, and the traditions of learning were very carefully kept up among them. Moreover, here and there, were private "academies," where a few young men, placed under some minister of learned reputation, studied university learning, and, unfettered by articles or creeds, discussed all questions with a thoughtful freedom, and nourished a spirit of liberty which trained up many sturdy patriots and reformers. In the early times of the Old Dissent, however, the ministers had not much to do with public reform. Their work was in the pulpit, the study, and the home. Men of long sermons and long prayers; great Scripturalists, arguing out their doctrines under many heads and subdivisions; much revered by their flocks, consulted on every matter of interest, having part in every household trouble or rejoicing; men to whom, in their black dress and great wig, the little children in those old Dissenting homes looked up with awe. Many of them took pupils; for the great grammar-schools were all in the hands of Churchmen, so that the Dissenting families needed schools to which their sons might go without losing the old feeling of fidelity to the cause to which their fathers had held so strongly. In the country places the ministers were generally poorer, and eked out their living by farming. But still, throughout the kingdom, both ministers and people of the Old Dissent were held in respect, and lived out their life still in something of the sober Puritan fashion of the older times which had passed away.

When we speak of the Old Dissent we must not

forget that it was not all of one kind. During the days of persecution, indeed, the different parties of Nonconformists had been drawn much together by their common sufferings, but there really were considerable differences among them, and hence the various sects which make up the Dissenting side of English religious life.

The chief bodies of Nonconformists at the time of the Toleration Act were, the Baptists, Independents, and Presbyterians. There was also the Society of Friends, but after their first generation of heroic suffering and noble testimony, they came little before the people in their religious work, and took comparatively little part in the public religious life of England. There were also, here and there, small groups of worshippers, remnants of some of the smaller sects of the Commonwealth time — Muggletonians, Ranters, and such like—who still kept together in a feeble way, but were gradually disappearing. But the strength of English Dissent, as an active religious power, was in the bodies first named—which gradually came to be known in the history of the time as "the three denominations."

Of these three, the Baptists were the most distinct. Their doctrine that only entire immersion was any real baptism, and that baptism ought not to be administered to infants, but only to persons old enough to make a personal profession of religion, kept them apart from their fellow-Nonconformists, almost as much as from the Church itself. The first Baptist church in England had been organized in 1633, and as early as 1644 a Baptist Confession of Faith had been put forth by seven churches in London. At first they were persecuted by the other Puritans, but as time went on this passed away, so that there were three Baptists among Oliver Cromwell's commission of "Triers," and among the Puritan clergy ejected on St. Bartholomew's day were about thirty of the same persuasion. The chief part of the Baptists, however, kept aloof from the churches. Whether Episcopalians or Presbyterians carried the day, there was no likelihood of the Church being widened so as to take them in. So they accepted the position of being separatists, and were building their little meeting-houses, and organizing little groups of worshippers meeting in private houses into regular churches, while the Presbyterians were still holding back from forming separate churches, and from building chapels, in the vain hope of being able in a few years to go back into the Church, from which they had been ejected in 1662. The Baptists, moreover, being obliged to stand for religious liberty, and being held together by a form which had nothing to do with special theological views, were more free than most in their discussion of some of the doctrines of the time, and while many of them had a good deal of sympathy with the peculiar views of the Quakers, some were even leaning towards Socinianism. For the most part they were of a somewhat humbler social standing than the Presbyterians and Independents, and so had fewer settled ministers among them, and had much more largely to depend upon the ministrations of their own members. It does not, indeed, follow that these were inferior in zeal or ability, and it must not be forgotten that among these humble preachers was John Bunyan. He had been released from Bedford Gaol by the "Indulgence" of 1672, and continued to be the head of the Baptist congregation in Bedford till his death in 1688. The Baptists themselves were not all united in one body; for some called themselves "Particular Baptists," holding the old Calvinistic doctrine that salvation was only possible to the particular persons who were "elect;" while others were "General Baptists," believing in salvation being open to all; and a few were called "Seventh-day Baptists," from their keeping the Sabbath according to the old Jewish custom, on the seventh day of the week instead of on the first.

The greater part of the Old Dissent, however, was comprised among the Presbyterians and Independents. They were not only the most numerous, but the most learned and the most wealthy, and thus had most social and political influence. Under the Commonwealth both these parties had been included in the Church; at the Restoration they had both alike been ejected; and through the many years of trouble and persecution which followed, they had stood together as brethren, had shared the same fortunes, and their differences had then appeared very trivial matters. So, when the era of toleration came, there were many places in which they united, and simply formed one congregation, and built one meeting-house. For, by this time, the English Presbyterians had come to be practically almost as "congregational" in their church government as the Independents. Government by presbyteries had never been able to be carried out at all fully, and though the Presbyterians still professed to stand for that, and kept their old name, they had been so long accustomed to act alone, or simply in friendly association with their neighbouring churches, that when the time came that they might, if they chose, have organized after a strict Presbyterian fashion, they had no longer any real desire to do so.

This made it easier for them to unite with the Independents, and at first it seemed as if the two bodies would gradually amalgamate, and their separate life be merged in one common name of "Protestant Dissenters."

This was not to be, however. It is true that their original differences had been gradually passing out of sight, but meanwhile other differences had been growing up which, though not very perceptible at first, gradually caused them to drift apart. In the earlier years of the Commonwealth, the Presbyterians had taken high ground for the duty of the civil government to uphold religious truth, and to punish and repress all departure from it, while the Independents had advocated the principle of toleration. But, in the course of time, the Presbyterians had become a good deal more liberal. Much variety of opinion had sprung up among them. The Calvinism with which they started had been softening down, and their leading men, especially the venerable Richard Baxter, had come to see that it would not do, and was not right, to draw the lines of religious truth too rigidly. Baxter was all for unity. He wanted to see one great Church in which all earnest Christians might join, and the thought of this, and the hope that it might some day be realized, accustomed the Presbyterians to lay as little stress as possible on differences of opinion. So much had this come to be the common temper among them, that they still retained a good deal of it, even when they found that their dream of comprehension was not to be realized in the national Church. On the other hand, the Independents, under the leadership of Dr. John Owen, a keen, logical, dogmatic divine, kept more closely to Calvinism, and generally held stricter views, and stood more firmly for the old ways, than their Presbyterian brethren.

In the general rejoicings at the toleration which had at last come, these differing tendencies were almost forgotten. Both parties felt so glad and so brotherly in their new freedom, that it seemed the most natural thing for them to unite. If the Church would not have them, they could at least have one another, and they would be the stronger together. So, at first, in many a large town and country village one Protestant Dissenting meeting-house was reared, by Presbyterians and Independents together.

When, however, it came to living and working steadily in union, their old differences soon began to make themselves felt. The Presbyterian element would have things left more free and open; did not like drawing rigid lines of membership; would let all who attended the services and supported them, join in the Communion, and have a voice in the affairs of the Church. The old Independents among them, on the other hand, wanted to keep the Communion and the management exclusively to "Church members," and were more particular about the soundness of the ministers, in the old doctrines of the Westminster Confession. So it came about, that within twenty or thirty years after the first founding of these united congregations, it commonly happened that the people of this stricter way of thinking withdrew, and formed separate congregations of their own under the Independent name, and on distinct Calvinistic principles. These very separations widened the differences between the two denominations. The Independents became more closely orthodox, and more careful in examining their members and their ministers; and, moreover, put stringent conditions in the trust deeds of their new chapels, to prevent any people ever getting possession of them, who did not continue to hold the same views as the founders; while the Presbyterians, left to themselves, became still less particular as to the exact doctrines held by their members or ministers, refused to have any creeds connected with their places of worship, and instead of tying up their chapel property to those who should continue to hold the same doctrines, usually settled the trust deeds simply "for the worship of Almighty God," leaving those who should come after them to form their own opinions, and to worship in their own way.

It was not, indeed, till much later in the last century that such differences entirely separated these bodies from association and fellowship; but even from a short time after the Act of Toleration they were gradually drifting apart, and "the three denominations" of the Old Dissent were more and more becoming three separate Churches.

CHAPTER XXXI.

THE AWAKENING OF THE PEOPLE—WHITEFIELD AND WESLEY.

FIFTY years wore away after the passing of the Act of Toleration, without any great event taking place in the religious life of England. They were fifty years of gradual weakening and decay, both to the Church and to the Dissenters. The Church had never recovered from that great self-inflicted blow of 1662, when two thousand of the ablest and most pious of the clergy were cast out. Some of the best clergymen had come nobly to the front at the time of the Revolution, and William and Mary had promoted good men to be bishops, but the mass of the clergy had lost ground throughout the country, and while the most learned seldom lived or worked in their parishes, a great many of the rank and file were mere hangers-on of the country squires—drinking and fox-hunting parsons, with very little religion about them. Meanwhile, the Nonconformists also had very much decayed in life and influence. The quiet times which had succeeded the days of persecution, told upon both the ministers and their flocks. The old zealous Puritan life had got chilled down into a quiet plodding respectability, which was content to go on without much progress or much effort. The old congregations still held together, and in the towns they were still powerful by the adhesion of the trading classes; but the common people had never taken very kindly to Puritanism, even when it was strong and zealous, and it produced still less impression upon them now that it was passing into a stage of formalism and feebleness.

Meantime, while Church and Dissent were thus alike, year by year, growing more powerless for any strong religious work, the need of some such work among the people was continually becoming more urgent. Great changes were coming over the face of the country. England, in those fifty years of peace and mainly of prosperity, had become quite a different country from what it had been in the days of the Tudors or the Stuarts. Trade had marvellously increased. The great manufacturing industries were springing up. Mines were being opened in places that before had been lonely country wastes. All these were drawing together large populations. Manchester, Liverpool, Birmingham, Newcastle, had formerly been little more than villages, but now were becoming large and crowded towns; while in many parts, both north and south, great colliery districts were growing up. Life was very hard and rough in these new places. There were no laws for regulating factories or collieries. Little apprentices of nine or ten years old were worked like slaves. Women laboured, almost naked, in the coal pits. Fighting, bear-baiting, drinking, were the only amusements the people knew. There were no day schools, except a few grammar-schools founded at the time of the Reformation, and the middle-class academies kept by the Nonconformist ministers. Sunday schools had not yet been thought of. Religiously these great new populations were utterly neglected. In many a place that had come to number its inhabitants by tens or scores of thousands, there was still simply the one little parish church which sufficed when it was a small country village. For fifty years hardly a new church had been built. Nor had any new chapels been built by the Dissenters, after the first outburst of zeal. They had enough to do to keep from declining; and though they worked on in a quiet, respectable, earnest way among their own people, they did very little for those great masses around them, who were growing up in a lost, neglected, brutal, ignorant life, such as in the present day we can hardly imagine.

And yet there were, here and there throughout the country, numbers of people of very deep, true piety. Religion was not dead. The nobility were for the most part indifferent to it or scoffers at it, and the tone of morality in fashionable circles was very coarse and low; while the masses of the people knew little about religion. But the middle and trading classes of the country were sound at heart, and here and there were country parishes in which good pious men and women kept alive the spirit, which was by-and-by to go forth and speak the word of life, and awaken the people to a better time.

Such a parish was that of Epworth, in Lincolnshire, where, during the first quarter of last century was living, as rector, the Rev. Samuel Wesley. Both he and his wife, though now warm adherents of the Church, had come of good Puritan stock, being the children of Nonconformist ministers who had been ejected in 1662; and they were persons of great piety, firmness, and tenderness.

Here in 1703 was born to them a little child whom they named John,—their second son. Brought up under a beautiful religious influence, which was deepened by a wonderful escape from being burnt to death when he was six years old, which his mother laid to heart as a special mercy from God calling for special care of his soul, John grew up a thoughtful, religious lad. He went to the Charterhouse School in London, and then, at seventeen, to Christ Church College, Oxford. Nothing special appeared in him here. He threw himself eagerly into his studies, and took a good position as a young man of keen logical mind and scholarly tastes. It was only after five years of this college life, and while he was preparing for ordination, that a change began to take place in him. He began to study religious books; Jeremy Taylor's "Holy Living and Holy Dying" and Law's "Serious Call," absorbed his leisure hours and gave him a new feeling of what a really religious life might be. He tells how it grew upon his heart, that it is impossible to be a Christian by halves. He had much inward distress. An old man whom he travelled many miles to see, chided him for his solitary life. "Sir," he said, "you seek to serve God and go to heaven. Remember you cannot serve Him alone. *The Bible knows nothing of solitary religion.*" John Wesley never forgot those words. They were the key-note of much of the most helpful work of his after-life. He went back to Oxford, and joined himself with his younger brother Charles and several others, in a little society for mutual help in religious life and work; and together they busied themselves in looking after the younger students, visiting the prisoners in the gaol, and taking care of the poor people in the workhouse. They soon became the scoff of their college; they were nicknamed the "holy club," the "Bible-bigots," and especially the "Methodists." But they were strengthened by their father, who told them not to mind it any more than "the crackling of thorns under a pot," and they kept right on. More and more they became absorbed in their work. To have money to spend on it, they lived on the hardest fare, spent as little as possible on dress, and when they needed to go to London tramped thither on foot!

The time came when John Wesley and his friends must leave Oxford. His father died. His friends wished him to apply for the living. But he dared not do so. He shrank from such a responsibility. "Two thousand souls!" he said, "I see not how any man living can take care of a hundred!" So he chose another opening, went out to the new Colony of Georgia; tried very hard to leaven the wild, hard, worldly life he found there with his own spirit—but failed; and came back to England, very sad and sick at heart. Like a true man, he laid the blame on himself. "Ah me," he wrote in his journal; "I went to America to convert the Indians, but who shall convert me?"

It was under the influence of some Moravian brethren that he at last found peace. It came to him at one of their meetings, as he heard them speaking of the change which God works in the believing heart. It seemed to him that, as if with a sudden bound of happy faith, his heart became all at once given up to complete and happy trust in Christ. Thenceforth he gave up brooding over his own condition, and thinking of his own state of mind, and simply gave himself up with a freed heart to the service of God in the world.

Such men were sorely needed just then. The life of the poor, in England, was very dark, ignorant, and neglected. Already, one of the little band of those who had prayed and worked together at Oxford—

George Whitefield—had felt the terrible need for something to be done, and, with such a power of preaching as had never been known in England before, was going up and down among the people. Whitefield was not either learned or original, but he had a noble voice, and a grand, rushing eloquence, and his very soul seemed on fire with his longing to win souls to a better life. The very first sermon he ever preached —in Gloucester Cathedral—produced an extraordinary effect. Some one complained to the bishop that it had driven some of the people mad with excitement; but the good bishop simply answered that he hoped the madness would last till the next Sunday. Then Whitefield went to London, and soon became the most famous preacher of his day. Crowds hung upon his words—many going with torches, before it was daylight, to make sure of good places in the churches where he was announced to preach. Benjamin Franklin went on one of these occasions, when there was to be a collection, half despising the popular excitement, and declaring he would not give anything. But even the sober-minded American was excited, and tells how he relented, and at first made up his mind that he would give the coppers he had in his pocket; then thought he would give the silver, and ended by pouring into the plate copper, silver, and gold—all that he had with him. George Whitefield's best work, however, was among the poor. By thousands and thousands they pressed around him, as he stood on some hill-side to preach; and sobs and groans told how deeply they were touched by his warnings and appeals. And yet Whitefield could do little permanently. The people wept, and repented,—and went back to their old lives. There was wanted some one who could not only convert men, but draw them together, strengthen them, organize them, build them up. This was to be the work of John Wesley.

Try to form some idea of Wesley as he was at this time—no raw inexperienced youth—this was in 1739, and he was thirty-six years of age, and older still in the deep experiences of life. A small, spare, wiry man, with a firm resolute mouth, and a bright piercing eye, a quick, commanding sort of way with him, but kept in check by the patient gentleness which his overmastering love of his fellow-creatures had infused into him—his whole presence that of an unmistakable gentleman and scholar. Add to this, a clear voice that could ring out like a trumpet, a simple direct style of speech, great readiness in argument; and all these powers held promptly and resolutely at the service of a fervent piety, and intense pity for all careless and sinful souls, which made him willing to face anything, to go through anything, so that he might turn them to a Christian life.

But he could not find his work all at once. The fact is, he was full of High-Church prejudices. He says, himself, that, at first, he should have thought the saving of souls almost a sin unless it were done in a church. But his work was too strong for the churches. His plain, searching sermons gave offence. "Sir, you must preach here no more," they said to him, in more than one place. Just then it was that Whitefield, being about to set out to America, wrote to him to come and take up his work among the colliers at Kingswood, near Bristol. Long and anxious was John Wesley's deliberation about it. It seemed like a call from God; but to go in that irregular way, and preach out of doors, seemed a dreadful cross to take up. However, it came more and more upon him that it *was* the will of God, and so he went; and, the day after Whitefield left he writes, "I submitted to be yet more vile, and proclaimed in the highways the glad tidings of salvation, speaking from a little eminence in a ground adjoining the city (Bristol) to about three thousand people."

Thus, the ice was broken, and Wesley was one of those who, having made up his mind that it was right to do a thing, would not do it by halves. Soon, he took a warmer place than Whitefield himself in the love of the people. From one place and another came urgent requests that he would go and speak among them, and little by little he was led on to that wonderful itinerant ministry of his. With a strange power he spoke to the crowds of rude people who everywhere gathered about him, touched their hearts with a sense of their sinful, miserable state, and showed them the hope that there was for them in the Gospel of Jesus Christ. It was not a Gospel of damnation that he preached, though often he spoke of the fears as well as of the hopes of religion; it was especially the Gospel of the infinite love of God, caring for every poor lost soul, and waiting to receive even the vilest who would repent and believe in Christ.

Such preaching would have been effective under any circumstances, but at that time its effect was tremendous. Of the people to whom he preached, thousands had never heard any preaching of religion at all. There were no Sunday schools, no missionaries or home-visitors in those days, and Wesley's word came with all the power of a new message from God to them. Hither and thither he went, as one opening or another presented itself. His first great journey was northward, through Derbyshire and Yorkshire, preaching everywhere as he went. On a Saturday night he came to Newcastle, and walking through the lower parts of the town, was awe-struck at the degradation which he saw. On the Sunday morning, at seven o'clock, he and John Taylor walked down to Sandgate, in the worst part of the town, and stopping at the end of the street, they began to sing the Hundredth Psalm. A few people came out to see what was the matter, and soon the crowd was gathering till there were twelve or fifteen hundred people. To these he preached, the people standing still, staring and astonished. When he had finished he cried—"I am John Wesley; at five this evening I shall preach here again." When the evening came, the hill-side was covered with the largest crowd he had ever seen; and though his voice could not be heard by half of them, such was the impression, that, when he had done, "the poor people," he says, "were ready to tread me under foot out of pure love and kindness." Years afterwards, when he had numbers of followers there, he still often speaks of them as "the wild, staring, loving society."

That is a good illustration of the way in which he went to work. But it was not only in these great preachings that his work was done. He was possessed by an overpowering anxiety for the souls of men, and he resolved to use perfect openness towards all whom he met. Not a day passed but brought him opportunities. Now it is a companion whom he falls in with on the road; now the ostler, or the hostess and servants of the inn where he is putting up, or the chance company gathered at the public table. Is there a little crowd loitering on the village green as he rides through? He stops, takes out his Bible, has a little service among them. At Epworth, the curate would not let him preach from his father's pulpit, so he stood in the churchyard and preached from his father's grave.

Wherever he thus came, he not only preached, but banded together those who would join him, into little societies. He had no idea of founding a new sect. These were to be merely little lay societies of members of the Church of England; they were to go to their parish church for the Communion, and to attend the Church services; but they were to meet together at other times to have prayer, and take counsel among themselves, and help each other to keep steadfast in this new religious life they had begun together. So their first meeting-rooms were not intended as churches, but only as places where they might gather together in their "classes;" and they had no ministers, only "class leaders" who might pray and talk with them, but on no account preach.

Gradually, however, the work outgrew these first humble ideas, and assumed the character of a vast, independent religious movement. The churches could not hold the crowds that began to resort to them, and in many cases the clergy were angry at this movement which shamed their own indolence, and, indeed, the formal services of the Church could never long have satisfied the strong religious feelings of those who had been aroused by Wesley's preachings. Little by little the idea of dependence on the Church of England passed away, and the societies began to meet for worship and preaching of their own. In much the same way John Wesley's objection to lay-preaching fell to the ground. When he first heard that Thomas Maxfield, one of his most earnest helpers, whom he had left to look after the Society in London, was preaching, he hurried back from a distant journey to stop such a shocking irregularity. But old Mrs. Wesley said to him, "John, take care what you do concerning that young man, for he is as surely called of God to preach as you are; go and hear him yourself." And so he went, and sat in a dark corner of the Moorfields Chapel; and when the sermon was over, he said, "It is the Lord, let him do what seemeth him good." From this time, lay-preaching became one of the great powers of Methodism; in these preachers Wesley himself was multiplied a hundred fold, and the societies became more strong and established.

For a little while at first, all went well; but as the movement began to spread and grow, and attract attention, gradually a fierce opposition arose. The clergy were jealous of this man, angry at his wonderful influence; they repelled his followers from the Communion; then they began to stir up persecution against him. Of course there were plenty of the mob everywhere, who resented the drawing away of their companions from their old ways, and were only too ready for disturbance and riot. Thus, at Colne, the clergyman, when Wesley was announced to be coming, put up the following notice: "Notice is hereby given that if any man is mindful to enlist into His Majesty's service under command of the Rev. George White for the defence of the Church of England, let him repair to the drumhead at the Cross, where each man shall have a pint of beer in advance, and other proper encouragement!" So "encouraged" the mob savagely beat Wesley and his followers, some of whom were thrown into the river. Thus, too, at Poole, there may still be seen among the churchwardens' accounts, the item: "Expenses at Ann

Gartrell's on driving the Methodists, nine shillings." In London the mob tried to unroof the Foundry Chapel, and threw wildfire and crackers into the meeting-room at Chelsea, but the magistrates there promptly did their duty and soon repressed these outrages. In the country, however, there was hardly any protection. At Wednesbury, in the Staffordshire "black country," a good society was gathered, and the clergyman, Mr. Egginton, at first was very kind and friendly; but by-and-by some irregularity occurring he became very bitter against them, and the magistrates taking part with him, the society was for months subject to constant outrages. When John Wesley was at Birmingham he heard of this, and as his custom was always to look danger in the face, he went straight there. He preached without hindrance; but afterwards a mob gathered about the house where he was, crying, "Bring out the minister, we *will* have the minister!" Getting the ringleaders into the house, however, Wesley soon calmed them, and by-and-by the crowd which had been raging for his life, became a sort of bodyguard to him. But then came upon them the Walsall mob, and his new friends were overpowered, and Wesley himself, unable to get a hearing, was in the midst of a rabble who beat him cruelly and tried to throw him down. Shop doors and house doors were closed against him; he was dragged back by the hair of his head, and the cry "Kill him!" arose. He thought the end was come, and broke out into prayer; when, struck to the heart by his look and words, the very man who just before had been the fiercest of his assailants, suddenly cried, "Sir, they shall not touch a hair of your head." This man had been a prize-fighter.

Incidents of this kind marked every step of the progress of Methodism. For years Wesley and his helpers went with their lives in their hands. John Nelson, of Birstall, was impressed for a soldier by the instigation of the vicar of the parish, who wanted him out of the way, and he was treated with shameful cruelty. But the brave man would not fight, and would not drill, and kept reproving the officers and men for swearing, so fearlessly, that at last they got tired of persecuting him, and he was set free.

No part of the story of the sufferings and labours of the early Methodists is more striking, than that of Wesley's preaching in Cornwall. Cornwall, in those times, seemed almost out of the world, and its people were rude and lawless, chiefly engaged in wrecking and smuggling. Wesley's principle was, to go not only where he was needed, but where he was *most* needed, so thither he went with John Nelson as his companion. At Falmouth the mob rose, and the house where he stayed was attacked by privateersmen, who broke in, filled the passage, and shouted to bring him out. Wesley stepped forward into the midst of them, saying, "Here I am! which of you has anything to say to me? To which of you have I done any wrong? To you? or you? or you?" and so he came bareheaded into the street, and went on speaking, till the captain swore that not a man should touch him. Nor were such outrages the only trial there; the people crowded to hear him, but no one offered him either food or shelter; sometimes he was refused either, even for money, and he and his companion had to pick blackberries for a meal. At St. Ives, John Nelson tells, "Mr. Wesley and I lay on the floor; he had my greatcoat for his pillow, and I had Burkitt's 'Notes on the New Testament' for mine. After being here near three weeks, one morning, about three o'clock, Mr. Wesley turned over, and finding me awake, clapped me on the side, saying, 'Brother Nelson, let us be of good cheer; I have one whole side yet, the skin is only off on one side!'"

Gradually, as is ever the case, the courage and sweetness with which all these things were borne, overcame opposition. The rough usage only lasted for a few years, and then John Wesley became a revered and honoured man. Still his work went on; his brother Charles was the hymn-writer for the new societies, but John was the life and soul of them, and as they kept increasing and multiplying until Methodism became one of the great powers of English life, he was still the leader and head. He grew into an old man; still he lived with the same simplicity and the same activity. When he was a student at Oxford, and his income was but £30, he lived on £28 and gave away £2. When he had become a fellow and tutor there, and his income was above £100, he still had lived on £28 and gave away the rest. And so when he was seventy years old, above his bare food and lodging he kept but £5 19*s*. for clothes, and gave away £593, the surplus of what his books brought him; and year by year he did the same to the end. His life was as active as it was simple and frugal. At eighty years old, he rose in the morning at four; travelled from thirty to sixty or seventy miles a day, on horseback, preached every day three or four times, and wherever he came was ceaselessly occupied, visiting the sick, talking with friends and inquirers, and superintending the societies. And eighty-one came, and eighty-two, and eighty-three, and he was still the same. "Lord, let me not live to be useless," was his prayer. Still, at eighty-six, he managed to go from place to place; and at eighty-seven he writes, "My eyes are dim, my movements are slow and weak; however, blessed be God, I do not slack my labours, I can preach and write still." So it was for yet another year; crowds packed the places where he was to preach, and listened breathlessly as the old, old man stood feebly up, supported by a minister on each side of him, and in his trembling tones, like one upon the threshold of eternity, pleaded that men should give their whole hearts to God, that his people should help each other, and keep to their old simple ways of prayer and song. And then at length came the last feebleness, and on March 2, 1791, a fortnight after preaching his last sermon—

"The weary springs of life stood still at last."

CHAPTER XXXII.

THE FREE INQUIRERS OF LAST CENTURY—THEOPHILUS LINDSEY.

One of the most interesting features in the story of religious life in the eighteenth century, is the movement which was continually going on, both outside of the Established Church and within it, towards a freer and more reasonable way of looking at religion. For, though it was an age of religious decay, and the Church of England was suffering from being so completely under the control of the State, there was a good deal of interest in religious questions. The clergy were not all mere farmers, or jolly "Church and King" squires; and though the more learned among them often knew more of Homer than of their Bibles—still, here and there were good and thoughtful men. who studied the great questions of religion, and were feeling their way to something better than the orthodoxy which had been settled by the Act of Uniformity, and embodied in the Prayer-book and the Thirty-nine Articles. If the awakening of the people to religious life, by Whitefield and the Wesleys, was the most important movement of the century, next to it must be ranked the movement, helped on by many men and many minds, by which the various doctrines of the Churches were investigated, and cleared of much that was weak and false, and the simple truths of religion were put in a clearer and stronger light.

This work was really begun by a class of men who are not generally set down as having much to do with the story of religion—and yet in reality religion owes a great deal to them. At the beginning of last century a number of writers gradually came into notice who are commonly known as "the English Freethinkers." The philosopher, John Locke, had, only a little while before, in the last years of the seventeenth century, published his work on "The Reasonableness of Christianity," in which, without attacking the doctrines of the Church, he had endeavoured to show that the essentials required by Jesus Christ himself were so few and reasonable, that all Christians might unite upon them. This work caused great discussion, and was bitterly attacked by many of the clergy, inasmuch as it really dealt a blow at the general system by which their Church was maintained in a sort of superiority to all others. But Locke's work was followed up by other writers, who, appealing to the same grounds of common sense, or, as they called it, "right reason," went much further than he had done, and openly attacked a great many of the Church doctrines. Thus, John Toland, in a work entitled "Christianity not Mysterious," protested against the so-called mysteries of the creeds with a boldness that raised a great outcry and caused his book to be publicly burnt; and for many years he was perpetually bringing out some new pamphlet or book of pungent criticism, on theological questions. Lord Shaftesbury, a cold, polished writer, though never directly attacking the Church, yet continually alluded to religion and the Bible, in his general writings, in a way which tended to overthrow the mysterious awe in which the clergy would have them kept. Dr. Matthew Tindall, in his "Christianity as old as Creation," based religion on human nature, and argued that Christianity was not an entirely new religion first revealed by Jesus Christ, but simply the everlasting truth of God, cleared by Christ from corruptions and traditions. Anthony Collins and Thomas Chubb are others of the same school. They have, all of them, a bad name, from the abuse that was heaped upon them by the clergy, and have usually been treated since, as they were treated in their own day, as enemies of Christianity. Yet, in reality they were, almost all of them, honest and earnest men, who were doing their best to free Christianity from doctrines which they believed to be no teachings of Christ, but mere corruptions of after ages. They were all sincere believers in God, and wrote about Christ with respect and reverence.

Though these men did not convert very many to their views, they did a great deal of good by arousing public attention to these religious subjects, and forcing the clergy to study them more carefully and to write about them. Some of the greatest works of Bishop Berkeley and Bishop Butler, among Churchmen, and of Dr. Nathaniel Lardner among the Presbyterians, were called forth by the writings of the Freethinkers. Thus the whole subject of religion and of the Bible was put in a new light, and began to be studied in a more reasonable and thorough way; and it may be said, that from this time, dates that more scholarly and scientific investigation of the doctrines and history of religion, which has ever since been carried on with increasing breadth and freedom.

It was not only outside the Church that such writers as Locke and Toland met with earnest readers. Their works found their way into the study of many a parsonage, and many thoughtful clergymen began to see that there was a great deal of truth in them. They set many a mind looking into doctrines which had been taken for granted, age after age, without any real foundation, and so gradually there came to be a number of clergymen who doubted or rejected this point or that. Many were beginning to see that the doctrine of the Trinity, as it was minutely laid down in the Athanasian Creed, was not really any teaching of Christ or his Apostles; while others came to have more reasonable views about the Bible, to see that it could not all be taken as the inspired word of God, but that mixed up with it is a good deal of allegory and tradition. For a time these new views did not create any difficulty. It was very easy for a clergyman to hold almost any opinion he liked on such matters, if he did not make much public stir about them. If he was only a good neighbour and a pleasant fellow, and not "Methodistical"—the one intolerable fault in the eyes of Churchmen—he might explain away the Athanasian Creed, or even leave it out altogether, and the neighbouring squires would think none the less of him, while the bishops were too fond of their ease to meddle unless there was some very urgent necessity. Thus there came to be a great deal of what was called "Latitudinarianism" in the Church. With some it was held in private; others made no secret of it; and many tales were told of the way in which one or another held up the creed to ridicule, or got over the difficulty of having to read it as part of the service. Some made the parish-clerk read the sentences which they would not read themselves. One clergyman, on being commanded to restore it to its place in the service, set it to the tune of a well-known hunting-song, and sang it; while another prefaced his reading by saying to the congregation, "This is the Creed of St.

Athanasius, and I am obliged to read it; but it is not my creed, and I hope it is not your creed!" Such evasions of the matter, however, did not raise the clergy in the estimation of the people; and to some of these "Latitudinarian" clergymen, of honest and thoughtful minds, it gradually became very painful to be constantly professing one doctrine in the Church service, while in reality they held something very different. It must be remembered that, by the Act of Uniformity, every clergyman was not only obliged to use the Prayer-book and read the Creeds, but, on entering into a living, he had to read the Articles as well, and solemnly declare his "unfeigned assent and consent" to everything contained therein; and it began to be asked, how could honest men, who had changed their opinions, continue to hold their livings in the face of having subscribed such a declaration. So, as time went on, it began to be questioned whether the terms of "subscription" should not be altered and made a little less strict, so as to meet the difficulties of these Latitudinarians.

Of these more thoughtful clergymen, and of the movement for making subscription a little easier so as to satisfy their consciences, there is no better representative than Theophilus Lindsey; certainly he is their noblest representative, because, when it was clearly seen that no change in the law would be made, he was the one—almost the only one—who felt that it was impossible honestly to remain in the Church, and who, therefore, bravely gave up his living and went out.

When Theophilus Lindsey first came to be known as one of these liberal clergymen, he was vicar of Catterick, a little parish in Yorkshire.

He was the son of a tradesman at Middlewich, in

Cheshire, where he was born in 1723. His training was not of the kind most likely to make a strong man, for his mother had been brought up by the old Countess of Huntingdon, and the great family were still very kind to her, sent her boy to school, and then to Cambridge, and used to have him amongst them in his vacations, at their mansion, as a sort of petted dependent, with my Lord This and my Lady That. Then, when he left the University, he was made domestic chaplain to the Duke of Somerset, and afterwards tutor to the young Duke of Northumberland, and finally settled in a comfortable family living. A kindly, scholarly, refined man, a favourite among them all, this was just the kind of lot which was about least likely to make a man deeply anxious in seeking the truth, or especially conscientious in suffering for it. His parish was just the kind of berth for the genteel clergyman of those days; there was plenty of good society, and his predecessor had been one of the easy-going school, a man who maintained a bowling green and kept open house for the neighbouring squires. But Theophilus Lindsey's was one of those natures that do not easily spoil. Through all his patronizing by noble personages, he kept his simplicity and his unworldliness. When he entered on the living, he quietly set himself there to the earnest, faithful life of a true minister of Christ. He, and his wife, the daughter of a grand Yorkshire archdeacon, but a lady like-minded with himself, began practising the utmost frugality, that they might have as much as possible to spare for doing good amongst the poor. In a little time, however, he changed this Dorsetshire living for the one at Catterick; and here he still worked on in the same fashion, preaching, visiting the sick, lending and giving books, helping the poor with medicines, beloved by and loving all. His ministry at Catterick is worth remembering, if only for the fact that here, in 1764, he opened the first Sunday School in England. Robert Raikes, of Gloucester, is usually named as the founder of Sunday Schools, but Raikes did not begin his school till 1780, while, sixteen years before, Lindsey was, every Sunday, in a room of his own house, gathering the poor children of his parish together for instruction.

During all this time, however, a cloud was rising up which was beginning to darken the good man's happiness. He was a deep student of the Scriptures; and it had begun to grow upon his mind, that there was no warrant in them for some of the doctrines which he had subscribed in the Church Articles, and which he had to acknowledge every time he read the Church Service. Especially was his mind disturbed on the subject of the Trinity. It was a question on which, years before, in his Dorsetshire living, he had not felt quite easy. Now, in his Yorkshire parish, with fuller study, he gradually became convinced that it was a mere corruption of Christianity, and that there is simply one Almighty God, He whom Christ addressed as the Heavenly Father. He consulted some of his brother clergymen about it. To his surprise he found that many of them thought as he did; but one and all made light of the matter, and advised him not to trouble himself about it! He found that his own father-in-law, Archdeacon Blackburne, shared his views, but the archdeacon had no idea of giving up his living for it; and Lindsey's friends urged upon him that most insidious argument of all, that, for the sake of the Church itself, he ought on no account to think of leaving it, but to stay in it and work with those who were trying to widen and reform it. His mind was not easy, but for the time he gave way; and finding that a number of clergymen were getting up a petition to Parliament for relief from subscription to the Articles, and for permission to make changes in the liturgy, he remained where he was and joined heartily in their movement. His father-in-law, Archdeacon Blackburne, had, a little while before, published a book called "The Confessional," in which he had argued very strongly against the setting up of confessions of faith in Protestant churches, and especially against requiring subscription to the Church Articles; and this led to a meeting of the clergy in London, and the formation of an association for petitioning Parliament and obtaining some change in the law. This association, from the place where it first met, was called "The Feathers' Tavern Association." Mr. Lindsey took charge of the petition which they drew up, and himself went with it up and down Yorkshire, endeavouring to get his brother clergymen to sign it. He had a very poor success, however. Most of them did not want any alteration, many bitterly attacked him, and of those who wished for some change, the greater number were so timid that they did not like to give their names. The result was, that the Feathers' Tavern Petition only received about 200 signatures from clergymen, with about fifty others, and though many of the clergymen were men of very high reputation, and though the petition was supported by some of the ablest members of Parliament, the House of Commons refused, by a vote of 217 to 71, even to receive it. The petitioners generally said they must try again, and keep on trying till they got the reform they wanted—anything rather than go out. Alone of them all, Theophilus Lindsey saw his duty, and did it; he saw clearly enough that there was no chance whatever of any change being made, and that it could not be right for him to go on repeating, Sunday by Sunday, prayers and creeds about the Trinity which he no longer believed; so, without taking any further counsel, he sent in his resignation to the bishop. Everything was against him; the bishop wrote him a long, kind letter, urging him to remain in the Church where he was. But his resolution was fixed, and he kept to it. His brother liberals protested; old Archdeacon Blackburne stormed; his aristocratic patrons laughed incredulously; his poor parishioners pleaded and wept, but all in vain. In December 1773 he gave up his vicarage and left Catterick. He had spent his income so freely in charity among the poor, that he had to sell his furniture and books in order to meet the expense of journeying to London; and he went forth into the world with just twenty pounds a year to fall back upon.

It is not easy to realize in these days all that such a change meant then. It was not merely poverty; it was not merely the change from a good living, in a pleasant country parsonage, to a poor London lodging, and no certain living at all; it was that he was so utterly alone. He avowed that he did not believe in the Trinity,—he was a Unitarian, and he wished to preach Unitarianism. A generation later there were scores of Unitarian congregations, which would have welcomed him to their pulpits, but at that time there was not a single one! The old Presbyterian congregations were mostly coming to that way of thinking; here and there a Presbyterian minister was openly preaching it, like Dr. Priestley, who was then minister of the Mill Hill congregation in Leeds, and whose friendship Mr. Lindsey had already made. But even among these Presbyterian congregations it was a strange and novel thing, and there was not one place of avowed Unitarian worship in the kingdom.

Theophilus Lindsey resolved to establish one. The mere project of such a thing aroused attention. To deny the Trinity was still a crime punishable by law; and though the law had for a long time not been enforced, still Lindsey's public proposal brought it to mind again; however, he went right on. He hired an old auction-room in a little street off the Strand, friends helped him with money—Dissenters, for the most part—hardly a penny did his old Church friends give him—and the room was fitted up as a chapel. But, even then, he and his supporters had hard work to persuade the Middlesex magistrates to license it for preaching; they did not dare to make any public announcement of its opening; serious fears were entertained of a disturbance, and for months it was known that an emissary of the Government attended to report what was said and done, to the authorities.

Lindsey's friends had prophesied that if he left the Church his usefulness would be gone, and that he could do far more to advance his views by remaining where he was, like the rest of them. Time showed who was right. Of all those Feathers' Tavern petitioners, the only one who made any mark upon the religious thought of the time was Theophilus Lindsey, the one who went out. The rest are forgotten. Their liberal views, contradicted by their own words every time they signed the Articles or repeated the Creeds, made little impression; Parliament never made any change in subscription, and the whole Latitudinarian movement gradually died away.

In that little auction-room, Lindsey, whom men might think wrong, but whom they respected as an honest man, succeeded beyond his expectations. That Essex

Street Chapel became a notable place; to it gathered numbers of the leading liberal thinkers of the time, barristers, members of Parliament, scientific men; and from the earnest, thoughtful, honest preaching of its minister went forth an influence that was carried to many a part of England, and not only taught men to think, but taught them to be more open and faithful in speaking out their thoughts. There, for twenty years, Theophilus Lindsey laboured on in a happy, prosperous work, till he was seventy years of age; and yet for fifteen years longer, he lived on among the same warm circle of friends, helping on the cause for which he had left the Church, till his death in 1808.

CHAPTER XXXIII.

THE MOVEMENT IN PRESBYTERIANISM—DR. PRIESTLEY.

The life of Joseph Priestley is not only interesting as that of one of the leading thinkers of his time, but as carrying us through one of the most curious stories of religious change, that the later history of religion in England has to show. It is the story of how the congregations of the old Presbyterian dissent, gradually passed from the Calvinism of their original founders, to the very different views which are now known as Unitarianism.

This change was the gradual work of above half a century. It has been already told, how, when the Act of Toleration enabled the Nonconformists to build meeting-houses, and form regular congregations, the English Presbyterians (who must never be confounded with the sect of the same name in Scotland) were already becoming rather less rigid in their orthodoxy, than the Independents and Baptists. They had to a great extent given up Calvinism; they did not like to tie down those who should come after them to hold any special doctrines, by insisting upon them in the trust-deeds of their meeting-houses; and, they were letting go the distinction of "Church-membership," and allowing all who attended the services to join in the communion. They were not yet Unitarians, indeed Unitarianism was still actually punishable by law; but the "Socinian controversy," which raged warmly, with hosts of tracts and pamphlets, about the end of the seventeenth century, left its mark upon them in making them unwilling to press hard in doctrinal matters on any one. The Independents blamed the Presbyterians very much for this laxity, and in many places where the two bodies had at first united, the Independents had withdrawn and formed separate congregations. Still, however, the two bodies acted publicly together, but the difference between them kept increasing, for the Independents became more and more strict in requiring a profession of faith from their ministers and members, while the Presbyterians were disposed to leave men to read the Scriptures for themselves, and form their own opinions about the truth without committing themselves to creeds or statements of doctrine. In 1719 there was a great debate in the Salters' Hall, London, which is one of the land-marks of the change. One of the ministers of the Dissenting meeting-house at Exeter had become an Arian, having ceased to believe in the Trinity, regarding Christ as more than Man indeed, but not as actually God. The Exeter congregation was divided on these subjects. So the question of whether, holding such opinions, he could remain their minister, was referred to the Dissenting ministers (including both Presbyterians and Independents) of London. Very long and earnest were the discussions held by these London ministers on the subject, at their chapel in the Salters' Hall, the Independents generally insisting that a man holding such opinions could not be a minister among them, and urging that all ministers must sign a declaration of belief in the Trinity. The Presbyterians, however, for the most part voted against any subscription or confession of faith at all. Most of them still believed in the doctrine, but they said that they had left the Church of England for conscience sake, and they would not give up their Christian liberty, or take it away from others. They set up, as the only rule that they would allow, the authority of Scripture, leaving each man to interpret the Bible for himself.

From the time of this great discussion, which was watched and talked of by Dissenters all through the country, the gradual change which was already going on among the Presbyterians became still more marked. As time went on, more and more of them became Arians. Even those who still held by the more orthodox views did not make them very prominent in their preaching, disusing the old language about the Trinity, and simply keeping to the words of Scripture. That was their great point: let every one read the Bible for himself, they said; keep to what Christ taught, and then there will not be so much to disagree upon, and people cannot go far wrong. Mr. Haynes, one of the ministers of the Presbyterian congregation in Sheffield, about 1755, was once spoken to by one of his congregation, who said he should like to hear some of "the *old* doctrine." "Yes, sir," the minister answered, "the older the better; mine is as old as the Apostles!"

It was just at this time that a young minister named Joseph Priestley was entering on a course which was by-and-by to make a good deal of noise in the world, and to exercise a great influence on these Presbyterian congregations.

Joseph Priestley was born in 1733, of a plain family of clothmakers at Fieldhead, near Leeds. They were a genuine old Puritan stock—strong Independents—the mother a woman of especially tender piety, and deep conscientiousness. Years after, Dr. Priestley used to tell how, when he was a child of seven years old, his mother made him take back a pin which he had brought away from his uncle's house. So he grew up through a grave Puritan training; instructed in the Westminster Catechism by his father; at school with the Parish clergyman, who taught him Latin and Greek, and on holiday afternoons learning Hebrew from the Dissenting minister—and dreaming of the time when he might perhaps be a minister. Strong diet, this, for a sensitive, thoughtful lad. One effect of it was, that, before he was well out of his childhood, being unable to feel what those about him described as "conversion," he got it into his head that he must be among the lost. Another effect was, that, having already begun to think for himself, he found himself unable to make sufficient profession of faith to be received as a communicant at the little meeting-house. He wanted to join, and the minister was willing, but the "elders" refused him, because he could not say that he believed that all the human race deserved the pains of Hell for ever, on account of Adam's sin! So he must not go to the Lord's table! That was how they managed matters in those days.

However, in due time he went to a little Dissenting academy at Daventry, where he studied for the ministry three years. A curious little school of theology it was, where one tutor was orthodox, and the other heretical—verging towards Arianism; and where every question was frankly discussed, between the tutors and the little group of students in a friendly, but perfectly free spirit.

At the age of twenty-two he left the academy, and entered on his ministry at Needham Market, a little country town in Suffolk. It was not a very hopeful beginning, for the people were stiff, and suspicious of heresy, and could only give him £30 a year. But he was glad even of this "day of small things," for he was not much of a preacher, and had an impediment in his speech; so he went hopefully to work, and did his best.

He had a hard time of it, however, and in three years was glad of a change. He was asked to Sheffield to preach "on trial," but the congregation there could discern nothing in him but a very ordinary man with a very bad delivery, and chose instead a flowery preacher from Diss, in Norfolk, while Joseph Priestley was glad to go to a small charge at Nantwich, in Cheshire. Thence, in three years more, he was called to a professorship in the Dissenting academy at Warrington, recently started by some of the more liberal Nonconformists.

These years, both of ministry and tutorship, were busy years to his mind. He was gifted with a rare love of knowledge, and a restless, persevering spirit of inquiry; and, from the beginning, he was spelling his way into all kinds of scientific and literary pursuits. Nothing came amiss to him. While keeping school at Nantwich, his mind fastened on some of the deeper subjects involved in grammar, and he wrote a treatise on "the Theory of Language." At Warrington, he was busy with history, laws, and criticism. Then, going to London, and being introduced to Dr. Price and Benjamin Franklin, he became deeply interested in electricity and chemistry. He began his experiments under great disadvantages, for he was very poor, and had to be content with imperfect, home-made apparatus, yet he became very eminent in these subjects. So his name kept rising among men of science. When Captain Cook was setting off on his second voyage of discovery, Priestley was asked to accompany him as the scientific observer of the expedition; and he would have gone, but he was objected to by some of the clergy on account of his religious opinions, and the appointment was cancelled!

The fact was that the same free and fearless spirit of investigation, which was leading him to new discoveries in science, was leading him also to new positions in religion. Severely truthful, unable to persuade himself that he held a doctrine unless he really did believe it, looking with a clear, unshrinking gaze into all the opinions which in his youth he had taken for granted, he found that in many things he could not believe as the most of people about him did. First, he rejected the doctrine of Original Sin, and ceased to believe that man's nature is so lost and ruined by inherited tendencies to evil, as the orthodoxy of the time made out. Then he searched into the doctrine of the Atonement, and could not find it in Scripture; it seemed to him to be the Bible teaching that men are forgiven for their own repentance and amendment, and not because of Christ's having been punished in their stead. Then, the doctrine of the Trinity was inquired into, and as he could not find it taught by Christ, he straightway investigates the rise of it some centuries after Christ's time, and denounces it as one of the corruptions of the Church. And yet, while he was thus busy, in some matters, pulling down, in others he was most earnestly building up. His scientific pursuits brought him much into acquaintance with the scientific men and philosophers of the time, and he found them almost all inclined to treat religion as an ignorant superstition. In Paris most of them were professed Atheists, and they told him that he "was the only person they had ever met with of whose understanding they had any opinion, who professed to believe Christianity." Priestley did a great deal of good among this kind of people, for he was never ashamed of his faith; he always stood up for Christianity. He gloried in maintaining that religion, properly regarded, was just as reasonable as science; and we find him turning from his treatises on Electricity or Oxygen to write addresses on Family Prayer, or "Letters to a philosophical unbeliever."

So his life went on, in its busy round of ever-widening usefulness. After six years at Warrington Academy, he was chosen minister of the great Dissenting congregation at Mill Hill, Leeds, where he spent about the same period, and among many warm friends counted that vicar of Catterick, Theophilus Lindsey, spoken of before, whose religious studies were already making him a little uncomfortable in his Church living. Then, for a while, Priestley found a happy home in the family of the Earl of Shelburne at Calne, as librarian there, and companion to the Earl, who was fond of science and literature, and glad to have so able a man pursuing his studies under his roof, or travelling with him on the continent.

All this time, Priestley—now Dr. Priestley, the University of Edinburgh having conferred its degree of LL.D. upon him—was becoming more and more eminent. He was constantly writing and publishing books, now on science, now on those new ideas of religion, which people were denouncing as Unitarianism, but which he maintained to be the simple Christianity of the New

Testament. And hence came the influence which he had over those congregations of the old Presbyterian Dissent, amongst which he was a minister; for, though he never became a very popular preacher, he was so widely known and respected as a man of science, that his opinions carried great weight, and his books were much read, and people listened with deep interest when he preached. To many, his doctrines seemed new and strange; and great discussion and controversy they caused among those quiet old Presbyterian congregations of the Old Dissent, which for half a century had been going on in their jog-trot way, gradually caring less and less about doctrines at all, and hardly knowing how far they had really got from the old orthodoxy. The Unitarians of the present day look back upon Dr. Priestley as the most old-fashioned of their teachers, but he was regarded then as an almost dangerous innovator. The old men shook their heads about those new notions of his; the Independents cried that this was what they had always prophesied that their Presbyterian neighbours would come to, with their open trusts and no creeds. But the Presbyterians were a strong, thoughtful sort of people, and had always held that men must read the Bible and think for themselves; and though some held back, the most part were true to their principles. Priestley's preaching, and Theophilus Lindsey's example, roused them up to look these questions of religious truth in the face; and the more they looked into them the more this Unitarianism seemed to them reasonable, and in agreement with the teachings of Christ; and, indeed, they found that it was very much the doctrine they had generally come to, and been really worshipping by for a long time past, though they had not known it. They did not like the name

"Unitarianism," but since that was the name by which these views were becoming known, they would not refuse it; and so, gradually, they came to be called Unitarians, though they still chiefly used their own old name of Presbyterians, and liked it better because it seemed less sectarian.

Dr. Priestley's ministry at Birmingham was during an eventful time. Those years from 1781 to 1791, were years of stir and change throughout the country. At first the American war was raging, and Priestley, with most of the liberal thinkers of the time, felt a strong sympathy with the struggling colonists. Then there was much agitation among Dissenters, against the "Test Act," by which it was still illegal for any one to hold any municipal office, unless he was a Churchman. Finally the French Revolution broke out, causing great excitement among the Tories and the clergy, against all Liberals who were supposed to sympathize with it. All these things together caused a very bitter feeling to spring up against outspoken men like Dr. Priestley. According to the Church and Tory papers, this quiet old minister, spending his days among his papers and books and scientific instruments, was a bloodthirsty revolutionist and an enemy of order and religion. In 1791 the rising excitement burst out in the memorable "Birmingham Riots." A great mob, excited by the clergy, and hounded on by the High-Church magistrates and gentry, burnt Priestley's meeting-house and then destroyed his home, with other houses of some of his leading friends. In danger of his life, he withdrew from Birmingham and went to London. But though his life was safe there, his happiness was gone. The prejudice of bigotry pursued him everywhere; the members of the Royal Society, his old scientific acquaintances, shunned him; his very name was dreaded, and those who bore it found it difficult to live. One of his sons was turned out of the firm in which he was a partner, on account of it. Another son wanted to learn farming with some eminent agriculturist, but no one would receive a Priestley. Persecuted and harassed, the old man found that, if he would end his days in peace, it must be in another country. It was a bitter thing for him, at sixty years of age, to seek new friendships and a new home; but with quiet fortitude he submitted to the necessity, and, in 1794, emigrated to America.

Thenceforth a quiet little Pennsylvanian village, Northumberland, was his home. He mingled little with the world outside; busy with his apparatus and his books, holding pleasant intercourse with Adams and Jefferson and other leading Americans, who greatly respected him, and corresponding with his old friends in England—ten years wore quietly away, and in 1804, at the age of seventy-one, he passed to his rest.

In his own day he was mobbed and suspected, and had to take refuge in exile. But a later generation has done more justice to his worth. A few years ago a statue of him was placed in the great library at Oxford; and later, another statue, representing him in the act of making his great discovery of oxygen, has been erected in Birmingham. Some day, when men have come to see how the world is saved more by earnest, honest thinking than by correct believing, he will be honoured even by those who may think his doctrines erroneous, as one of the purest and noblest of those who, in spite of all opposition, have tried to see and to teach the simple truth of Christ.

CHAPTER XXXIV.

THE NEW DISSENT—FOREIGN MISSIONS.

The good work which was done by Wesley and Whitefield was not confined to the awakening of the people. Almost as important was the awakening of the Churches.

During the middle part of last century the "Old Dissent" was sinking more and more into religious lethargy. The spirit of the old Puritanism had almost passed away. In the large towns the Presbyterian congregations were still powerful, and their ministers, grave, scholarly men in wig and gown, were greatly respected and maintained in comfort, and the same was true, though, perhaps, in rather less degree, of the Independents and Baptists. But in the country places the Dissenting congregations were mostly small and weak, and the ministers poorly supported. The more learned of them eked out their living by keeping schools. Almost all of them farmed a little land. Many, especially among the Baptists, lived in the greatest need; struggling on, on incomes of twenty or thirty pounds a year, now and then helped out by a grant of a few pounds from some of the Dissenting Trust Funds for the support of "poor and godly ministers," and, some of them, glad to make a few shillings by some handicraft.

But gradually a new spirit awoke among the Dissenters. They felt the rush of Wesley's new movement. At first they disliked it, shrank from it, some even opposed it. The Baptists could not do with it, because it took no notice of their special doctrine. The Independents shook their heads over its preaching of a salvation freely open to all who would repent and accept Christ, and fell back upon their Calvinism with its salvation only for the elect. As for the Presbyterians, their old stiff, scholarly respectability was repelled by what they called the ranting ways of the new movement and its rude pioneers. Probably, deeper than any of these special objections, lay a dislike to be disturbed, and an unwillingness to admit the rebuke which there was for them, both in this new work and in its success.

However, this temper gradually gave way to something better. There were, in all the bodies of Dissenters, many sincere and religious men who had long mourned over the decay of the old Puritan spirit; and as soon as they saw how deep and genuine Wesley's work was, they welcomed it and opened their hearts to its inspiration. Gradually, throughout the Old Dissent, there was a stirring of the dry bones, and an earnest reviving of religious life.

Among the Presbyterians, as we have seen, this took the direction of a new interest in religious truth and doctrine, and, catching the spirit of Priestley and Lindsey, it threw its energies very largely into controversy, and only at a much later time began to do much in the way of simple Gospel-work among the people. But among the Baptists and Independents, a deep religious life and an earnest spirit of religious activity began to make itself felt. Many of those who had been converted by the new preachers of Methodism joined these bodies. Their preachings and prayings took a more fervent tone. They began to revive the conferences and prayer-meetings of the Puritan times. Their district and county associations were stirred with new questions, about what they could do for the salvation of the new, busy, modern world, to the needs of which they were at length awaking. Among all denominations Sunday-schools began to be started, at first to give the neglected children of the poor a chance to learn reading and writing, but in course of time becoming more and more a means of interesting the young in religion. New colleges were established, to educate young men for the ministry, the old injustice of none but Churchmen being admitted to the old Universities of Oxford and Cambridge being still continued. With activity in religious matters, a new activity in public and political affairs began to spring up. The Dissenters began to be no longer satisfied with the mere toleration which had been granted them at the Revolution. It was complained of as an injustice that Dissenting ministers should have to subscribe to thirty-five of the articles of the Church of England, and in 1779 this was done away. Many of the Dissenters began to be known among the most outspoken reformers of all public abuses. Thus, gradually, a new Dissent, more active and aggressive, sprang up, and has gone on increasing in zeal, earnestness and power till the present day.

Among the fruits of this new and revived earnestness of Dissent must be ranked the growth of the missionary spirit, and the establishment of the great Foreign Missions, which now are doing their work in almost every heathen land throughout the world.

Up to nearly the close of the eighteenth century

foreign missions had been hardly thought of in England. Cromwell had indeed a great project for "a council for the Protestant religion," which should do for the reformed religion what the congregation "*de Propaganda fide*"—the great Catholic missionary power—did for Rome. But Cromwell was too busy with state affairs to be able to attend to missions, and the project came to nothing.

The next movement in the direction of missionary labour was the formation, in 1701, of the "Society for the Propagation of the Gospel in Foreign Parts;" but this was especially intended to help in establishing Church of England worship in the colonies; and though, as a second object, was included the conversion of "the native inhabitants of these countries," little was done in this direction. It was by this society that John Wesley was sent out to Georgia in 1735. He endeavoured to preach among the Indians, but had little success, and for the most part the agents of the "S. P. G.," as it has come to be usually called, were merely clergymen to the colonists.

The real awakening of England to the duty of doing something for the spread of the Gospel among the numberless peoples of the great heathen world, is due to the Baptists, and recalls a very interesting story of religious faithfulness and perseverance.

It was in 1784 that the Nottingham Baptist Association resolved on holding monthly "concerts for prayer" at the chapels of the district in rotation. Among those who met at these little gatherings was William Carey, pastor of the little village chapel at Moulton, a man who had just been rather unwillingly recognized as a minister at all, having been only a village shoemaker, who, from doing a little as a lay-preacher, had gradually found himself drawn to give up his life to the ministry. It was not by any worldly prospects that he was drawn, for his people could only raise him eleven pounds a year, and he was often nearly starving. So it was hard work for Carey to get much hearing among them at all, and hardest of all when they found that he was a man of one idea, and that one idea—which had come to his mind in reading Captain Cook's travels—was, the duty of English Christians to the heathen world. When it came to be his turn to introduce a subject, and he opened to the conference "the duty of Christians to attempt the spread of the Gospel among heathen nations," old Mr. Ryland, one of the seniors of the district, sprang to his feet and cried out, "Young man, sit down; when God pleases to convert the heathen he will do it without your aid or mine." Only one of the brethren, Andrew Fuller, of Kettering, took his part, and even he was staggered at the idea, and all he could say was, "If the Lord should make windows in heaven, such a thing might be!" William Carey, however, would not be beaten off. He drew up a pamphlet on the subject, and showed it about among the ministers. With threadbare dress, often for weeks without being able to taste meat, and with little enough even of bread, he yet forgot all but his one possessing idea, and went from one to another, and year after year kept pressing it upon them. It was seven years before he succeeded in winning over a sufficient number to his way of thinking, to get anything done; but at last in 1791, he felt that the tone of the meeting was with him, and at the next association, in the spring of 1792, he put all the power of his soul into a last fervent appeal. The key-note of his discourse was: "Expect great things; attempt great things!" For the moment the audience were held spell-bound; but after the service the question came up, what could be done about it, and then the difficulties and obstacles occurred. It is impossible for us to realize now-a-days how great those difficulties then were. The heathen world was not known then as it is now. The idea of trying to carry Christianity into those vast unknown regions, might well appal a little gathering of poor country ministers! Indecision seemed likely to carry the day; when Mr. Carey seized old Mr. Fuller's hand in an agony of distress, and asked if they were again going to part without doing anything. This appeal was irresistible, and a resolution was passed for a plan to be prepared against their autumn meeting.

At that Autumn meeting, at Kettering, October 2, 1792, twelve ministers were present. They did not know what to do; they were ignorant of any opening for missionary work; they had neither funds, nor influence; but Mr. Carey's enthusiasm carried all before it, and "the Baptist Missionary Society," was constistuted. A Committee of five was appointed, of whom Carey was one, Mr. Fuller being Secretary; and a subscription was raised—which amounted to £13. 2s. 6d.! Other sums, however, soon began to come in. The London ministers and congregations indeed, would have nothing to do with the Society, looking down upon it as a wild scheme of some obscure country ministers; but Birmingham sent £70, and other churches followed.

What were they to do, however? The heathen country with which England seemed most connected at that time was India, and the wealth that England was deriving thence seemed to make it all the more a duty to do something for the Christianizing of its people.

But India was then under the control of the East India Company, and the Directors of that Company did not want the natives meddled with, and had absolutely forbidden all their ships (and no others could go thither) to take any missionaries over! The very difficulty, however, only brought out the duty in a clearer light. It seemed shocking that, for fear of trade being a little injured, the millions of Hindoos should be kept from hearing of the Gospel. So the Baptist Missionary Society resolved to begin their work in India.

But obstacles stood in the way, in every direction. Carey was willing to go; said he, at one of their meetings, when Mr. Fuller had said that India was like a great *mine* of souls, "I will go down, if you will hold the rope." But no vessel would take them. Once he and his companion, a Mr. Thomas—who had been in Calcutta before, and was relied upon as knowing all about the country—embarked on board an Indiaman; but just before sailing the captain received an anonymous warning that they were "unlicensed persons," and they had to land again at an hour's notice. At last they got a passage in a Danish ship, and in Nov., 1793, they landed in Calcutta. Here, however, worse difficulties arose. They were soon without funds, for Mr. Thomas, who turned out to be a thriftless enthusiast, sold the goods they had brought with them, at a loss. They had to move twenty-five miles up the river, and lived there in great poverty. Mrs. Carey was constantly reproaching her husband for having come out, and, moreover, she and the children were very ill. Yet, through all, Mr. Carey never lost sight of the object for which he had come out. At every spare moment he was studying Hindustani, and as often as he could he went to Calcutta, and with a native interpreter frequented the places of public resort, and tried his best to interest the natives in the Gospel. For years the Mission struggled on in this way. For a time he got a situation in charge of an Indigo factory, at a salary of £240 a year, of which he devoted a large part to the services of the Mission. Alas, it did not seem as if the Mission was to come to much. Perhaps Mr. Carey had underrated those he wanted to convert. Like many others who have gone out to Eastern countries, he had regarded them as poor ignorant creatures sunk in debasing superstitions, and lost unless converted to Christianity. In reality, he found them keenly intellectual, strongly attached to their old religion, and very well able to argue for it, and just as persuaded that it was divine as he was of the divineness of the Gospel. However, he did what he could. He went about preaching in the neighbouring villages, established a school for native children, and translated the New Testament into Bengali.

After five years things became more hopeful. Two helpers came out to him, William Ward and Joshua Marshman, and they were offered a shelter at Serampore, where the Danes, who were favourable to missionary work, had a settlement and fort. There, accordingly, they all settled with their families, and, Mr. Ward having been a printer, they began to set the type for their Bengali New Testament. A few converts, too, began to show themselves, chiefly of the lower castes at first, but at length they won over to join them several of the "writer" caste, and then their work began to attract more attention.

From that time the Baptist Missions have gone steadily on; until, now, instead of that one little station at Serampore with one or two lonely workers, they have above two hundred stations in different parts of the world, and some seventy English missionaries, with three times that number of native preachers and pastors. Their work was often opposed, and is still often sneered at, for it is carried on under great difficulties, and the results seem always disproportionately small; but slowly yet surely it is making way. In time, Dr. Carey and his helpers, Mr. Ward and Mr. Marshman, became widely known and respected in India. Dr. Carey, however, never forgot the days of his struggles and poverty. His biographer tells how, one day when he was dining with the Governor-General of India, and one of the officers present asked another whether he had not once been a shoemaker, Dr. Carey happened to hear it, and, stepping forward, replied, "No sir—only a cobbler!"

The Baptist Missionary Society was not the only result of Carey's labours. When once he had aroused the conscience of English Christians to the duty of trying to spread the Gospel, many others besides the Baptists began to think of missionary work. Only three years after the formation of the Baptist Missionary Society, there was a large gathering of other Christian people in London to try to form some plan of missionary work, in which various bodies of Christians might join, and the result was the formation of the "London Missionary Society." At intervals of a few years similar Societies were formed in Scotland, and by the Church of England, the Wesleyans, and other religious bodies, and gradually the "London Missionary Society" came to represent especially the Independents, or "Congregationalists," as during the present century they have gradually come to call themselves. The work, which this Society has done, has been a very noble one. In Tahiti, and many an island group in the Southern world; in Madagascar, which under the labours of Rev. Wm. Ellis, has become a Christian island; in South Africa, where the noble-hearted Moffatt spent his long life, and in the labours of David Livingstone, whom this Society first sent out on his wanderings, good, more than can be told, has been accomplished.

It is sometimes said, that it is a pity for such vast sums as those raised by these great Missionary Societies, to be spent upon the heathen abroad, when there are so many heathen at home, needing help and teaching. But let it be remembered that these very bodies which have been doing most abroad, have also been doing most at home. The new Dissent has carried out that revived religious life which, in its first impulse, sent Dr. Carey to far-away India, in many a noble effort among the neglected classes of England. The first definite idea of a "Mission to the Poor" was formed, indeed, by Dr. Tuckerman, a Unitarian clergyman of Boston, U.S., who for many years devoted himself entirely to it; and when he came over to England in 1835, many of the English Unitarian congregations (who had never attempted foreign Missionary work) gladly took up his idea, and "Domestic Missions" as they were called—in distinction from Foreign Missions—were established in London, Manchester, Liverpool, and other large towns. But since that time the necessity of Town Missions has been felt by all Churches, and by none have they been more earnestly and liberally carried out, than by those Churches which also have been most active abroad.

CHAPTER XXXV.

EDWARD IRVING.

Here and there in some of our large towns may be seen a little church not much frequented, very little known by the people around, very seldom making much attempt to attract notice, calling itself the "Catholic Apostolic Church," but more commonly spoken of as "Irvingites." They have a cathedral in London, and at times the world wonders to hear of their rich ritual and curious orders of ministry, "Prophets," "Apostles," "Evangelists," besides the ordinary pastors of the congregations who are called "Angels." In general doctrine they are very orthodox, yet they never seem to have anything to do with other Christian bodies, but keep on their own quiet way, looking for the end of all things as near at hand.

These little churches, now scarcely noticed by the world, are the visible memorial of a man, and of a religious awakening, which in their day were among the most remarkable incidents in this later part of the story of religion in England. We may doubt whether these Irvingite churches have any important work to do, for, indeed, they are the outcome of a life which had come to its weakest time. But Edward Irving himself must never be forgotten by those who love to trace the workings of intense and lofty religious enthusiasm.

Edrawd Irving was born at Annan, in Dumfriesshire,

in 1792, the child of one of the old families of those parts—shrewd, strong-hearted folk, not wealthy, but thrifty and frugal, after the usual character of those Lowland Scotchmen. At the parish school he got the beginnings of his education; but stronger influences than those of school grew upon him in the old traditions of the Covenanters, which made every cottage and farm-house through the whole country-side a training place, where the boy's wondering heart learnt many a thought of mystic and heroic piety which helped to make him what he afterwards became.

Then he went to Edinburgh University, while still only a lad of thirteen,—he and an elder brother of fifteen years, to live in a little lodging there, all by themselves; very poor, like many a student in those Scotch Universities, but getting along somehow, and the carrier bringing them in, every now and then, a box from home with oatmeal in it and a cheese, and—rarer luxury—a ham. Five years of this, and then, a fine grown man, though only eighteen, and full of health, vigour, and hopefulness, he began teaching to help his own living, entering himself meanwhile as a "partial divinity student," and going in every now and then for examinations.

For two years he was master of a little school at Haddington, and then was promoted to a rather higher sort of "academy" at Kirkcaldy. And all the time he was growing—growing in body, till he was almost a giant, with a mighty strength in him, full of health and spirits, fond of long rambles over the hills and moors; growing in heart and mind, always learning, and loving to teach, and thinking of the days when his divinity studentship should be over, and he might enter on that grander work he longed for, of a preacher.

The Scottish Presbyterians are careful about the candidates for their ministry, and so it took six years of this "partial studentship" before he was ready for his final "trials for license," and these took six months more, examinations, and essays, and preachings before the presbytery of his neighbourhood; and then at last he was "licensed to preach the Gospel among the churches," though not yet ordained, for, as he used to tell, "our Church ordaineth no man without a flock."

He was now what is called a probationer, and longed very earnestly for the higher work. But it was not to be; he was doomed to long disappointment. The fact is that the great power that there was in him was of a kind that takes long to ripen. At Annan, indeed, where he preached his first sermon, a little incident won the people to him. In the middle of the sermon, by some sudden movement he let his manuscript fall over from the pulpit into the precentor's desk below; every one trembled for him, but quietly reaching out with his long arms, he gathered up the papers, and thrusting them into his pocket, he went right on without them, to the delight and admiration of his friends. But at Kirkcaldy the people complained that he had "ower muckle grann'er." He soared above them with his rich high-sounding sentences; so they shook their heads, and were not very well pleased when they saw him in the pulpit, and for some years he had to go quietly on with his schooling.

A curious mingling of different qualities there was in his life at this time. Very lofty thoughts of religion were in him, and yet curious stories are told of his fiery impatience, and of outbreaks of the old Adam in that great frame of his. Once when he and a friend were out on a walking expedition, they came to a little road-side inn, and after ordering dinner, they laid their knapsacks in a corner of the one small sitting-room, and went out for a stroll; when they returned, what was their surprise to find the room occupied by another party, who not only insisted on keeping it, but would not even let them share the table. Irving strode forward to the window, flung it wide open, and then turning round, said to his friend, "Will you toss out, or knock down?" They had their share of the room!

Gradually he got restless in his school keeping. He with a great longing longed for the work he had been so many years preparing for. Moreover another school was opened in Kirkcaldy, to which was appointed as teacher a man afterwards even greater than Irving, —Thomas Carlyle. So, in 1818, Irving left his teaching, and going back to Edinburgh lingered about there, studying, and especially writing sermons. For at this time he burnt all his old sermons, and set to work anew. These years, during which he had been a listener to the dull, humdrum preaching usual in the country places of Scotland, had stirred him with a deep discontent with the ordinary ways in which religion was presented to men. He felt it was so noble a theme, and ought to be much more than it seemed to be, both to those who preached and to those who listened; he felt it might be put to the world, so that men of the strongest minds and highest culture should love it and feel its power, instead of passing it by as so many of them were doing. He longed for the opportunity to attempt this, and, as he put it to a friend, "to make a demonstration for a higher style of Christianity, something more magnanimous, more heroical, than this age affects." And so he burnt all his first sermons and tried to shape out these high thoughts into something worthier.

But no work came yet; he preached here and there, but no church called him. He began to grow very sad in a feeling that there was no place for him in Scotland. Plans came into his mind of wandering away into the East, as a missionary of the cross. But when he had lingered a year in Edinburgh, suddenly an invitation came to him to become assistant to Dr. Chalmers in his great Glasgow church.

Two years he laboured there; happy years they were in many ways, for he loved that great man, and loved the work he was trying to do in his dense parish of poor people. The fashionable church-goers, indeed, did not think much of him; Chalmers was their great man. It was a trying thing to be curate to the most famous preacher in Scotland; and often on the Sabbath morning when it was Irving's turn to preach, he would meet groups of people coming, turning back from the church-door and saying to one another, "It's no himsel' to-day!" But among the poor he found great joy; he threw himself into his mission-work among them, with a simple, unconventional eagerness and kindness which won their hearty love, not unmingled with awe. And still, though he loved his work and his leader with perfect loyalty, he could not help hungering for some field, however small, in which he might labour after his own thought.

At last the opportunity came. There was in London a certain "Caledonian Chapel" which had fallen into difficulties, and been forsaken for more popular and fashionable churches; but in which a handful of earnest Scotch Presbyterians were still holding together, hoping for better things. They heard of Irving, and invited him to come among them. They could offer him hardly any maintenance, but he did not hesitate a moment. He believed in the Gospel with a chivalrous faith, believed that if he worked truly for it the Lord would somehow take care of him. He was willing to go, he said, even though he should have to labour with his hands for a livelihood; and so to London he went, and began his ministry among them on the second Sabbath in July, 1822.

Almost at once, the marvellous power of the man began to show itself. One friend told another. The little Caledonian Chapel saw its first fifty adherents increased to hundreds. It began to be whispered in society that there was a new Scotch preacher come there, like no one else in London. David Wilkie and Sir Thomas Lawrence the great painters went there, and went again. Zacchary Macaulay and Allan Cunningham were among his regular hearers. Sir James Mackintosh was drawn thither, and one sentence in a prayer, in which Irving, pleading for a poor family of orphans, spoke of them as "thrown upon the fatherhood of God," so struck him that he repeated it to Canning; and the statesman went also, and was so impressed that he alluded to this new preacher in one of his great speeches. Soon the narrow streets about Hatton Garden saw such throngs every Sunday, that the little church with its five or six hundred sittings became too small to hold a fifth of those who sought places, and admission had to be by ticket. Now, at last, Irving had the opportunity he had longed and waited for. His critics assailed him for not preaching to the poor. No one loved the poor more than he. His fellow mission-workers in the Glasgow courts and lanes, had never seen such tender reverent love for the poor as he had shown. He who would carry the pack of a wearied pedler, or a poor woman's child; he, who could never enter a poor man's garret without the old salutation, "Peace be to this house," uttered with such an affectionate earnestness that no one who heard him could ever forget it, was not the man to be unmindful of the poor. But he had another work in hand just now. He wanted to preach to educated men. He wanted to draw to worship the classes who at that time were indifferent to it. He wanted to make scholars and thinkers bow down before that mighty revelation which he saw in the Gospels. And he succeeded. It was not merely to a large congregation that he preached. Through that crowd of eager listeners, who filled the seats and thronged every foot of standing-room, he reached a far wider audience, and awoke an interest in religion, a new sense of its truth and glory and power, in thousands who could seldom or never hear his voice.

Of course, such a success brought criticism and enmity. Men said that he was vain. The newspapers made fun of his antique Scripture-fashion of speaking, as pompous and pretentious. Let those who have formed any such idea of the man, read the Life of him by Mrs. Oliphant, and they will find how untrue all this is, and with what a single-hearted, enthusiastic piety he threw himself into all his work. He had indeed a strong consciousness of the power which was in him, and a great, thankful delight in it; and with his heart all aglow with the old Bible spirit, which he was ever drinking in, and with the feeling of that "more heroical Christianity" he read of there, it took such possession of him that it moulded even his very speech. He felt the awfulness of being set apart to speak the word of the Lord to men. The sense of it would not let him go. He never entered a house without that old salutation of "Peace!" When the little children came to him, as they loved to do, his first greeting always was "The Lord bless thee and keep thee!" This was no affectation in him. It was the overflowing piety of a strong, unconventional nature. Said one, of him, "In God he lived and moved and had his being. Not one act but was done in prayer. Every blessing was received with thanksgiving to God. Every friend was dismissed with a parting benediction." He could not even take one of his long excursions on foot, in his yearly visits to the old Scotch home, "without," as he writes in his journal for his wife, "calling at every shepherd's house along the route, to obtain an opportunity of admonishing mother and children of their mortality." And all was done in such simplicity of anxious love, that in him it seemed beautiful and natural. Nor was it only in these smaller matters that the spirit came out. When he was invited to preach for one of the great Foreign Missionary societies, instead of the usual kind of appeal based on the work and reports of the society, he astonished his audience by a picture of what a missionary for Christ might be now, if he should take up his work in the spirit of ancient apostleship—a picture drawn with such startling vividness, and set forth with such eagerness as held the crowded church in rapt stillness for hours, but grievously offended the plain business managers of the Society, who had looked for a good appeal for funds.

It was in his preaching that his life seemed to come to its climax and glory, but yet his preaching was only a small part of his work. To his home—a small house at Pentonville—came, day by day, a never ceasing succession of friends and visitors: old friends from Annan or Kirkcaldy; poor lads from the Glasgow mission-parish wanting counsel or work; religious enthusiasts with some new theory of prophecy; and people, numberless, of all sorts and conditions, who had been aroused to a deeper interest in religion by his preaching, and craved for closer communion with this helpful friend who seemed to be always walking in the light. From ten to three every day he kept sacredly for his study; but the rest of his time was one long, busy ministry of loving pastoral guidance and prayer.

Such was Edward Irving, at his best, for the first five or six years after his removal to London. His people built for him a great church in Regent Square, which was opened with great rejoicing and hope. His name was spread over the country, and wherever he went multitudes thronged to hear him. It seemed as if he was to be that which he had dreamed of—the instrument of arousing the strength and thought of society, from indifference and contempt for Christianity, to an earnest religious life.

It is a very sad task to trace the steps by which this grand influence became drawn into channels which gradually belittled it, and which changed Edward Irving from this noble leader of souls, into the victim of a strange, fanatical delusion.

It is one more illustration of the mischief which comes of confounding together the letter and the spirit of the Bible, and trying to treat every part of that grand Hebrew literature, as the very words of God. Let it be once clearly understood that the word of the Lord came through the words of men; that the gradually unfolding light of divine thought and truth comes down to us, winding like a golden thread through ancient poetry and tradition and psalm and history, and we cannot value it too highly, or study it too earnestly. But Irving started with the idea that every word was alike divine and authoritative; only, unlike most of those about him, he not only upheld this, but really *held it*, believed it in his very soul, and set himself to act upon it. So, a while after settling in London, the study of prophecy took hold of him; and, reading Isaiah, and Ezekiel, and Revelation with that intense conviction that every word was to come true, he became possessed with the belief in the speedy coming of Christ to make an end of the present life of the world, and usher in the Millennium. At once this weakened his hold upon practical men. Yet it gave such a new, almost prophetic fervour to the appeals of his preaching, that still the old crowds gathered about him for a time; and when he went to Scotland, for a preaching mission to proclaim "the coming of the Lord," the excitement everywhere was intense. In Edinburgh the largest church in the city was crowded, morning by morning, at six o'clock, and, as he made his way through the western Lowlands, immense numbers gathered about him at every stopping-place where he could preach. But his best influence was already gone. Dr. Chalmers said the change in him was "woful." Some of his most thoughtful friends began to turn away from this mysterious allegorizing, in which his preaching was losing itself. In London, the new church, though always full, was no longer crowded, and those who held with him were less and less the thinkers, and more and more the enthusiasts.

By-and-by, this enthusiasm, dwelling continually on the signs of the latter days, and looking everywhere with eager excitement for new signs from God, took a still stranger form. Strange broken utterances of ecstacy, from among the congregation, began to interrupt his preachings; solemn warnings and exhortations were shouted forth in the intervals of the service, and the awe-struck hearers remembered the "unknown tongues" of the day of Pentecost, and took these for the voices of the spirit. Irving himself never felt any such power, but this, in his deep humility, he thought was because he was not worthy. But he believed that those who were so affected were earnest and truthful people, and he could find no other explanation of these voices, but that it was—even as they said themselves—that the gift of tongues was revived.

This was the beginning of the end. His soberer friends gradually fell away from him. They were deeply troubled, for they all loved him as man has rarely been loved; but it seemed to them that he was giving way to a miserable and mischievous infatuation, and one by one they drew away, and at last the very church, which only five years before had been built for him with such joyful hope, was closed against him by the trustees.

Even in weakness and delusion, Irving was still great and true. Once convinced that the manifestations were genuine, nothing could change, nothing could shake him. His followers found a large, bare room for their temporary church, and thence they went forth to proclaim in the streets that great tidings of the coming of the Lord, which was now doubly assured to them by these strange signs. The attacks of the newspapers, the insults of scoffers, the coldness of his old friends, the tearful entreaties of his kindred, could not move him. His heart was grieved and torn, his health was broken, but it seemed to him the will of God, and he went right on. Not a word of complaint or reproach fell from him. Never did his face shine with a purer or tenderer enthusiasm than as he stood up in some vacant place off the London streets and preached to the crowds that gathered about him. It was on one of those occasions that Mrs. Oliphant tells how he was interrupted by the cry of a little child that had got lost in the throng. "Give me the child," he said, and as it was handed from one to another above the heads of the crowd, he stretched out his arms for it, and in a moment it was nestling with perfect confidence against his broad shoulder, happy and contented, and, so with the little one in his arms, he went on preaching with as much ease and freedom as before; and after prayer and blessing, in which he did not forget "the little child," he gave it back to the parents, who had seen it, as he intended, from the time he took it up.

With that touching little scene we will leave him. Indeed, he had not much longer to carry on that work, which had thus been so sadly turned aside and dwarfed. With broken, failing health he struggled on awhile; simple-hearted, unselfish, devoted as ever; meekly submitting himself to the smaller men whose voices, professing to be the voice of the Spirit, now guided and organized the new Society. And then, travelling slowly northward, staying here and there with old friends to whom he seemed in his failing strength the same Edward Irving they had known years before, he just managed to reach Glasgow, and there, in December, 1834, died. Almost to the end he had believed it was God's will that he should recover, for it was on the bidding of one of the "voices" that he had come northward for a special mission, and he could not think that God's word would fail. But no fear mingled with his dying thoughts, and when at length the death hour came, the last words that reached the friends about him were, "if I die, I die unto the Lord. Amen!"

CHAPTER XXXVI.

THE FREE CHURCH OF SCOTLAND—DR. CHALMERS.

WHILE we recall with admiration the noble sacrifices of our forefathers, and their sufferings for religious truth or religious liberty, let us not forget that within our own times has taken place one of the finest movements of religious heroism. This is what is commonly called the "Disruption" in the Established Church of Scotland, in which, in 1843, four hundred and seventy of the clergy of that Church gave up their livings, and went forth, with Dr. Chalmers at their head, to form the Free Church of Scotland.

The "established religion" of Scotland is Presbyterianism. It is one of the curiosities of religion in Great Britain, that the clergy and bishops of the Church of England are mere Dissenters as soon as they cross the Tweed! This dates from the Revolution of 1688, which finally overthrew the Stuarts, and put an end to the attempt which they had made to have the Church of Scotland Episcopalian, like that of England. Though only the Covenanters had actively resisted that attempt, the whole people were really against it, except the nobles and lairds who liked the plan of the English Church because it gave them the power of appointing the clergy to the livings. The real religion of Scotland was the old Calvinistic Presbyterianism of John Knox, and with the advent of William III. and toleration this was restored and the people were left to choose their own parish ministers. So thoroughly was this regarded as a final settlement that when, a few years afterwards, in 1707, England and Scotland were made into one kingdom by the Act of Union, a special statute was passed enacting that the Presbyterian Church government of Scotland should remain as it was without any alteration. Unfortunately this agreement was not kept. When once the Union was accomplished, the feelings of the common people of Scotland were little cared for. It was the lairds and the nobles who were influential in Parliament and with Government, and these were greedy for their old powers of Church patronage. The consequence was that within five years after the Union the old scandal of patronage was re-established by law. The feeling aroused by this change, however, was so bitter that for some time it was not acted upon, but gradually the proprietors began to assert their "rights." Many sad scenes were then witnessed, for often the nominees of the lairds were so unpopular that it was only by the help of guards of soldiers that they could be forced upon the unwilling parishes. As time passed on the feeling became so strong that secession after secession took place. In 1733, the Rev. Ebenezer Erskine, of Sterling, left the Church, and being joined by several other clergymen, set up the "Associate Presbytery," which soon grew into what was called the "Secession Kirk," and kept increasing till it numbered several hundred congregations. About thirty years later another similar movement took place. The Rev. Thomas Gillespie, Minister of Carnock, near Dunfermline, refusing to take part in inducting a minister into a parish where he was extremely unpopular, was expelled from the Church by the General Assembly (which was in the hands of the patrons and their nominees), and, with several others, formed what was called the "Relief Church." This also steadily grew, till it numbered above a hundred congregations in different parts of Scotland. Of course, however, these secessions left the Established Kirk more completely in the power of those who were favourable to patronage, since those who were opposed to it withdrew to join the "Voluntaries" as these "Secession" and "Relief" churches were called.* So for a long time, within the Kirk itself, there was no further movement; the patrons appointed whomsoever they pleased to the livings, and of course ministers who obtained settlements in that way were not likely to oppose. Still, the system was so wrong and mischievous that gradually a party grew up again in opposition to it, those belonging to this party being called "Evangelicals;" and they rapidly increased in numbers. It was a time—at the beginning of this century—when religious life was reviving among the people, but the revived life sought for the churches of the Voluntaries, where men could have a voice in choosing their own ministers. The most earnest men in the Establishment felt this keenly, and more and more of them joined the Evangelical party. The spirit of reform was very active throughout both countries at this time, and the leaders of the anti-patronage movement believed they had only to agitate in an earnest spirit and let the people of England and Scotland see the real rights of the matter, to have the law altered. So they petitioned Parliament, and such numbers of petitions were sent in that at last in 1832 the House of Commons appointed a Committee of Inquiry. Then, having at last come to outnumber

* These two movements were amalgamated in 1847, forming the United Presbyterian Church.

the "Moderates" (as the other party, who favoured Patronage, called themselves) in the General Assembly, the Evangelicals passed a "Veto Act" declaring that it was contrary to the fundamental law of the Church for any pastor to be intruded on a congregation against the will of the people. It was very doubtful if this act was legal, but so strong had the feeling throughout Scotland become, that for five years no "patron" ventured to disregard it, and it was generally believed that the question was practically settled.

Throughout all this later movement the chief leader of this reforming party in the Scottish Kirk was a clergyman who had come to be known, not only as the most eloquent man in Scotland, but as one of the noblest Christian workers of these modern days—Dr. Chalmers, whose life up to this time must now be sketched.

Thomas Chalmers was born in 1780, at Anstruther, in Fifeshire, the son of a busy tradesman there—so busy that his son got but a poor, half-neglected education, both as child and boy. When about fifteen years old, however, the lad went to the University of St. Andrews, and there the study of mathematics took hold of him, and from that time learning was one of the great delights of his life. He became a divinity student, and at nineteen was licensed to the ministry. He was not much of a minister as yet, however, but was an eager, impetuous youth, full of a wilful and undisciplined power. Yet there were already signs of the future man, as, for instance, when we find him rebelling against the cautious advice of one of his divinity tutors, who, while teaching a rather modified sort of Calvinism, counselled his students not to say much about it in the pulpit! "If it be truth, why not be aboveboard with it?" burst out

Chalmers, and from that time he never could be brought to pay much attention to that tutor. Something, too, of the rich flowery eloquence which afterwards distinguished him was beginning to show itself, and they tell how on the days when it was young Chalmers's turn to lead the college prayers, Divinity Hall would be filled with town's-people come in to listen.

First, as assistant in the village kirk at Cavers, and then, after a year or two, as pastor at Kilmany, some nine miles from St. Andrews, he began his ministry. At first, however, his heart was more in teaching than in preaching. He thought two days a week quite enough for his parish, he said, and he gave most of his time to an appointment which he got as Assistant Mathematical Professor at St. Andrews University. His teaching made a strange commotion, for such grand rhetoric as that in which he lectured was quite unusual on such a dry subject; but when he was remonstrated with, his fiery spirit flashed up, and he appealed from the authorities to the students, and of course lost his lectureship. Straightway he set up opposition lectures on his own account, adding chemistry to mathematics; first bearding the University and then the Presbytery; fully persuaded that he was fighting the battle of injured scholarship and human liberty, and attacking those quiet dignitaries with a magnificent eloquence that must occasionally have created some amusement as well as astonishment. And yet people could not help admiring him. Every one recognized the pure, noble spirit of the man; and gradually he gave way to wiser influences, and after a few years we find him settled earnestly down to his parish work at Kilmany, and giving up all his college engagements in order to devote himself wholly to his ministry. A serious illness, too, came upon him. For nearly a year he was laid by from work, and that long time of quiet thought was like a new birth to him. When he took up his ministry again, it was with a trembling earnestness, and an all-absorbing sense of God and eternity, which gave to that grand rolling rhetoric of his just the fire which it had needed, and which made it thenceforth irresistible. No more complaints now about his giving too scanty a portion of his time to his parish! Formerly a story had been repeated, of how an old parishioner had said, "I find you aye busy, sir, with one thing or another, but come when I may I never find you at your studies for the Sabbath;" and the minister's answer had been, "Oh, an hour or two on the Saturday evening is quite enough for that!" "But now," says his biographer, "the change had come," and the same old man on entering the manse often found Mr. Chalmers poring eagerly over the pages of the Bible. The difference was too striking to escape notice. "I never come in now, sir, but I find you aye at your Bible." "All too little, John, all too little!" was the significant reply. Thenceforth, all that restless power of his strong nature was thrown into his parish work. He lived among his people, visiting the sick and going much from house to house in earnest pastoral teaching, while his fervent, passionate preaching filled the church with eager crowds of listeners. Gradually his fame spread far and wide, until it reached Glasgow, and he was elected to the great Tron Church there. He had great hesitation about going, for he dreaded the multitude of small engagements with which a minister's life in a great city is always invaded, but at last he accepted, and twelve years after his ordination at

Kilmany he began his ministry in the great Glasgow church.

At once his preaching took the city by storm. It was very different to what people were used to, for old Scotch Presbyterians hated "read" sermons, and yet his were every word written, and *read*. But, as an old woman said in answer to this objection,—"*It's fell reading, yon!*" He wrote just as he would have spoken, with a grand careless wealth of language, every idea being put again and again in varied forms—very wearisome to read, but, delivered with his overmastering rush of earnestness and fervour, it carried people away like a whirlwind. Hearers often used to start from their seats in the excitement of it. Sober-minded professors from the University stood up, leaning forward in tears. The very reporters sometimes stopped writing, carried away by the passion of his eloquence. Wherever he went, eager crowds pressed in to hear him. When he visited London, the street in front of the church became so completely blocked, before the building was full, that a way in had to be made by a plank to one of the windows. Of all the sermons he preached in those days, perhaps those which have been most famous are the series of "Astronomical Discourses," in which he dwelt upon the wonders of the heavens, which his mathematical studies had made familiar to him, and carried on the thoughts which they suggested towards the glorification of the Creator.

But Dr. Chalmers was much more than a preacher. No sooner had he entered on that great city parish, in which he had undertaken to be God's minister, than its terrible state touched him very deeply. It included in it much of the worst part of the old town, and the ignorance and immorality which he found were just appalling. He determined to go through it himself and know all about it. With one of his elders accompanying him, he went from house to house throughout the whole dense parish. At first, rather to his surprise, he was very cordially received, but he soon found that it was because he was connected with so many city charities, and as soon as the people had got him in their houses they began to appeal for help. This, he felt, would not do; it would utterly spoil his religious work; so he at once gave up his connection with every charity, and let it be known that he had nothing to give. For the moment this led to a somewhat cooler reception, but, as the people got to know the man, they loved him for himself and for his religious work among them. Then he divided the parish into districts, got a number of visitors to help him, and established a considerable number of small Sabbath schools. Inspiring his helpers with his own enthusiasm, he accomplished one of the noblest missionary works of modern times. In order to be able to grapple thoroughly with the problem of pauperism, he got a new parish carved out for him, with a population of ten thousand, and arranged with the authorities that this parish, St. John's, should be entirely left, for the care of its poor, to him and to his church. He was determined to revive the old Scottish plan of having the poor looked after by visitors from his church, and their relief met by the offerings in the poor's boxes at the church-doors. For the time he succeeded wonderfully. Breaking up the parish into small districts, he got every household visited and known; the children were sent to school; the people were taught to help each other; non-attendants at church were drawn in to worship; and the relief expenditure, which when he undertook the parish had been £1,400 a year, in four years was reduced to £280.

A few years, however, of this work, into which he threw the whole of his great power and energy, began to tell upon his health. He longed for some quieter scene of labour, and after eight years of that intense strain of popular city-life he suddenly, to the great grief of Glasgow, gave up his parish and his work there, to become Professor of Moral Philosophy in his old University at St. Andrews. He was too famous, however, to be left there in peace, and after three or four years he was, in 1828, called to Edinburgh to be Professor of Theology in the University. This was a position of very great influence. He was free from the cares of a parish, and could give the whole of his great powers to helping on every movement of the time for advancing civilization or Christianity.

It was now that we find him drawn into that position of leadership among the reformers of the Kirk of Scotland, which gave him the greatest work of his life. Edinburgh was the centre of that National Church. There its General Assembly always met in state. There the "Evangelical" party were, year by year, fighting that battle which has been described, for the right of the parishes to appoint their own ministers. Dr. Chalmers was a very strong advocate of the system of an established church, but all the more was he zealous against such an abuse as that of the clergy being appointed by some lay-patron without the people having any choice; so he threw himself very earnestly into the struggle. Greatly he rejoiced when at last his reforming party became the majority in the General Assembly and got the "Veto Act" safely passed, and the whole question, as they thought, practically settled.

It was only for a few years, however, that this settlement was allowed to remain unchallenged. In 1839 a case, which afterwards became very famous, arose at Auchterarder, where the patron, Lord Kinnoull, insisted on appointing a parish minister against whom the people had given their veto. The Patron went to law, and then it was found that the Veto Act of the General Assembly could not stand against the iniquitous Patronage Act passed by Parliament in 1712. From court to court the case was carried, but the parishioners were finally worsted, and then other patrons gained courage to assert their "rights," and the reforming party found themselves powerless. Then they tried to get the law altered. Perhaps if the whole Church had been of one mind they would have succeeded; but the laird and patron classes, and many of the ministers they had appointed, were on the other side, and Parliament was perplexed between the statements and counterstatements. Moreover, as Parliament was mainly composed of English Churchmen, who were accustomed to seeing church-livings given away, and even bought and sold, in England much more shamelessly than in Scotland, they were not likely to feel very strongly the hardship of Scottish patronage; and the result was that at last the Government refused to make any change whatever in the law.

It was a sad day for Dr. Chalmers and his fellow-reformers when, after all their long struggle, they at length found that all hope of any amendment of the law was at an end. They loved their Church with a deep and passionate love. They were no sectaries or Voluntaries. They believed in the principle of an established church, but they dared not remain in a Church in which such a shameful and unchristian thing was to be maintained, as that the right of appointing the clergy should be regarded as a matter of property, to be bought and sold with the great estates. So, when at last it became clear that there was no hope of reform, they no longer hesitated. That could not now be their Church. When the General Assembly opened, May the 18th, 1843, there was great excitement in Edinburgh, for it was known that on that day the final step would be taken. It was not known, however, how many would take it. It had been scoffingly prophesied that, when it came to the point, not six would give up their livings.

On the morning of the opening of the Assembly, the reformers were all present in their places, and waited till prayer had been offered and the Roll was about to be made up. Then they presented a solemn protest, and rising, headed by Dr. Welch and Dr. Chalmers, they withdrew from the Assembly. When they had all withdrawn, it was found that 470 clergymen, nearly half of the entire body, had left. Crowds lined the streets and thronged balconies and windows, and great cheers went up as they passed along to the hall which had been prepared for them to reassemble in. When some one rushed in to tell Lord Jeffrey, he exclaimed: "I am proud of my country; there's not another country upon earth where such a deed could have been done."

Such was the origin of the Free Church of Scotland. But that conspicuous act of withdrawal gives little idea of the hardships and sufferings through which the Church, so founded, had to rise into an organized and working institution. When those 470 ministers went home, it was—to be ejected from their comfortable manses, to find themselves without incomes, without churches, without homes. In many a parish, of course, there were so many who sympathized with the seceding minister that he had no lack of help till a new congregation could be organized. In the large towns, the Voluntaries and Dissenters lent their chapels. But in many of the poorer country districts the ministers were put to great suffering. The landowners were bitterly against them. Humble labouring people who would fain have befriended them were threatened. In several cases exposure and privation brought aged ministers to their death. Then the lairds would not grant land to build the new "Free Churches" upon. They met in the open air; but they were driven from the fields, they were driven even from the high road. In some places the only spot where they could meet, without the patron being able to molest them, was on the sea-shore, below high-water mark, when the tide was out! But they were Scotchmen. The memories of the Puritans and the Covenanters were revived. The more they were persecuted the closer they held together, and the more friends came forward to help them. Money came from England and even from America. Most of all, they themselves gave, as people who knew that by themselves must their upbuilding be wrought. In a few months many thousands of pounds were raised, churches were erected, and the Free Church of Scotland arose, the monument of one of the noblest protests for religious liberty that has been seen in modern times.

From the story of that Free Church, which has ever since gone steadily forward increasing in numbers and in influence, till it has become the strong and energetic body that it is to-day, we turn back to the life of the man who was its leading spirit. Dr. Chalmers was unwearied in his efforts to carry it through its difficulties. He wrote and lectured, procured help for needy ministers, raised money for the multitude of new churches that had to be built, organized the great Sustentation Fund, and then settled down to give the remaining years of his life to the training of the students in the new "Free Church College."

And yet this is not all. It is very beautiful to see how, through all the excitement of this great church-struggle, his heart was still given to the simple cause of helping the poor. In those four years which were all he was to have after the "Disruption," as that movement was called, he did one of the most beautiful works of his life. He was still, as in his earlier ministry at Glasgow, feeling the burden of the misery and sin of the great cities, and longing to do something more for it before he died. But what could he do? He could not undertake a church again, his life was too busily occupied.

What he did was this: He chose out one of the worst districts in Edinburgh—the West-port, as it was called—a nest of narrow, squalid wynds and courts clustering about one main street, which was only rather more public in its wretchedness and vice. The district which he mapped out contained about 400 families, some 2,000 people in all, of whom half were either beggars or thieves, and not above a fourth connected with any church whatever. He divided this neighbourhood into twenty districts, each containing about twenty families. Over each of these districts a visitor was appointed—some were men, some were women—whose duty it was to visit each family once each week. At their first going round, a slip of paper was left with each family explaining the object of the visiting; and then, by leaving tracts, by conversation, sometimes by reading the Bible or engaging in prayer, the visitors endeavoured to become friends to the people, and to lead them to send their children to school and take an interest in religion. He laid especial stress on avoiding almsgiving as far as possible, and even when he opened a school in the midst of the district he insisted that it should not be gratuitous. Every Saturday evening all the visitors met together—Dr. Chalmers meeting with them when his failing health permitted—to talk over their work, and to keep up the interest and spirit of it. Nothing could well be simpler than this work, and yet in the end it changed the whole character of the district, and won it from squalor, ignorance, and vice, to decency, morality, and Christianity. After a time it became a sort of missionary parish. On February 19th, 1847, a little "West-port Church" was opened for worship, and Dr. Chalmers administered the Communion to 132 Communicants, of whom no fewer than 100 were from this poor district. He wrote of that as "the most joyful event of his life." It was almost the last public event of his life too. One Saturday night, only three months later, he was happily among his household, though in failing health. When the Sabbath morning came, they found him dead. He had passed quietly away in the night.

CHAPTER XXXVII.

TOLERATION, LIBERTY, EQUALITY.

BEFORE bringing our story to a close, let us trace a few of the more important steps by which the great struggles of the past have been followed up in more recent times, and the "Religious Toleration" obtained at the Revolution has been widened out into "Religious Liberty," and even carried a good way towards "Religious Equality."

These later steps of progress have not, indeed, been marked by any heroic stories of conflict or martyrdom, but they recall many a peaceful struggle with the voice and the pen, and many a long endeavour, renewed year after year, to win a hearing for justice and right. Few peoples have such a noble chronicle of bloodless victories to recall, and they should not all be forgotten.

The Dissenters of 1689, after all the persecutión they had suffered, were thankful enough for the Act of Toleration. And yet, as we have seen, it was a very imperfect measure. It gave no toleration at all, either to Roman Catholics, or to those who denied the Trinity. It only allowed other Dissenters to worship on condition of their subscribing thirty-five out of the "Thirty-nine Articles," and even those who did this were still shut out (by the Test and Corporation Act, which still remained in force) from holding any office either under

Government or in a city, except on condition of taking the Sacrament in the Church of England. Yet even this small toleration went too far for some. There were still statesmen and bishops who could not give up the idea of forcing Catholics and Dissenters into the Church of England. In 1699 fresh laws were passed against Catholics; priests, for saying mass, were made liable to perpetual imprisonment, and a reward of £100 was offered to informers against them; and it was made illegal for Catholics to hold or purchase land, to undertake any work of education at home, or to send their children to be educated abroad. It is difficult to realize that such an atrocious law could be passed after the era of toleration, but a Church and Tory reaction had set in. Thus in the same spirit, in 1711 an "Occasional Conformity" Act was aimed at Dissenters, making it illegal for them to take the Sacrament at church unless they usually worshipped there; and in 1714 the still more infamous Schism Act was passed, making it illegal for any Nonconformist to keep even a private school! In a few years, indeed, these two last acts were repealed, but the Catholics remained under the same injustice still. In Ireland their condition was still worse. There, no Catholic could vote at an election, or serve in the army or navy, or practise as a lawyer, while the law was that any priest performing a marriage service between a Protestant and a Catholic should be hanged!

Gradually, however, the tide turned again, and more liberal counsels have ever since been gradually making way. Dissenters took their place among their fellow citizens; first they were elected to offices in the great cities, and no one liked to enforce the law against them. Then in 1728 an Act of Indemnity was passed, relieving any who were thus holding office, from any fine or punishment; and this was repeated every year, but the Test and Corporation Act was still kept on the statute-book. One exception must be made to the statement that no one liked to enforce that act. The Corporation of London made a bye-law, fining all persons who refused to serve as sheriff £400, or, if elected by the citizens, £600, and then elected Dissenters year after year, devoting the fines to the rebuilding of the Mansion House. A curious illustration of how London had gone back from the spirit of religious liberty, of which the city had once been the stronghold! When £15,000 had been extorted in this way, however, the bye-law was resisted, and in 1767 the House of Lords finally confirmed the refusal.

During the latter half of the eighteenth century Dissenters became bolder in claiming their rights, and began to protest against being obliged to subscribe the Church Articles at all, in order to enjoy toleration. In 1779 this was altered, and instead of subscribing the Articles, Dissenters had to make the following declaration: "I, ——— ———, do solemnly declare that I am a Christian and a Protestant Dissenter, and that I take the Holy Scriptures, both of the Old and New Testament, as they are generally received in Protestant countries, for the rule of my faith and practice."

In 1778 many of the worst penalties against Catholicism in Ireland and England, especially those of the Act of 1699, were repealed. The people, however, were hardly prepared for this. The old traditional dread of Popery still lingered among the masses, and was sometimes fanned into a flame by fanatics of higher position. Even these concessions of 1778 to the Catholics of England and Ireland aroused a storm of Protestant rage; and when, the following year, it was proposed to extend them to Scotland, the storm became a tempest. Great riots took place in Edinburgh, a fierce agitation was set on foot throughout the kingdom; and the whole came to its height in June, 1780, when the great "No Popery" riots, headed by Lord George Gordon, a half-crazy fanatic, held London in a reign of terror for three days.* Such violence, however, discredited the cause it was intended to serve. The Catholics became bolder, and began to agitate for complete emancipation from all the old repressive or disqualifying laws. When the Act of Union between the two countries was passed in 1800, it was only consented to, in Ireland, on condition of the Prime Minister of the day, William Pitt, undertaking that all these laws against the Catholics should be forthwith repealed. When the Union was accomplished, however, Mr. Pitt found that he had promised more than he was able to perform, for the king, George III., took one of his fits of obstinacy, and, in spite of all that the minister could do, the disabilities remained for another generation.

But all through that generation, the change of feeling was going on which was at last to do away even with the last of these old remnants of persecution. About 1812 and 1813, several alterations in the law were made which showed how the change was working. The old penal laws against the Quakers, and the Five-mile Act and Conventicle Act, by which the Nonconformists had been harassed in the time of Charles II., had always remained on the statute-book, though the Act of Toleration had practically made them a dead letter. In 1812, however, it came to be felt that it was a scandal to

* The story of those riots is well told in Dickens's "Barnaby Rudge."

have such laws remaining, even in name, and they were finally and entirely repealed. The following year, Mr. William Smith, M.P. for Norwich, pointed out that there was a similar old Act by which it was a punishable crime to deny the doctrine of the Trinity, and this too was repealed.

From this time the great question of religious liberty, for many years, was that of what was called "Catholic Emancipation," the doing away with the old laws which pressed hardly upon the Catholics and shut them out from public service. There was no real reason in the world, why these old laws should be kept up. The power of the Pope had long ceased to trouble any one in England; the government was perfectly secure; and yet the old prejudices still held the king and the Tories, and every now and then the old alarm cry of "No Popery," carried the rabble with them. But the movement steadily went forward. Alike in Ireland and England, the Catholics were constantly protesting against being treated differently from the people of any other religion. Hardly a session of Parliament passed without the question being introduced. The Catholics themselves were moderate and reasonable, much more so than they have since become. At one time it was seriously declared in Parliament by Henry Grattan, the champion of Catholic liberty, that the Catholics of Ireland were willing to allow the king a veto on the appointment of Catholic bishops.* In 1821, the feeling in favour of granting justice to the Catholics had gathered such strength, that at last a Catholic Emancipation Bill was passed in the House of Commons. From this time, almost year by year, the Commons kept passing the bill, while the Lords threw it out.

* In 1808. "Pictorial History of England," vol. vi. p. 771.

This raised a strong feeling in the country against the House of Lords, and at last in 1829 the popular outcry became too strong, and the great Catholic Emancipation Act was passed.

Perhaps this final victory was rendered easier by the fact that in the previous year the old "Test and Corporation" Acts were entirely done away. Curiously enough, in doing away with this wrong, another was unintentionally created. For the Commons, instead of the old "Test," substituted a simple declaration to be made by any one taking office, that he would not use his power or influence to the injury of the Established Church; the Lords added that this declaration must be made "on the true faith of a Christian;" and in a little while it was found that these words prevented Jews from taking offices which previously they had been able to hold. So there had to be another struggle by-and-by over this, and it was not till 1845 that the exclusion of Jews was removed, so far as to allow them to be magistrates or town-councillors, and in 1858 they were admitted to Parliament.

The next important step in the progress of religious liberty, after the Roman Catholics had been put upon a level with their fellow-citizens, was the passage of an Act allowing Dissenters to marry in their own places of worship. By the ancient common law of England, people could be married anywhere, even in private houses. This led, however, to very great abuses, and in 1757 it was altered, and it was required that all marriages should take place in a parish church. There was one exception, for the Government knew that the Quakers would consent to nothing of the kind, and so they were still allowed to marry in their Meetings. Gradually it came to be felt as a great hardship by other Dissenters to have to marry in the Established Church. Some avoided this by going to Scotland, where the old law still prevailed; others went to church, but handed in a protest to the clergyman. At last, in 1836, a reform of the law took place, enabling people to be married in any place of worship duly registered for the purpose, or even at the registrar's office if they preferred.

The open discussion which took place in the course of all these changes, gradually aroused feelings which could not be satisfied without still further changes. The Dissenters began to ask why there should be any difference at all between people of different religions; why the Episcopal Church should be in a position to say how far people of other forms of religion should, or should not, be tolerated; why they should have to plead for liberty to do this or that, according to their own religious convictions; why they should be obliged in any way to have special respect or consideration for the Church of England, more than for any other sect. Especially did these questions arise in connection with the matter of "church-rates." From very early times, it had been the practice for the people in each parish to meet every year in "vestry," and agree to some rate for the repairs of the church, and in the course of ages this rate had come to have the force of law. There had been no great hardship in this, so long as the parishioners were all of the same faith; but after the people of England had come to be divided into different religious bodies, it became a great injustice. The Church of England was felt to be, after all, only one of those bodies, even if it was as large as all the rest of them put together. Besides, if the Church of England was the largest, surely its members could all the better bear the burden of supporting their own places of worship. Gradually this feeling grew, until many Dissenters, the Quakers especially, entirely refused to pay church-rates, and every year more and more of the parishes became scenes of bitter contention, the Church people endeavouring to levy a rate and the Dissenters using every means to prevent it. In many of the large towns the Church people were outvoted in the vestry meetings, and no rate could be had. From the year 1818, rates were given up in Sheffield, and from 1833 in Manchester. In 1834, the scandal caused by the struggles on the subject became so great, that the Government took up the matter, and introduced a bill for the abolition of church rates. It was not carried, but it gave such a stimulus to the subject that from that time it never rested, and at length, in 1868, they were virtually abolished by an act making their payment entirely voluntary.

Aside from the main course of the progress of religious liberty which has been thus traced, an episode took place in 1844 which, though at first affecting only a single group of congregations, is likely to be hereafter of wider value than it has at present—the passing of the "Dissenters' Chapels Act." It has been already told how the English Presbyterian congregations had gradually come to hold Unitarian opinions during the past century, and most of their ancient chapels having been left untrammelled by any doctrinal tests, they still continued to enjoy the places of worship and other property which had come down to them from previous generations. When, in 1813, the penal statutes against Unitarians were done away, it was supposed that all that was necessary to confirm them in their rights and properties was done; but some time afterwards it was discovered that, in reality, their title to all endowments which had been left to these Presbyterian congregations before that time, was liable to be disputed. The ground taken was, that as Unitarianism had been illegal till 1813, to endow it had been also illegal, and that therefore it could not be supposed that property given previous to that year could be rightly held by Unitarians. The courts decided that such was the law, and some very considerable property, especially a large endowment for the support of "poor and godly ministers," left by a wealthy Presbyterian lady of Charles II.'s time—the "Lady Hewley Fund"—was taken out of the hands of the Unitarian Presbyterians. But this was not all. They saw themselves further threatened with the loss of almost all their chapels and property (at least all which were in existence prior to 1813)—chapels in which their fathers, through many generations of unbroken dissent, had worshipped, funds which they had left for the support of those chapels, and burial grounds in which they had been interred. The Government of the day, however, stepped in, and insisted that it would be a great wrong to allow anything of this kind; that these congregations ought not to be disturbed in the enjoyment of the property which they had peaceably inherited, merely because the members had in course of time changed their opinions. Many in the more orthodox Churches were very bitter, and endeavoured to prevent any settlement being made; but the leading statesmen of both parties united in passing (in 1844) the "Dissenters' Chapels Act." By this act it was provided that, except where a trust-deed has expressly limited the use of a place of worship to persons holding some particular religious doctrine, those who have enjoyed it for twenty-five years shall be regarded as its rightful possessors. At the time this act was bitterly denounced by the Baptists and Independents; but of late years they have begun to see that changes of opinion are not so impossible, even within their own borders, as they then thought; and many of them are now contending that trust-deeds ought to be left free, so that the congregation of one time may not be prevented by the restrictions of a past generation, from worshipping in the way they think best.

Perhaps the most remarkable extension of the principle of religious liberty in these later days, however, is the opening of the ancient Universities of England to Dissenters. From 1834, many thoughtful men in the Universities themselves had contended that it was alike absurd and wrong to limit the advantages of Oxford and Cambridge to those who could sign the "Thirty-nine Articles;" and Dissenters protested against it as a great injustice. At Oxford, Dissenters were shut out from even becoming students; at Cambridge they were able to enter as students, but were excluded from receiving any degree, however eminent and successful they might have been in their classes. It was in 1834 that the question first came before Parliament, and from that time it was seldom allowed to rest. The struggle was long, but the end was sure. In the year 1854 a great step forward was made, in the opening of Oxford to Dissenting students, and a greater one yet in the admission, two years later, of Dissenters to degrees at Cambridge. Even this, however, was not sufficient. A Dissenter might take his degree, but he might not hold a "fellowship," without in some way acknowledging himself a member of the Church of England. Yet, year by year, among those who stood highest on the degree list, and who therefore, if Churchmen, would have been appointed to fellowships as a matter of course, were some Dissenters. Earnest men, among whom must be mentioned James Heywood, a worthy descendant of an old Puritan family who suffered at the time of the ejection, kept calling attention to the subject, and at length (in 1871) this last trace of exclusion was removed, and all tests for admission to offices and degrees in the Universities were finally done away.

Thus, step by step, has the religious liberty of the English people kept broadening down, "from precedent to precedent," until at the present time it may be said to be complete. All sects can now worship God as they think right. All people can now live out their own religious life in whatever way seems best to them—or, if they do not believe in religion at all, they may let it alone, and there is no law to molest them.

Some ask—what more, then, is wanted? The answer is: not only religious *liberty* but religious *equality*. Dissenters have gradually come to see that not only ought every Church to have perfect freedom to live out its own life in its own way, but that the law ought not even to make any difference between them, ought not to patronize, or favour, or establish one, and ought not to interfere with any. At present, the long growth of religious liberty has brought about this curious result: that whereas in old times the Episcopalians interfered with the worship of Dissenters, now the only power of interference with each other's worship is exactly the other way. The Episcopalian Church, being under the control of Parliament, its worship and its creed are regulated by a body which includes Jews and Catholics and Dissenters as well as Church people. Many sincere Church people feel this to be a great grievance, and are beginning to demand that they shall have the same liberty that people of other Churches enjoy, to control their own worship. The difficulty really arises from the fact that the Episcopalian Church is in possession of the whole ancient religious property of the country; this property rightly belongs to the nation as a whole, and not to the members of any one sect. As a fact, for instance, our magnificent cathedrals were built for the religious use of the whole nation, when all the nation was Catholic; and now that the nation is divided into many different Churches it is not right that those ancient monuments should be monopolized by any single one of these.

Thus the struggle has passed from one about Religious Liberty, to one for Religious Equality. What will be the end of it, this story of the past leaves little doubt. But the end is not yet.

CHAPTER XXXVIII.

CONCLUSION—THE CHURCHES TO-DAY.

The story of the religious life of the past is told. Step by step we have traced the mighty changes, which have brought this England of ours from the dark beginnings of history in old heathen times, and from the early Christian days when only one Church existed, to this nineteenth century, with its full religious liberty, and the multitude of sects and churches which have grown up with that liberty. We have seen the faint traditions of British Druidism yielding place to traditions, not much less faint, of British Christianity. We have seen that British Christianity overwhelmed by barbarous races, and these in turn, by-and-by, converted to the same Christian faith. We have seen that rude primitive Church changing, as wave after wave of conquest passed over the land; becoming more settled, more organized, more powerful, enriched with nobler buildings, until we stood in that old Catholic England the traces of which are all about us in ruined abbey, and parish church, and magnificent cathedral. Then we watched the beginnings of new and nobler thoughts about religious things, the sufferings of little bands of heretics, the struggles of great reformers, the seething and strife and confusion of the Reformation. And thence we have traced the different currents of religious tendency, into which that Reformation set the mind and heart of our

English people flowing; the steady flow of Puritanism increasing till, for a time, it even became the main stream, and this dividing, and still dividing; and gradually, all attempts to bring these back into one great channel of a national Episcopal Church, breaking down and abandoned, and all left, now almost for a century, to find their own level and to be what they are,—no one of them the whole of the mighty river of Life, but all of them parts of it.

It only remains to trace something of the later course of all these ever-branching and winding streams of religious life, and connect them with the actual state of things which we have around us to-day.

Foremost among the religious bodies of the country stands the ancient Established Church, which has been changed so often:—Catholic to begin with; semi-Catholic under Henry VIII.; severely Protestant under Edward VI.; Catholic again under Mary; Episcopalian under Elizabeth; Presbyterian under the Commonwealth; Episcopalian again under Charles II.; and now, in the present day,—what? Divided among three sections, Low Church, High Church, and Broad Church, which are just as different from each other as any three sects, and yet each of which insists that it is the true Church of England, the real representative of its position and faith. One thing is plain:—that the progress of that religious liberty which has more and more placed the Established Church on a level with all other Churches, and left that Church, like the rest, to its own voluntary efforts, has not weakened it but strengthened it. The Established Church never was so active, earnest, and living as it is to-day. Its clergy never numbered so many learned men, was never so active in good works, was never so much respected among the people;

its churches never were so well supported, its services never were so reverently and impressively conducted, as they are now. The revival began with the influence which Wesley's movement had upon English religious life. He awakened the Church of England, even though the first result of that awakening was to oppose him. Many clergymen who were touched by his movement were not prepared to go out of the Church, but remained in, and from them grew up the great Evangelical party, commonly called the "Low Church." In the latter part of last century and the beginning of this, the Evangelical party was the life of the Church of England, such men as Milner and Newton among the clergy, Wilberforce and Zacchary Macaulay among the laity, setting a tone of fervent methodistic piety, and doing much to elevate the life of the country. As this party began to fall into the formality and partisanship which too often are the death of movements at first very living, a new "High Church" party grew up, first at Oxford, and gradually spread through the Church. At first they were called "Tractarians," from a series of "Tracts for the Times," in which, about 1832, they began to advocate their views; later on, from their greatest leader, Dr. Pusey, they were known as "Puseyites," and in the present day they are usually named "Ritualists," from the importance they attach to matters of ritual, and also from the extraordinary nature of the ritual—almost like that of the Roman Catholic mass—with which they have astonished the Church. The leading idea of the High Church party is that which Archbishop Laud held, in the time of Charles I.: to restore the Church to its old position as one of the branches of the great Catholic Church, but without acknowledging the Pope. So, they have been very zealous in restoring many of the usages of early times, and, let it not be forgotten, in restoring the churches and cathedrals to their old dignity and splendour. Like the great Evangelical party, however, they have suffered decline; many of their ablest leaders, such as the saintly-minded John Henry Newman and F. W. Faber, have gone over to the Romish Church, and the present Ritualists, with their extravagant imitations of Romanism, are losing the hold upon society which was gained by such men as Pusey and Keble. Besides these two parties there is a third, commonly known as the "Broad Church." These are the Liberals of the Church. Like the Latitudinarians of the last century, they want the Church widened, so that men may remain in it even though they no longer believe many of the doctrines of the Articles and the Prayer-book; and as it has become extremely difficult to enforce the old Church-law against a clergyman who reads the creeds and the liturgy, however much he may disbelieve them, they continue to hold their places, and certainly form a useful element among the other parties. They are not very numerous; but a party which has been able to count among its leaders such men as the late F. D. Maurice and Rowland Williams, Dean Stanley, Stopford Brooke, Bishop Colenso, and Professor Jowett, must always be a power for good in the country. Such differences as those which divide these parties must always exist, where men are in earnest and think for themselves, and they are a token of the vitality of the Church. The only question is—and it is a question which thinking people are asking more and more—why should these three parties be specially encouraged and provided for by the State, and kept up as an "established" Church? Why should not they all work out their own life and thought in their own way, as the other churches of the country have to do?

Next in historical importance come the representatatives of the old English Puritanism, the Baptists and the Independents. Both of these bodies are large and powerful, and though they have both drifted a long way from the hard Calvinism with which they alike started, they are still generally "Orthodox" in opinion.

The Baptists are a very large and influential body. The original division into General Baptists and Particular Baptists has been already mentioned as existing for two hundred years back. The General Baptists have also been divided, for during the last century the tone of thought among them was gradually changing, very much as it was doing among the old English Presbyterian congregations, until many of them had become Arian and even Unitarian, and there were two parties among them. Those who remained Orthodox, finding it impossible to arrest the change, and being outnumbered, withdrew in a body from the old "General Baptist Assembly" in the year 1770, and formed the "New Connexion of General Baptists." The older body has gradually become still more decidedly Unitarian, and its congregations are usually associated with the other Unitarian Churches, though still retaining their ancient Baptist rite, and the organization of their ancient Assembly.

The main body of the Baptists, however, are the Particular Baptists, still technically so called, though they have in practice for the most part dropped the old Calvinistic idea, which first gave them their name, that salvation is only possible to the elect in particular. Their great preacher, Charles H. Spurgeon, is one of the leaders of religious life in England, and there are few congregations anywhere doing a nobler work than that of his great Tabernacle. Their congregations are all independent in their organization, but are for the most part associated together in the Baptist Union.

The "Independents"—who now generally prefer the name "Congregationalists"—form perhaps the strongest religious denomination in the kingdom, after the Established Church. No Church has furnished more sturdy, public-spirited workers for the various political and social reforms of the age. They have been foremost, too, in the movement for placing the Episcopal Church on the same footing as the rest, and so bringing about religious equality. Edward Miall, who has been the leader of this movement, is a man who has the respect even of opponents, and their leading preachers, such as Henry Allon, Alexander Raleigh, Newman Hall, R. W. Dale, are men of the highest reputation through all Churches.

The movement which has been already described as taking place about a hundred years ago among the old English Presbyterian congregations, has very much changed their character, and led to the gradual disuse of their old name, though some of their congregations, and many of their district associations, still cling to it. Of late, the congregations which have been founded in England, as offshoots of the Presbyterian Churches in Scotland, have taken to calling themselves "the English Presbyterians," which tends to some confusion, as the two bodies in England and Scotland were not of the same origin, never had much in common, and have had very different histories. The English Presbyterians, from the time when they ceased to have the political power and ascendency which is always mischievous to Churches, have had a very noble history of thoughtful and progressive freedom, which ought never to be forgotten. That freedom led them, in the course of generations of development, to a position which the word "Unitarian" fairly describes; but they are still free: the churches and chapels which they build to-day are not tied down to the use of Unitarians, but are founded simply "for the worship of Almighty God," just as those were which they have inherited from their Presbyterian ancestors; so that those who come after them may be perfectly free to follow whatever, from generation to generation, may seem to be the truth of God. These Unitarian-Presbyterians, are not a very numerous body, but of late years they have been much more active, and have been increasing. They have always held a high place for thoughtfulness, liberality, and public spirit. Their leading minister, James Martineau, is revered all over the world as a religious teacher of singular power, and as the strongest exponent of a spiritual philosophy against the materialistic tendencies of the day.

The Society of Friends holds a curious position among the Churches, not doing—hardly even attempting to do—much, in the way of influencing the religious thought of the time, and yet respected by all men for the charity, uprightness, and activity in good works, of its members. Having no formal statement of belief, there has always been a good deal of variety in their religious opinions. In 1827 these differences of opinion among the American Friends led to a division, about half of their number, under the leadership of Elias Hicks, rejecting most of the doctrines of Orthodoxy; and this movement caused great excitement among the English Friends, who were very much influenced by the late Joseph John Gurney, and from that time have taken a more distinctly Orthodox ground. In many ways, however, they have been growing more liberal; they have largely given up their peculiarities of dress and speech; and, of late, have been very active in Sunday School work and in endeavouring to make their religious life helpful to the poor.

The great Methodist Church, founded by John Wesley, is hardly now what it was in his day. It has become a much more powerful and much more wealthy body; its ministers are better educated, and its services have less of excitement about them, but it has hardly kept that hold upon the mass of the people by which it won its place, and if it has gained in calm respectability, it has lost in fervour and power. Yet it is still a mighty religious agency among the people, and has been the parent of many offshoot churches, which have, in reality, to be regarded as results of the work of the Wesleys. The constitution of the original body, its government by a conference of ministers only, has led to most of these secessions. Thus, as early as 1797, the "Methodist New Connexion" split off on this ground, and set up a conference composed equally of ministers and laymen. In 1810 there was a great deal of disturbance, arising from the feeling, on the part of some of the zealous Methodists, that Conference was falling away from the simpler ways of the early Methodist times. Camp meetings had been discouraged, and some wanted these restored, and also wished to see women admitted to preach, and at last out of these disputes grew the "Primitive Methodist" body. This Primitive Methodism has really taken up that rough-and-ready work among the poorest classes, which the parent Wesleyan society has rather let go; and it has increased until it has become the most extensive of the Methodist offshoot churches. In the same year another separation took place on the ground that there ought not to be a paid ministry, and the body of "Independent Methodists" was formed. In 1815 a lay-preacher named Bryan became the founder of another body generally known as "Bryanites," but who called themselves "Bible Christians." In 1834 the feeling on the part of various ministers, that the power exercised by the "Legal Hundred" who formed the Conference, was tyrannical and wrong, led to much disputing, and the ministers who complained were expelled, and set up the "Wesleyan Association;" and an exactly similar cause, in 1849, led to the establishment of the "Wesleyan Reform Association;" and these two bodies were amalgamated a few years since under the name of the "United Methodist Free Church," and have become a very large and active body. All these offshoot churches retain very much the general character of the original society, drawing their members much together in class-meetings and prayer-meetings, and doing a vast work by the "power of the pence." There is also another body called the "Welsh Calvinistic Methodists," but this, it is worth remembering, is not an offshoot from Methodism, but a parallel growth which originated at the same time. In Wales the religious movement which Whitefield and Wesley started remained Calvinistic, and never joined the English societies, but formed this distinct but kindred Church.

Any account of the churches of to-day would be incomplete without some mention of a sect which, though never large in numbers, holds a position of great respect in England, and some of the teachings of which have largely entered into the religious thought of the time. Swedenborg himself, indeed, hardly belongs to the religious story of England, but it is in England that his doctrines have chiefly taken root. Many of those who most deeply value the religious writings of Emanuel Swedenborg, doubt whether they are suited to become the rallying ground of a sect, and whether they would not have been best left, as Swedenborg himself left them, to leaven the thought of all churches. Swedenborg himself made no attempt to found a new sect, and it was not till 1788, the centenary of his birth, and when he had been dead sixteen years, that his followers first organized themselves under Robert Hindmarsh, a London printer, who was their first minister, as "the New Church signified by the New Jerusalem in the Revelation." Their views are too subtle and mystical for it to be surprising that they have not become popular, but wherever there are Swedenborgian societies they are distinguished for an earnest, thoughtful, religious life.

No mere catalogue of the various denominations, such as have been mentioned, would exhaust the many curious forms into which the free religious spirit of England keeps branching out. George Eliot, in her beautiful story of "Silas Marner," has given a sketch of a little community which she calls the Church of God in Lantern Yard. There are few towns which have not here and there, in small obscure chapels or little upper rooms, just such little groups of religious people as she has imagined; taking no sect name, perhaps claiming to be unsectarian, yet drawn together by sympathy in some peculiar view, which sunders them from all the Churches of the time. Many of these call themselves Bible Christians; there are a number of such groups in different places taking this name, yet in no way connected with each other. Perhaps the most important of these minor groupings of the religious life is that which is commonly known as the "Plymouth Brethren." It began among some extreme Evangelicals in Plymouth and Dublin, who drew out of the Church of England to try to set up a simpler religious life and ministry more like that of the primitive Christian Church. The most remarkable of these people was a young Irish clergyman named Darby; he had been educated for the law, but came under very strong religious impressions, and gave up his worldly prospects, entered the Church, took a poor curacy among the mountains of Wicklow, and threw himself into his work among the peasantry there with singular self-devotion. He lived in a poor, bare hut; he dressed in the roughest clothes, utterly neglecting appearances; he took nothing but the coarsest food, and spent his days in wandering from cabin to cabin, ministering among the poorest of the people, by whom, even by the Catholics, he was venerated almost as a saint. The influence of his character drew many of a higher class to him for advice and guidance, and after a time he left the Established Church, and visited different parts of England as the missionary of a higher, more Evangelical piety. Under his influence little groups of people, mostly of the higher classes, gathered together in a simple brotherly communion which caused them to be called "Plymouth Brethren," though they themselves refused any name but that of Christians. They adopted no creed, but yet were intensely Orthodox, and to a large extent were believers in the speedy reappearance of Christ on the earth.

Apart from all these various workings of the free religious spirit which has been leavening English society ever since the Reformation, holding no fellowship with any, not even recognizing any as churches at all, stands the old Roman Catholic Church and priesthood. Nominally it is the representative of the ancient Church of this country as it was before the Reformation, but in reality it has come to be more and more a foreign religion, the representative not of the old English Catholicism but of the modern Roman hierarchy. Up to a recent period the character of Catholicism in England was given by the old steady-going Catholic families, who had held quietly to their faith for many generations, but who were Englishmen first of all, and generally on the side of freedom and progress. After emancipation was once secured, however, the character of the Roman Catholic Church in England rapidly changed; it became much more Romish and much more aggressive; foreign priests were sent over, monasteries were established, stronger efforts were made to keep Catholics from in any way recognizing, or having any part whatever with, the religious doings of other bodies; and their old patriotism began to be lost in the struggle to gain special advantages for their own Church and priesthood. All this has made Romanism little more than a branch of a foreign Church on English soil; a large and strong branch, with many high-minded, learned men connected with it, and gathering many people to itself, and yet withal only making them alien to the spirit and sympathies of English life. Yet there is much about its working that is very noble; it keeps hold of multitudes, especially of the poor Irish immigrants in the great cities, in a way no other religious body could do, and does much to make them temperate. And though in ordinary times it does less for the poor than almost any other Church, in seasons of sickness or pestilence its priests carry the last Sacrament into scenes of disease and death, with an unflinching and heroic faithfulness which all must revere.

Such, then, is the endless variety of the Religious Life which is about us, in this England of ours, to-day. Everywhere variety, in many parts controversy, here and there bitterness and disputing; even in the Church which most professes uniformity, the same differences as elsewhere, and only the more bitter because of the attempt to keep them together. To some people, all these differences seem a token of weakness and decay, and the Catholics point at them as evidences that private judgment is a mischievous blunder, and that Protestantism, with its religious freedom, is a wreck going visibly to pieces. But it is not so, really. These very differences are a token of life, not of death; of restless vitality, not of feebleness and decay. In these different ways men have been feeling after higher truth and more helpful faith. They have come already to a larger charity, and wider, heartier brotherhood. There is more fellowship among the churches, more mutual respect. The different sects are beginning to think of each other—as they are—as the varying outcome of the one great Spirit which works in all men; and though it is hardly likely that the time is very close at hand when all their differences shall have ceased to be, the time is rapidly nearing when they will cease to be any hurtful barrier. That was a fine saying of Thomas Binney's, that he did not look to see all the walls between the Churches done away, but he did want them to be lowered, so that all good men might shake hands over them.

Surely *that* "good time coming" is *not* far off!

u/

NOTE BY THE PUBLISHERS.

The Author wishes the following paragraph to be added to what he has said about Foreign Missions in CHAPTER XXXIV.:—

The earliest idea of a Foreign Mission seems to have originated with John Eliot and Oliver Cromwell; for when, in 1643, the Rev. John Eliot sent word home about the intercourse he was beginning to have with the Indians, great interest was aroused in the mind of Cromwell, and in 1649 a "corporation" was formed by Act of Parliament "For the Promoting and Propagating the Gospel of Jesus Christ in New England." A curious series of eleven "Eliot Tracts" is still extant, giving accounts of work among the Indians. At the Restoration, this "New England Company" became defunct, but was shortly reconstituted by an Order in Council, and has been quietly in operation from that day to this, though, since the revolution of 1776, confined in its operations to the provinces of British America.